Abandoned Places

Abandoned Places

A photographic exploration of more than 100 places we have left behind

KIERON CONNOLLY

METRO BOOKS
New York

METRO BOOKS
New York

An Imprint of Sterling Publishing
1166 Avenue of the Americas
New York, NY 10036

METRO BOOKS and the distinctive Metro Books logo are trademarks
of Sterling Publishing Co., Inc.

© 2016 by Amber Books Ltd.

All rights reserved. No part of this publication may be reproduced, stored in a retrieval system
or transmitted in any form or by any means (including electronic, mechanical, photocopying,
recording, or otherwise) without prior written permission from the publisher.

Editorial and design by
Amber Books Ltd
74–77 White Lion Street
London N1 9PF
www.amberbooks.co.uk

Project Editor: Sarah Uttridge
Designer: Mark Batley
Picture Research: Terry Forshaw

ISBN: 978-1-4351-6306-5

For information about custom editions, special sales, and premium and corporate purchases,
please contact Sterling Special Sales at 800-805-5489 or specialsales@sterlingpublishing.com.

Manufactured in China

2 4 6 8 10 9 7 5 3 1

www.sterlingpublishing.com

Contents

Introduction	6
Industrial Places	8
Public Buildings	36
Ghost Towns & Cities	78
Military & Scientific Buildings	120
Recreational & Retail Buildings	148
Transport	184
Picture Credits	224

Introduction

Who would be interested in a crumbling factory, a deserted hospital or a derelict mining town long after the gold rush has peaked, we might initially wonder. And then we realize: we would. Because dilapidated buildings, railways and ghost towns have gained a new value in their decrepitude simply by being old, weathered and unmodernized by the decorator's paintbrush. Through them we glimpse the past – as journalist Murray Kempton wrote: 'Nothing preserves except neglect'. Places of seemingly little value become attractions, not for what they do but for what they no longer do. But there's another gain. In the absence of humanity, nature reclaims its own. Trees grow through buildings and roads are grassed over. Wildlife returns, too. Varosha in Northern Cyprus was once a fashionable beach resort. Today it is a ghost town. There's still a nightlife, just not one that involves people. Now that it's secluded, sea turtles have returned to climb the beach and lay their eggs in the quiet sand. *Abandoned Places* celebrates these strange landscapes.

ABOVE:
The Courthouse in Plymouth, Montserrat.
The town was abandoned after it was buried
in volcanic ash in 1995.
RIGHT:
Five centuries of abandonment. A tree grows around
a building in the city of Angkor, Cambodia.

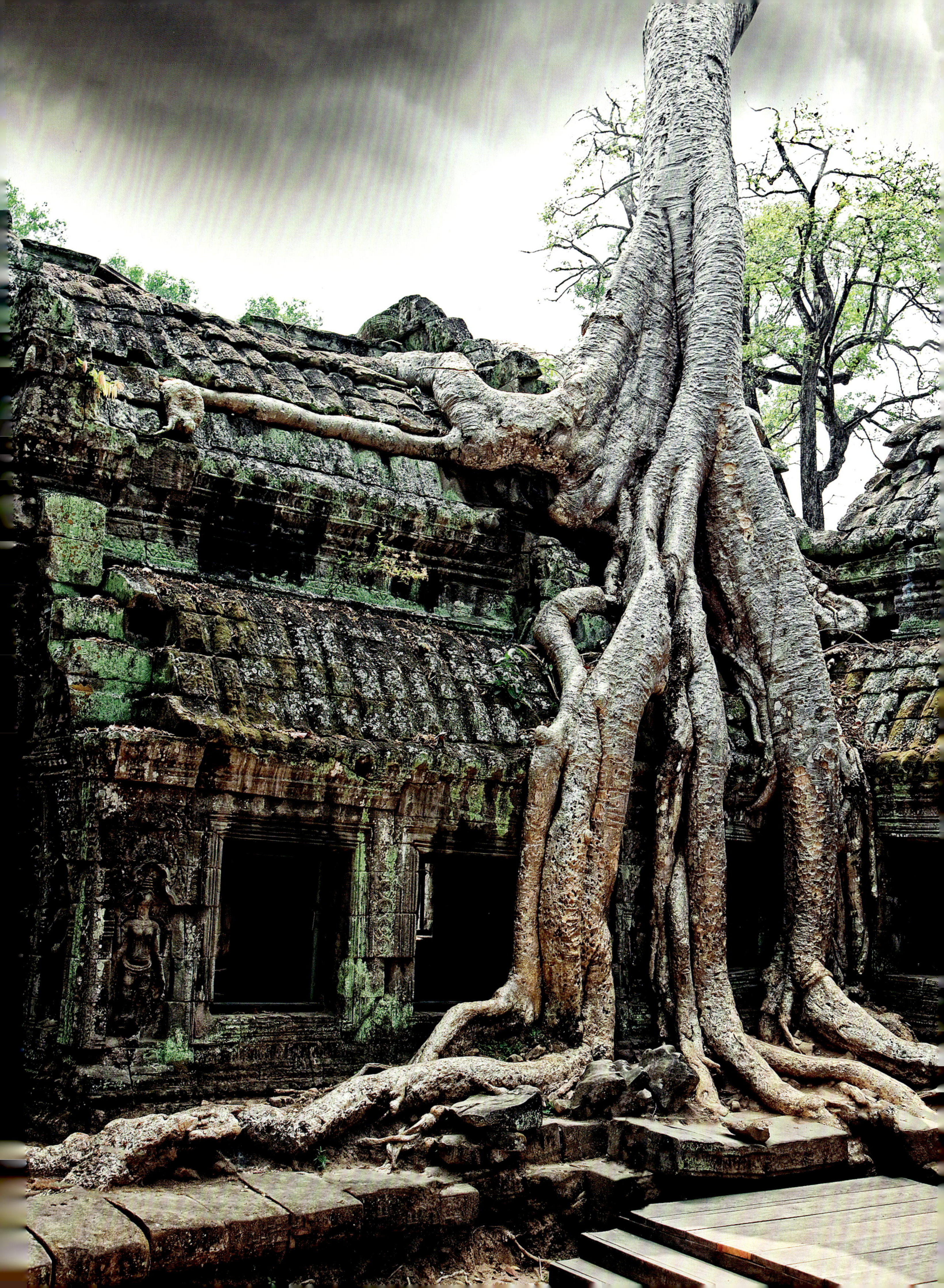

PROTECTION
NEUTRAL
EARTHING
66 K.V.
NEUTRAL EARTHING
66K.V. & 22K.V.

Industrial Places

At the beginning of the 20th century, the saltpetre works at Humberstone in Chile's Atacama Desert were most unlikely, in that remote, hot and dusty climate, to be regarded as holding any cultural or historical value. Essential in the production of fertilizers, yes, but not something anyone would have thought of preserving. A century later, however, and almost 50 years after they were closed, Humberstone, and its neighbouring settlement Santa Laura, became UNESCO World Heritage Sites. The wrecks of sheds and unmoveable rolling stock were saved, because today we find something interesting, beautiful and unusual about them – something that wasn't there before. So it is with many of the industrial places featured in these pages. Power stations and gasworks, gold mines and car factories may have been originally built for purely functional purposes. But whether because of their design, as with London's underground reservoirs, or the stories that they can tell, such as the collapse of Detroit through abandoned factories, or perhaps simply the stamp that they leave on the landscape, like the vast opencast mine at Mirny, they come to fascinate us long after they've ceased functioning. The exception to this would be the Aral Sea, one of the world's worst ecological disasters. Certainly not beautiful or celebrated, the drying up of almost all of the world's fourth-largest lake has become its own memorial to a brutal, reckless irrigation scheme.

LEFT:
Control Room A, Battersea Power Station, London, England
With art deco interiors and Giles Gilbert Scott's brick-cathedral style exterior, this coal-fired power station on the River Thames has long been a much-loved London landmark. In operation between 1933 and 1983, it later lay unused but under protected status for 30 years, until redevelopment to turn it into a residential complex began in 2013.

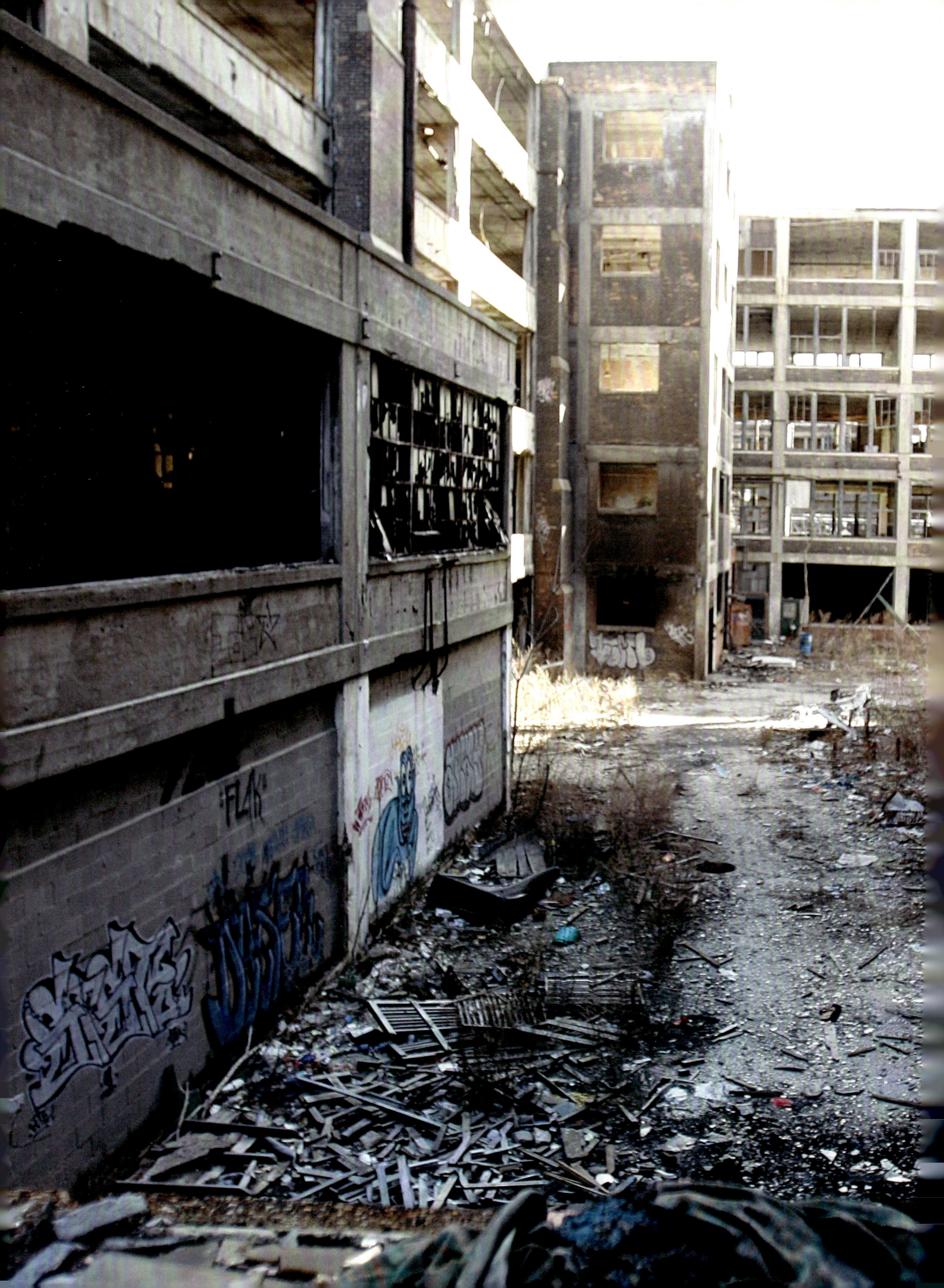
FL4K

LEFT:
Packard Automotive Plant, Detroit, Michigan, USA
Completed in 1911, the Packard Automotive Plant produced Packards and later Studebakers until it closed in 1958. Other businesses used the premises until the 1990s, but, with the collapse of Detroit's dominant motor industry, it fell into ruin. Bought in 2013, the plant is now undergoing renovation.

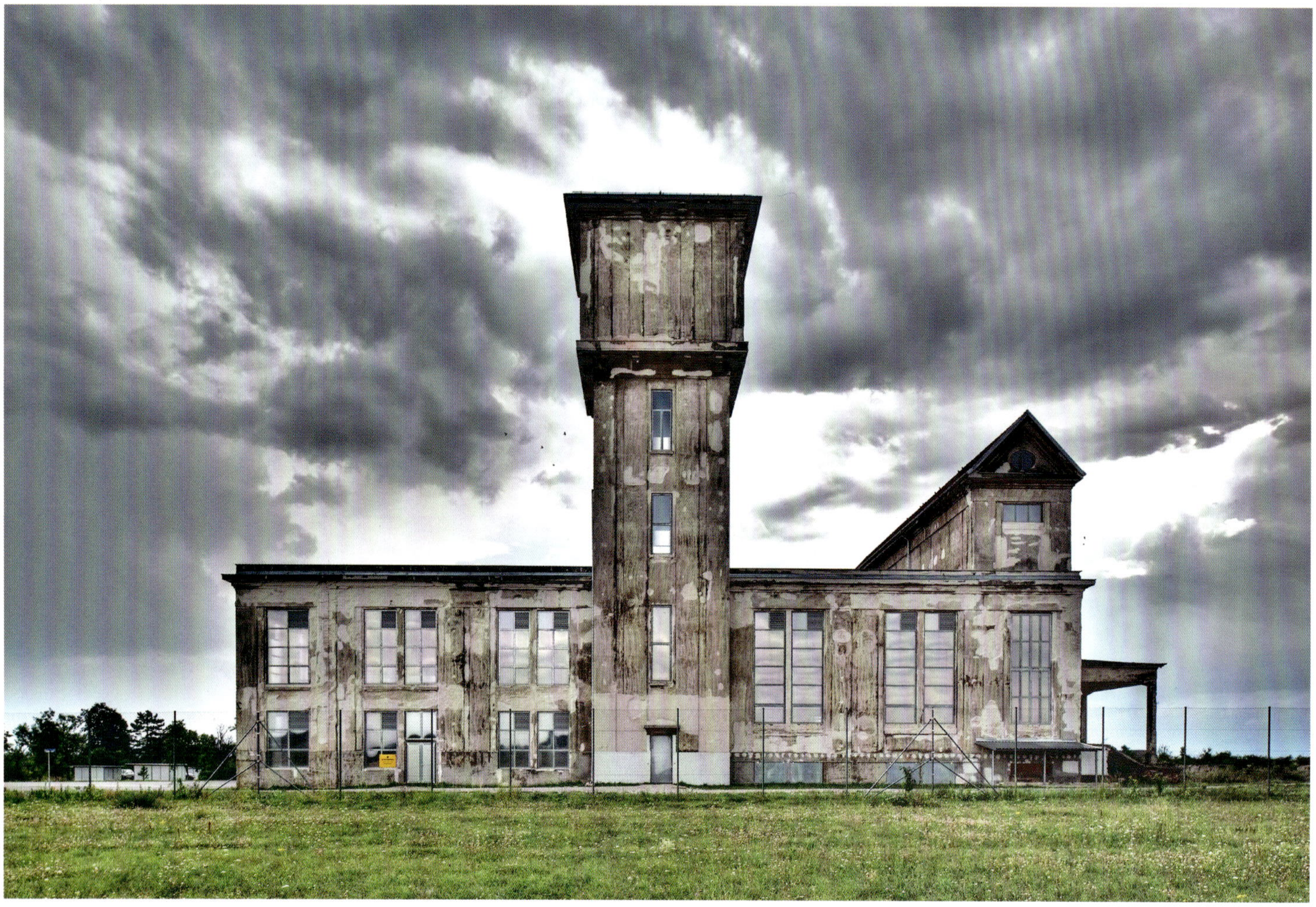

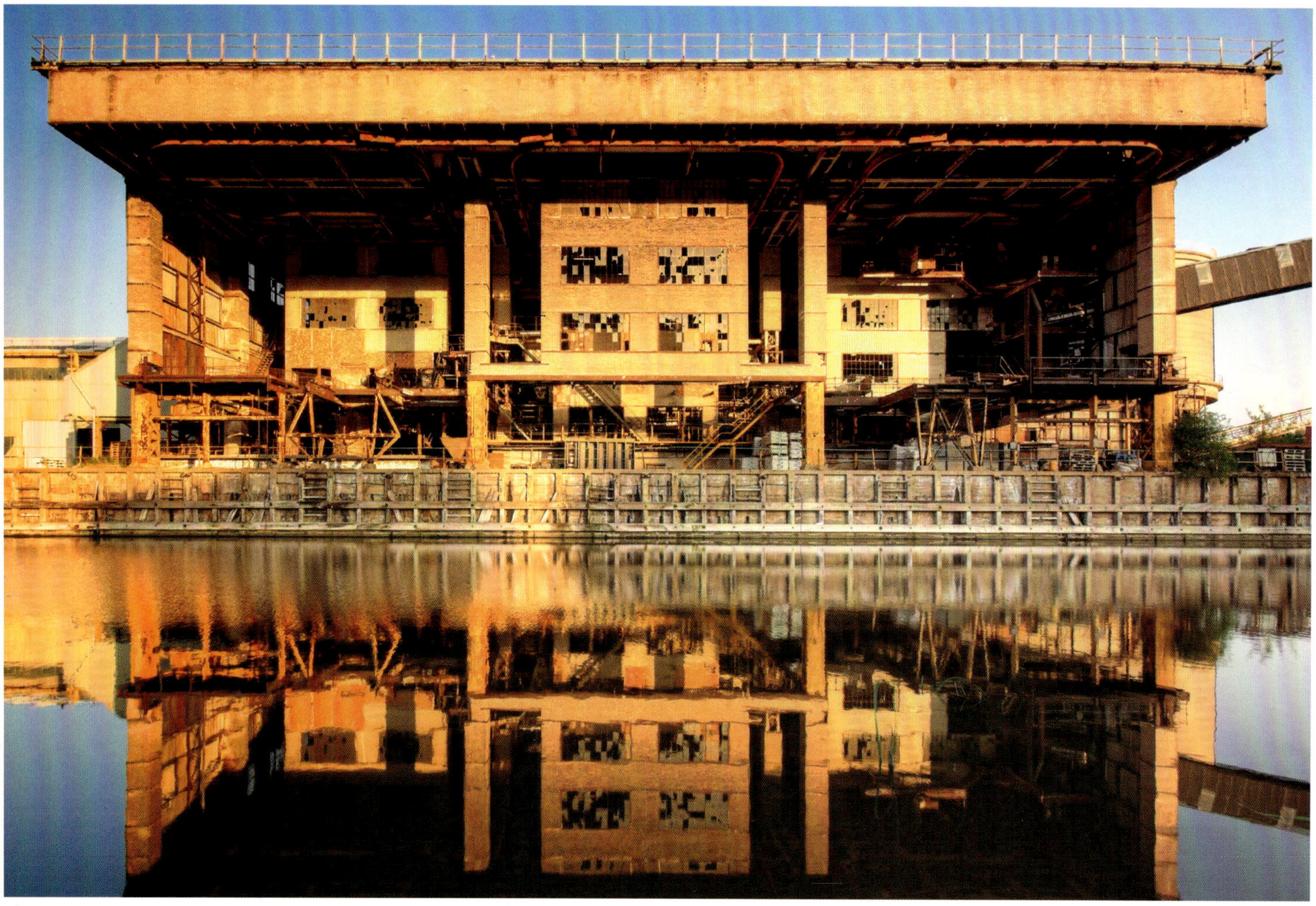

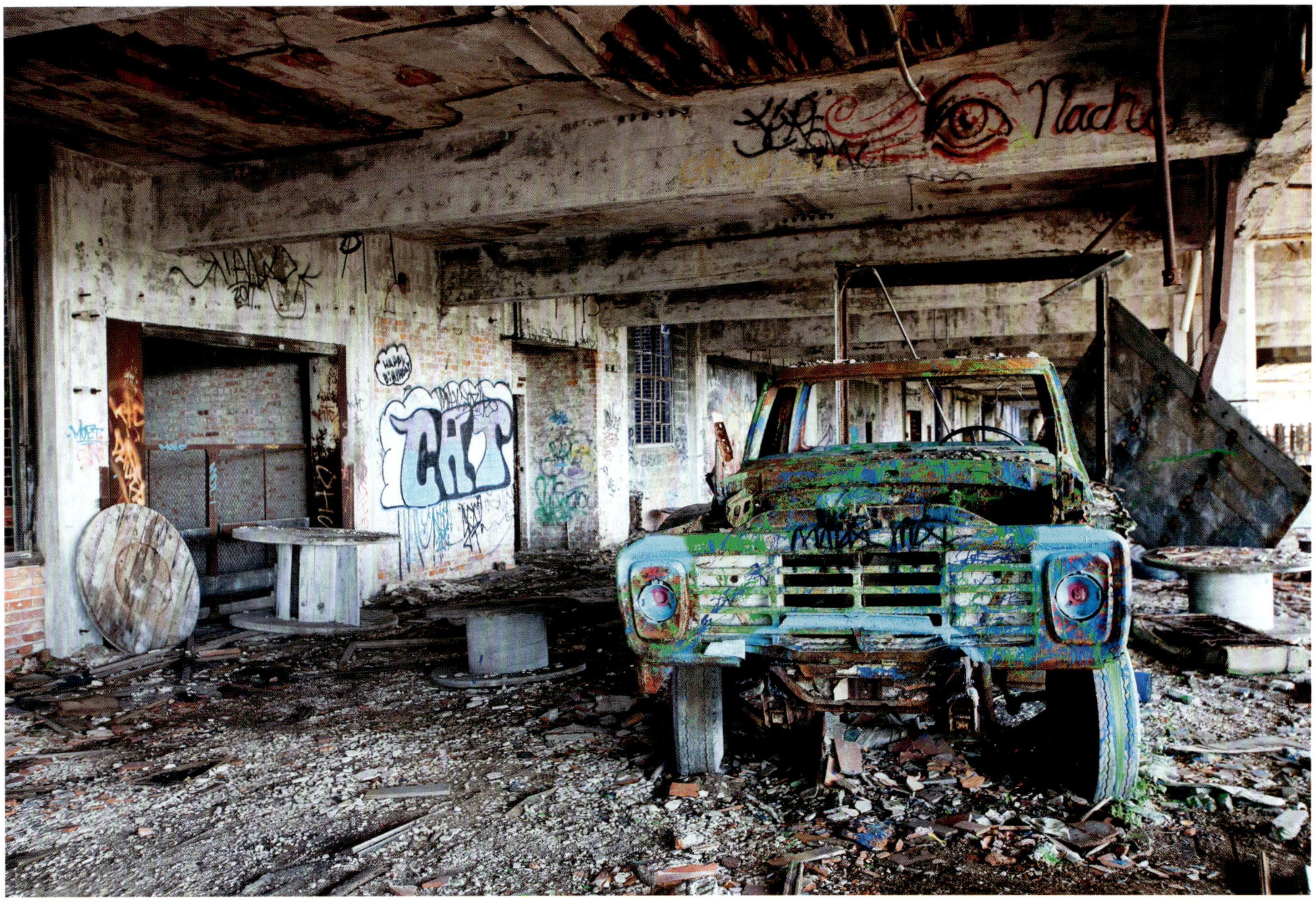
CAT

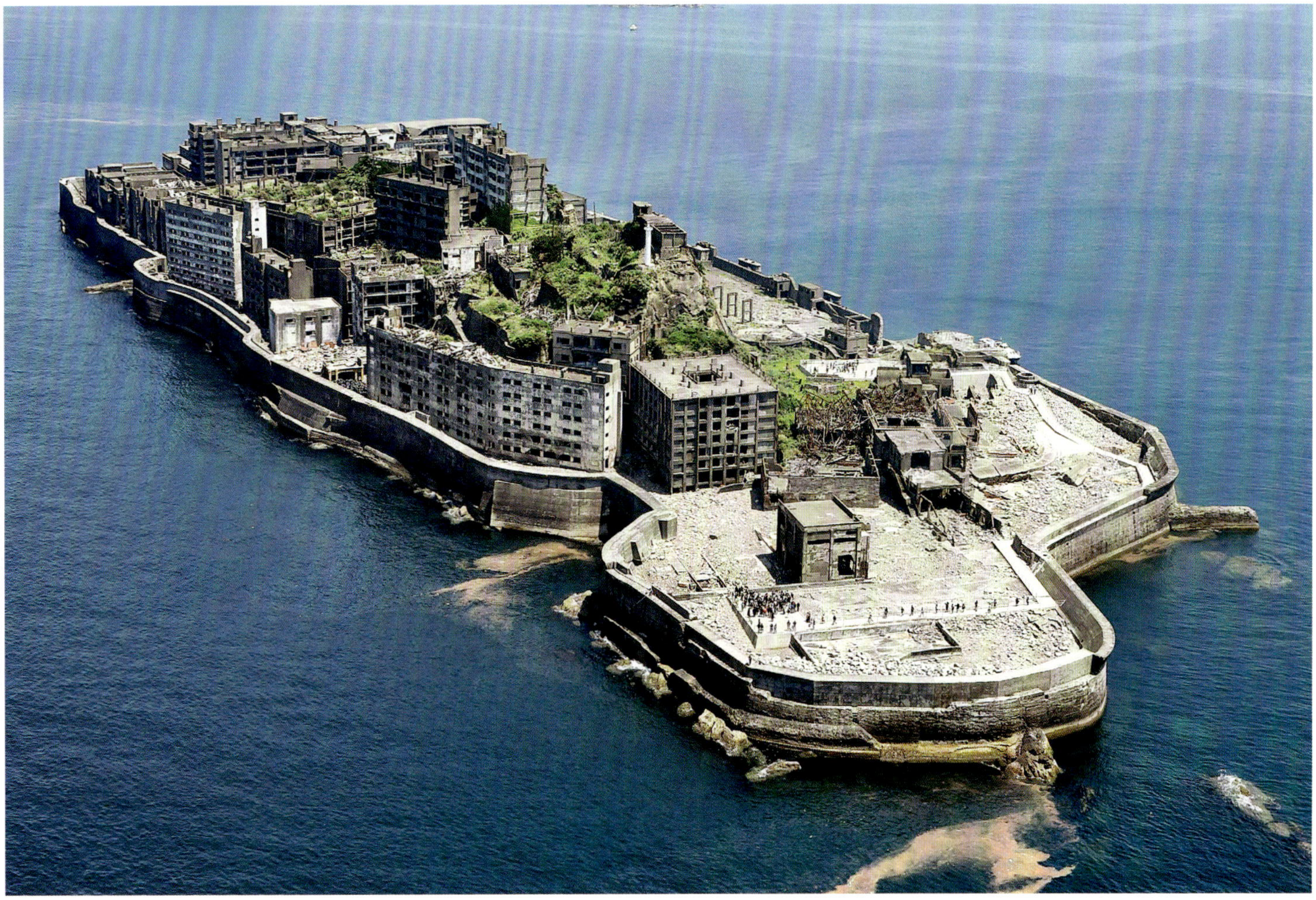

PREVIOUS PAGE:

TOP LEFT:
Tritol Munitions Factory, Eggendorf, Austria
The Tritol factory got its name from what it produced: the explosive TNT, or, to give its full name, trinitrotoluene. Built during World War I to provide munitions for Austro-Hungary, by 1993 it was no longer in use. Its dilapidated buildings were taken over by the Austrian Army, who use it as a military training ground.

BOTTOM LEFT:
Winnington, Northwich, Cheshire, England
Used in the production of glass, soda ash – also known as washing soda or sodium carbonate – was made on this site for more than 140 years. This photograph was taken in 2008; by 2014, the whole complex had closed down.

TOP RIGHT:
Packard Automotive Plant, Detroit, Michigan, USA
Something's lost, but something's gained: after the last tenants moved out in the 1990s, the urban explorers and graffiti artists gradually found their way in. The building may look a ruin, but it was built using the innovative Kahn System of reinforced concrete, and, more than a century after its construction, it remains structurally sound.

BOTTOM RIGHT:
Hashima, Japan
Hashima was used as the villain's base in the 2012 James Bond film *Skyfall*. Situated 9 miles (15km) off the coast from Nagasaki, the island was developed in 1887 as a mine to access undersea coal reserves. By 1959, more than 5,000 people were living and working there, but with coal supplies nearing depletion, the mine was closed in 1974, after which the residents soon left the island.

RIGHT:
Rotunda, Wola Gasworks, Warsaw, Poland
Opened in 1888, destroyed during World War II but rebuilt later, the Wola Gasworks finally closed in the early 1970s when the city switched to using natural gas supplies. Today, part of the gasworks is a museum, but other areas, such as the rotunda, remain dilapidated.

14

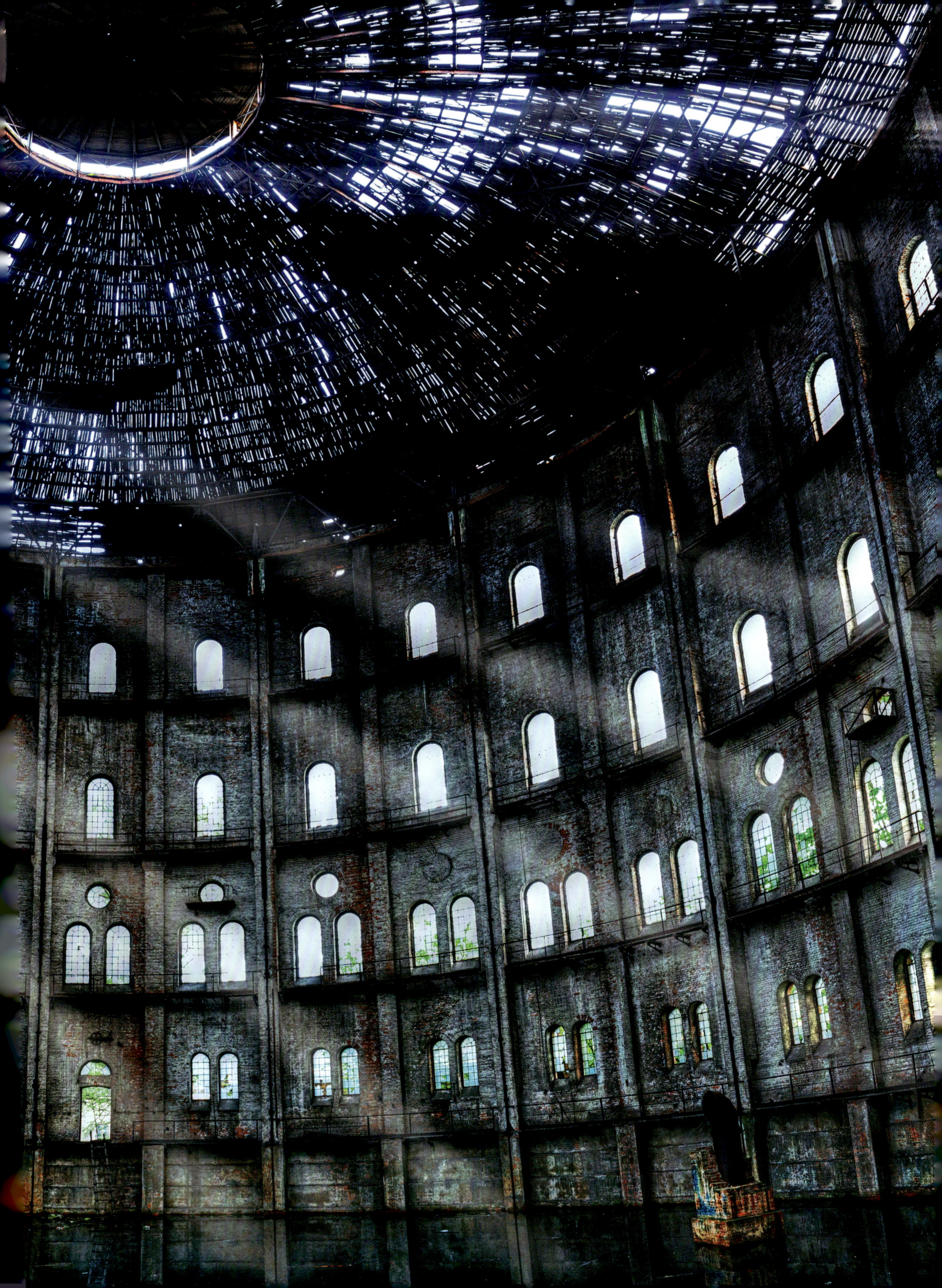

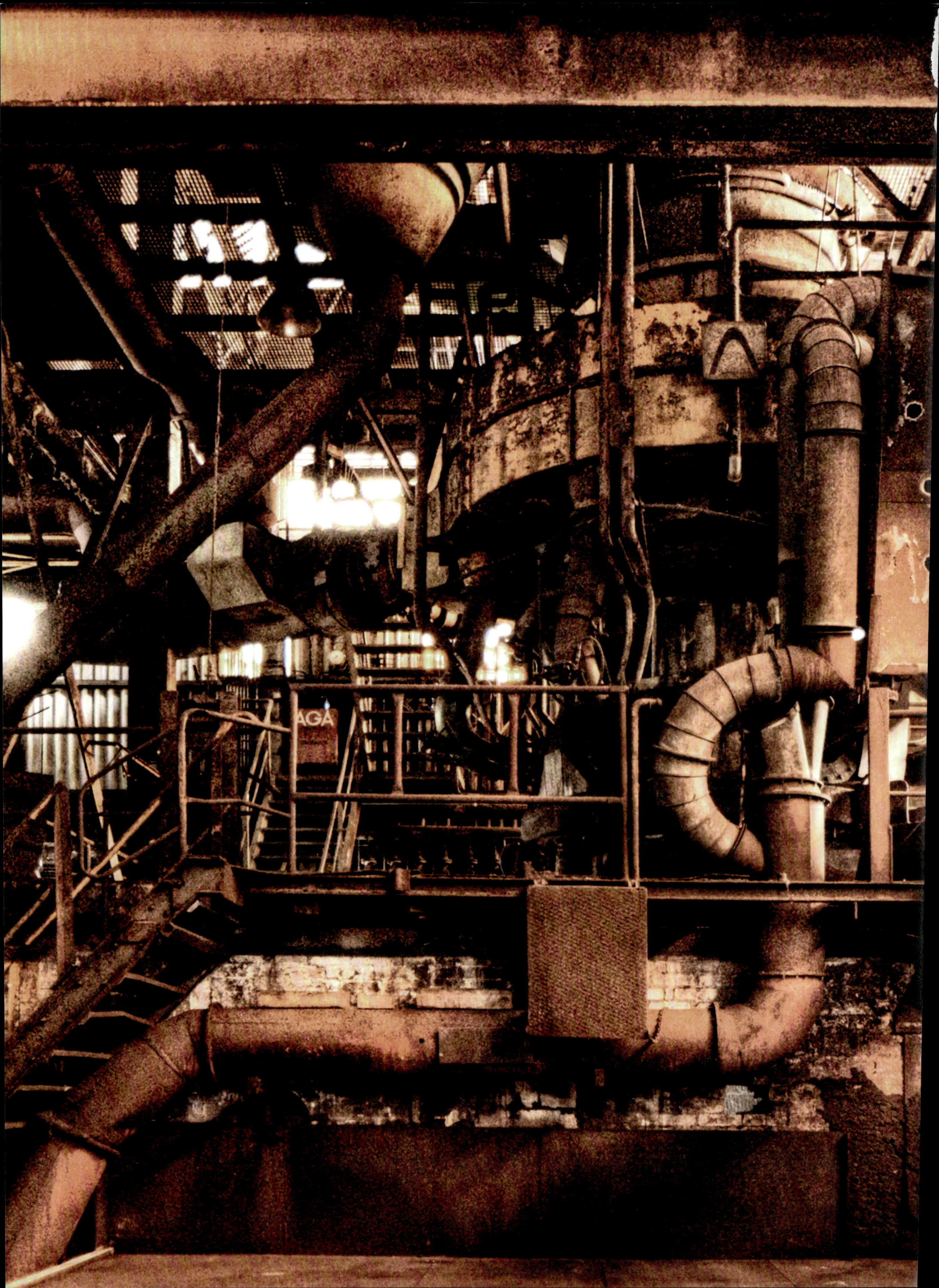
AGA

LEFT:
Carlshütte Foundry, Büdelsdorf, Schleswig-Holstein, Germany
Opened in 1827 and closed in 1997, the Carlshütte foundry was once the largest ironworks in northern Germany, producing, among other things, furnaces and cast-iron baths. Today the enormous foundry halls serve as an art gallery and arts centre, while the surrounding land is used as a sculpture park.

OVERLEAF:
TOP LEFT:
Washroom in factory, Laupheim, Baden-Württemberg, Germany
Photographed in 2011, the factory has now been demolished.

BOTTOM LEFT:
Control Room A, Battersea Power Station, London, England
A power station control room with an ornate art deco ceiling. Battersea Power Station is actually two power stations side by side, Battersea A and Battersea B. Work on Battersea A began in 1929 and was completed in 1935. It was in operation until 1975, when it closed due to falling productivity and rising operational costs.

TOP RIGHT:
Fisher Body Plant 21, Detroit, Michigan, USA
Fisher Body, an automobile coachbuilder founded in Detroit in 1908, provided the bodies for Ford, Buick, Cadillac and many other American cars. Opened in 1919, this factory was in operation until 1984, although production was suspended during the Great Depression. In World War II military aircraft were made here.

BOTTOM RIGHT:
Underground reservoir, London, England
Built in the 19th century to store drinking water for the city, such reservoirs are now empty and no longer used. But, untouched by human interference, their beautiful brickwork has been preserved.

DIRECT COUPLED EXCITER
STANDBY EXCITER
CARNABY STREET 2
MORETON STREET 2
CARNABY STREET 3
MORETON STREET 3
REACTOR 6
BUS COUPLER 6

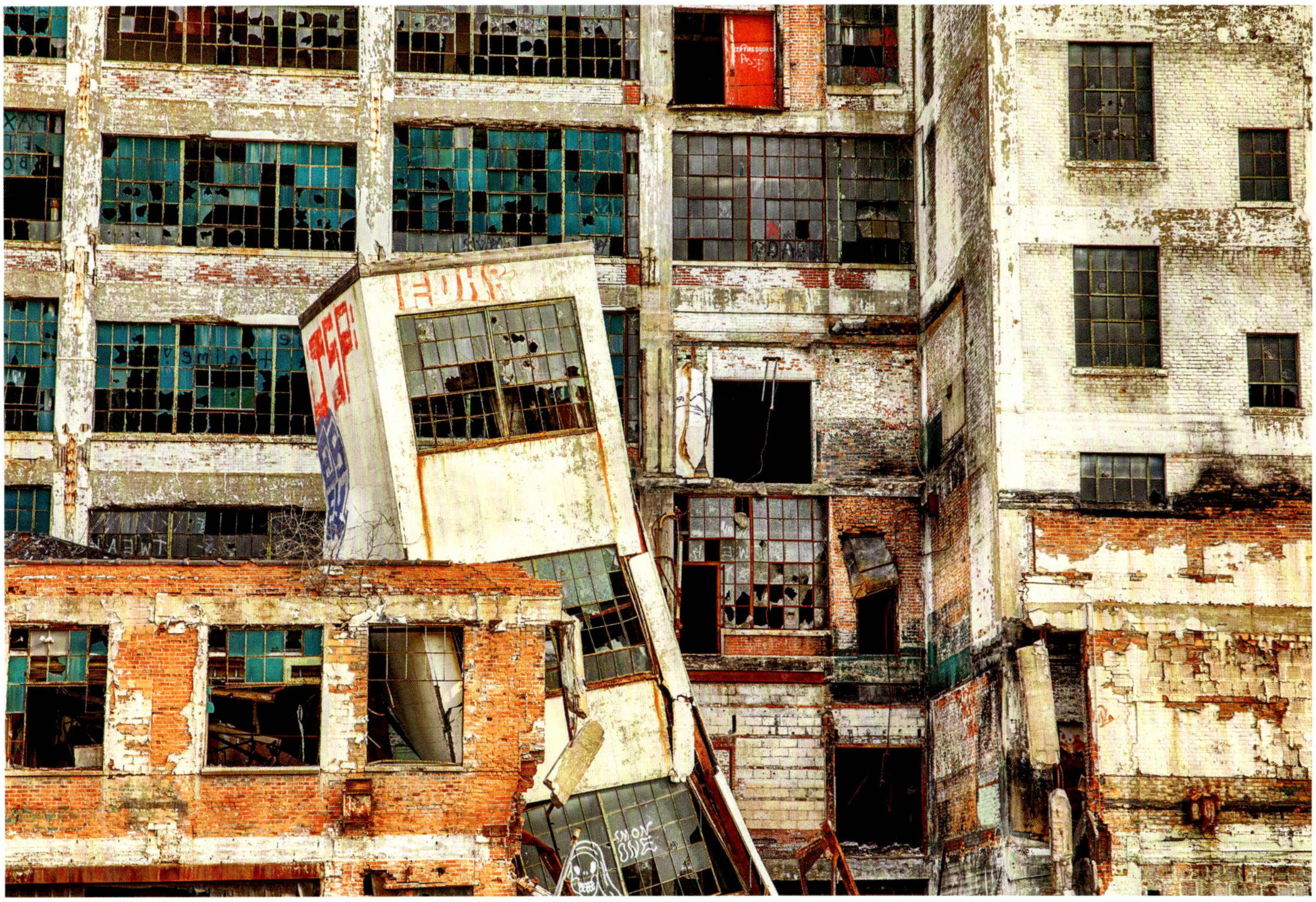

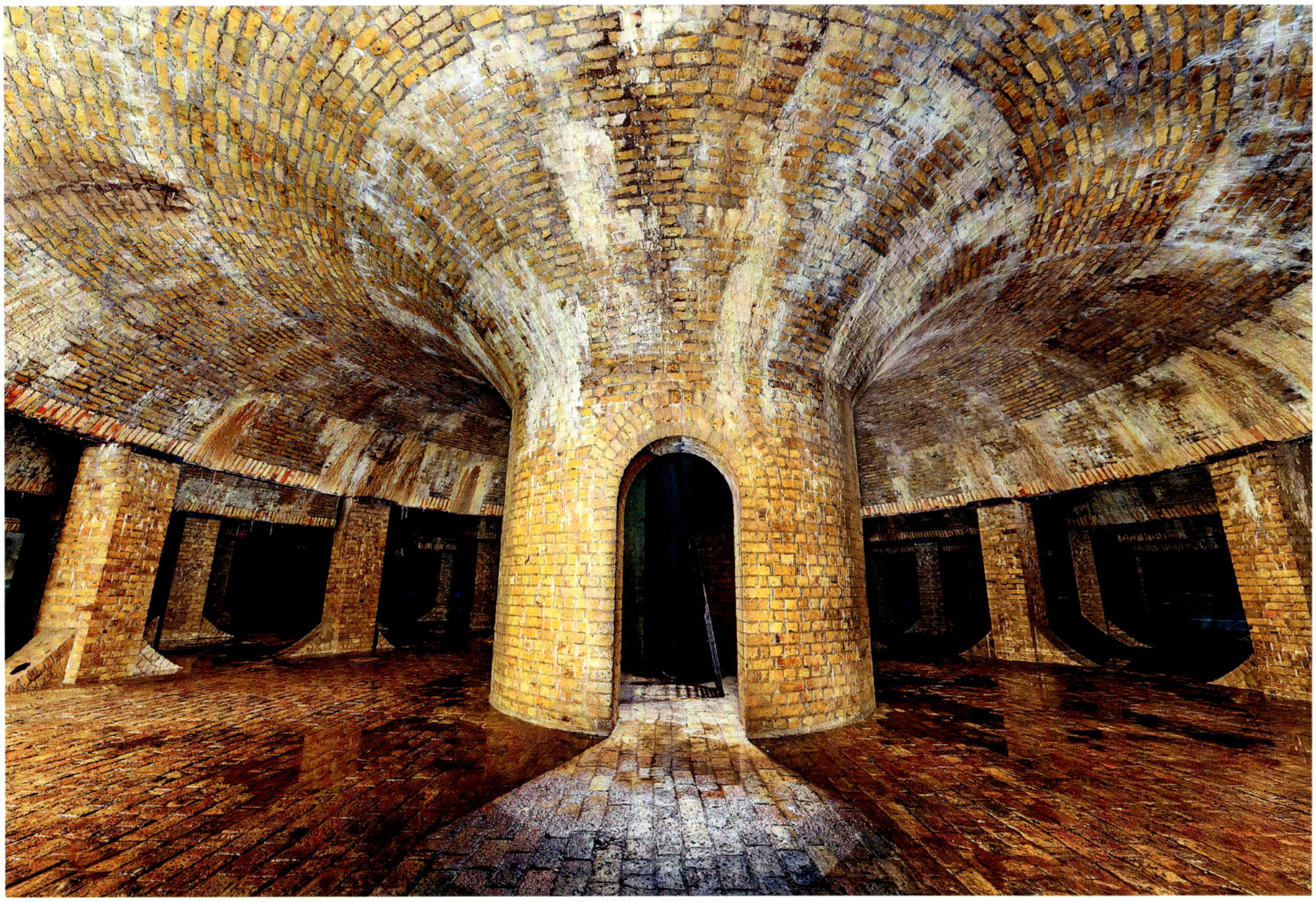

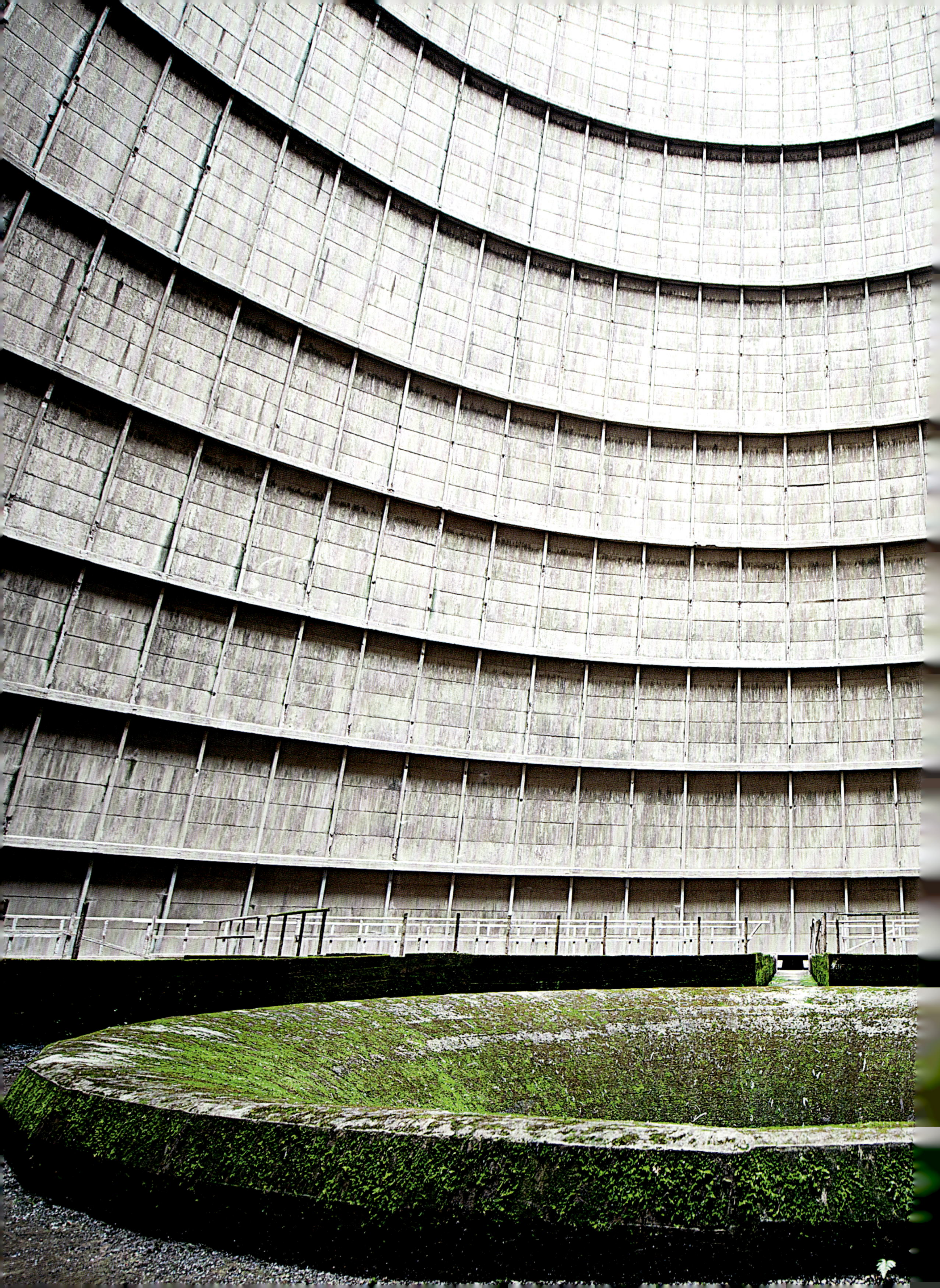

LEFT:

Cooling Tower, Charleroi, Belgium

When it was finished in 1921, the coal-fired power station at Charleroi was one of the largest in Belgium. In recent decades, however, a study revealed that it was responsible for 10 per cent of Belgium's carbon dioxide emissions, and it was closed in 2007.

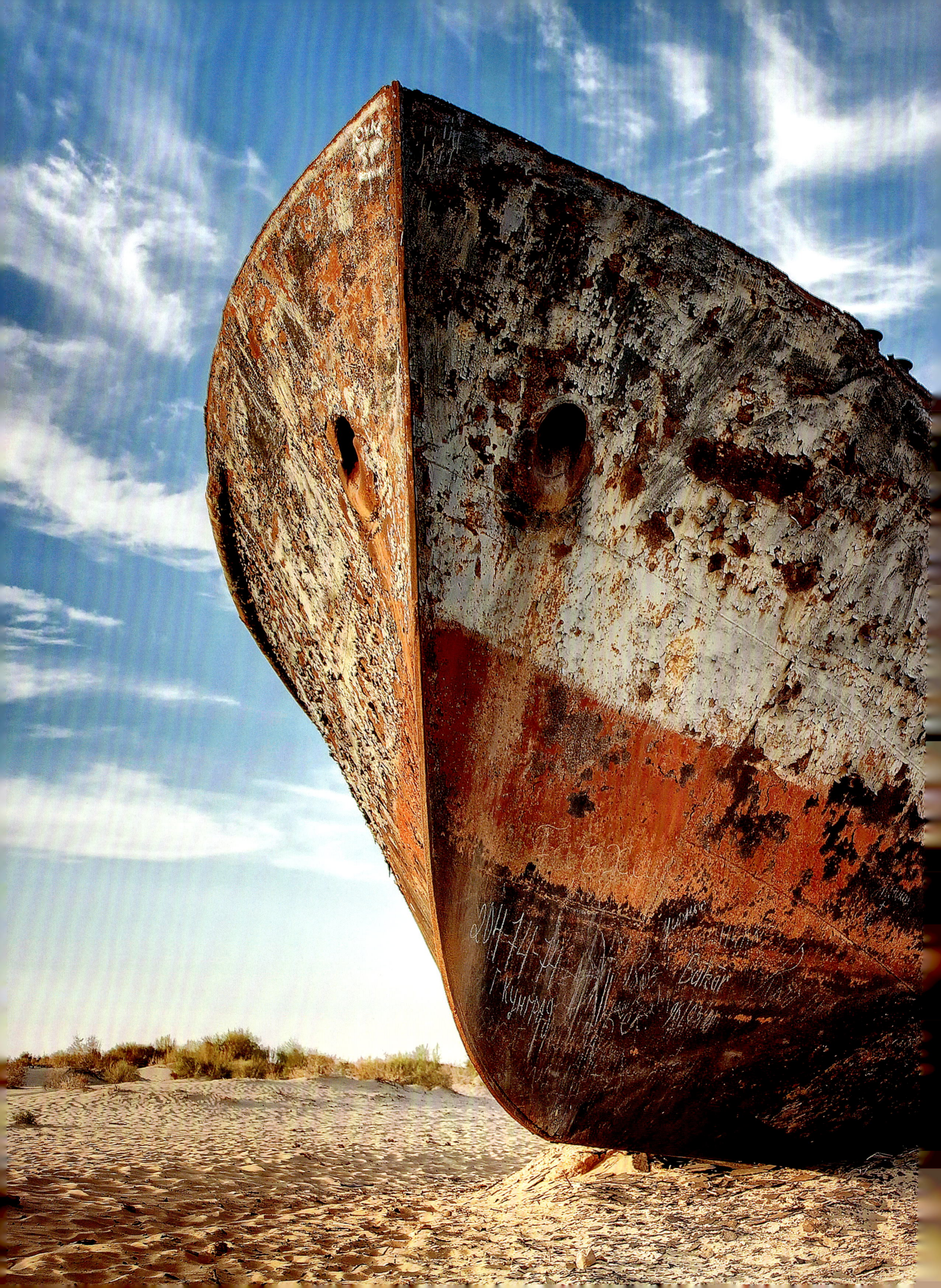

The Aral Sea, Kazakhstan and Uzbekistan
In an effort to bring more water to the cotton fields of the Uzbek desert in the 1960s, Soviet scientists embarked on a policy of diverting the rivers flowing into the Aral Sea, which, at the time, was the fourth-largest lake in the world. As a consequence, the Aral Sea is now one-tenth its former size, and rusting fishing boats and merchant ships are beached at inland ports miles from any water – with the water that does remain being too salty for animals or plant life. It's even saltier than the Dead Sea.

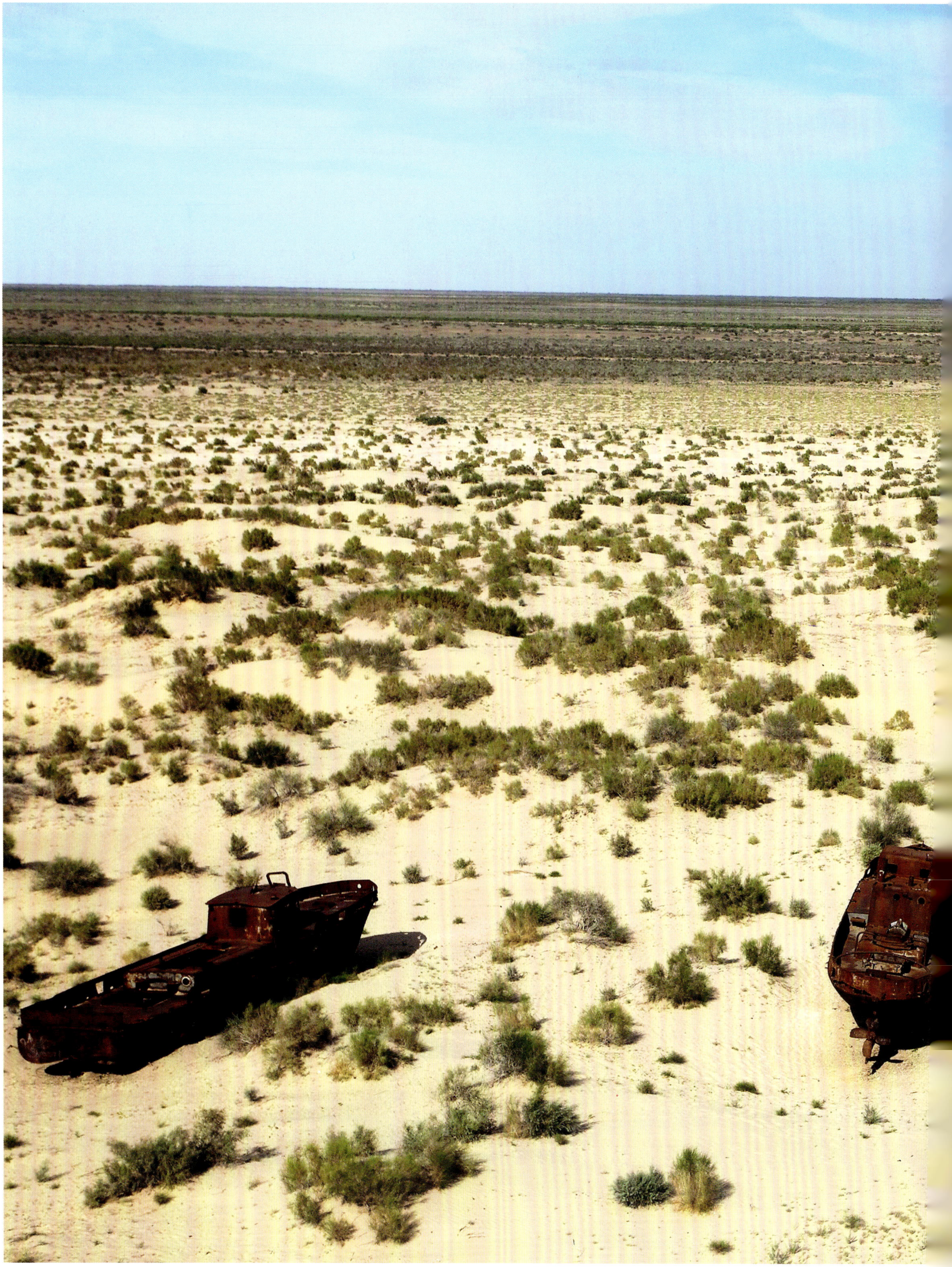

The Aral Sea, Kazakhstan and Uzbekistan
The drying up of the seabed has changed the local climate, with winters colder and summers hotter, while also releasing a dust of cancer-causing chemicals. In 2014, the sea's eastern basin, once deep underwater, was named the Aralkum Desert.

Santa Laura and Humberstone, Atacama Desert, Chile
Although the Atacama Desert is the driest non-polar place in the world, in 1872 work began at Santa Laura and neighbouring La Palma (later renamed Humberstone) to extract saltpetre for use in fertilizers. Quickly towns developed around the works until in 1960 COSATAN, the parent company, collapsed and they were abandoned. In 2005, the ghost towns were declared UNESCO World Heritage Sites.

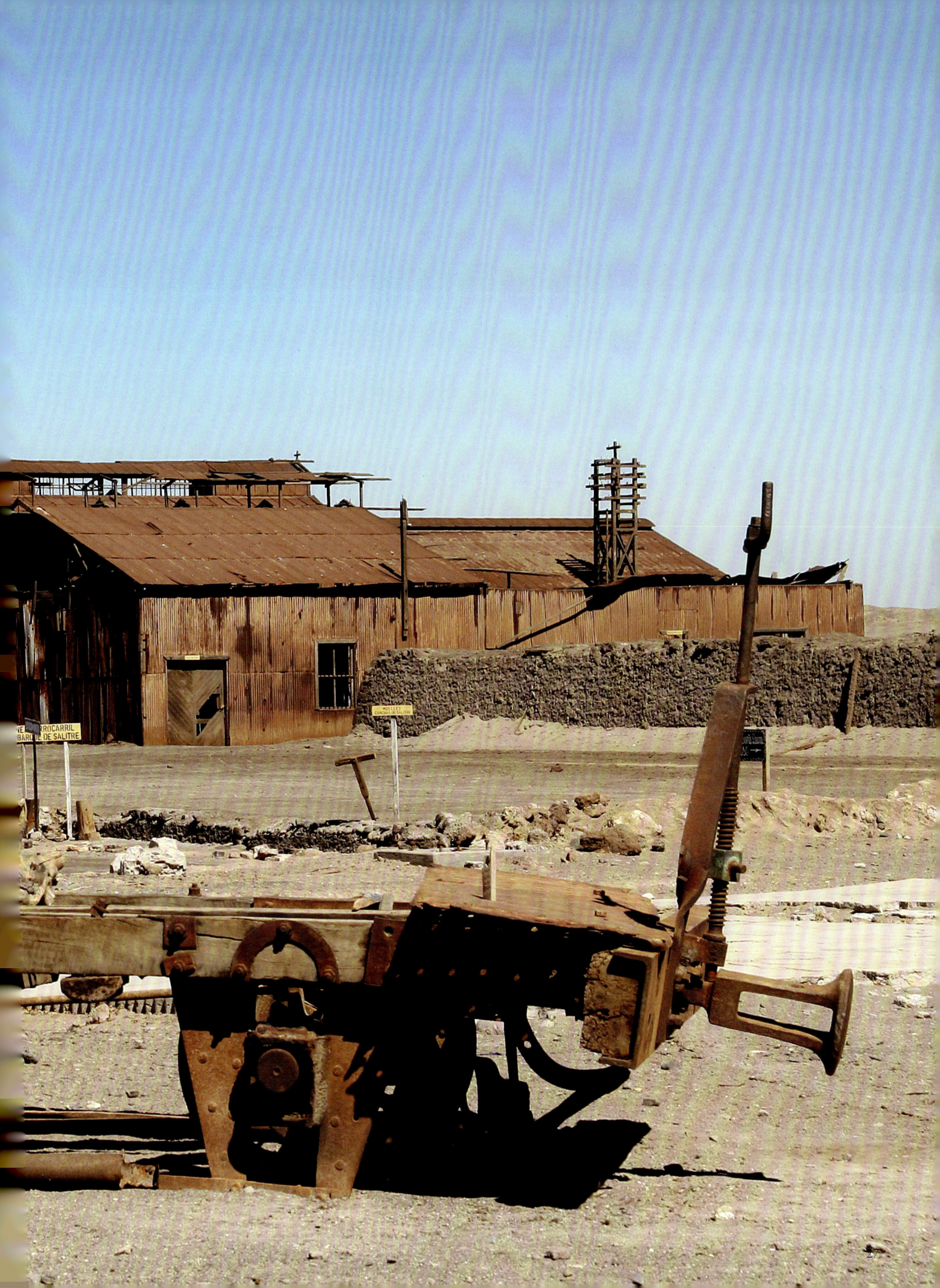
DE SALITRE

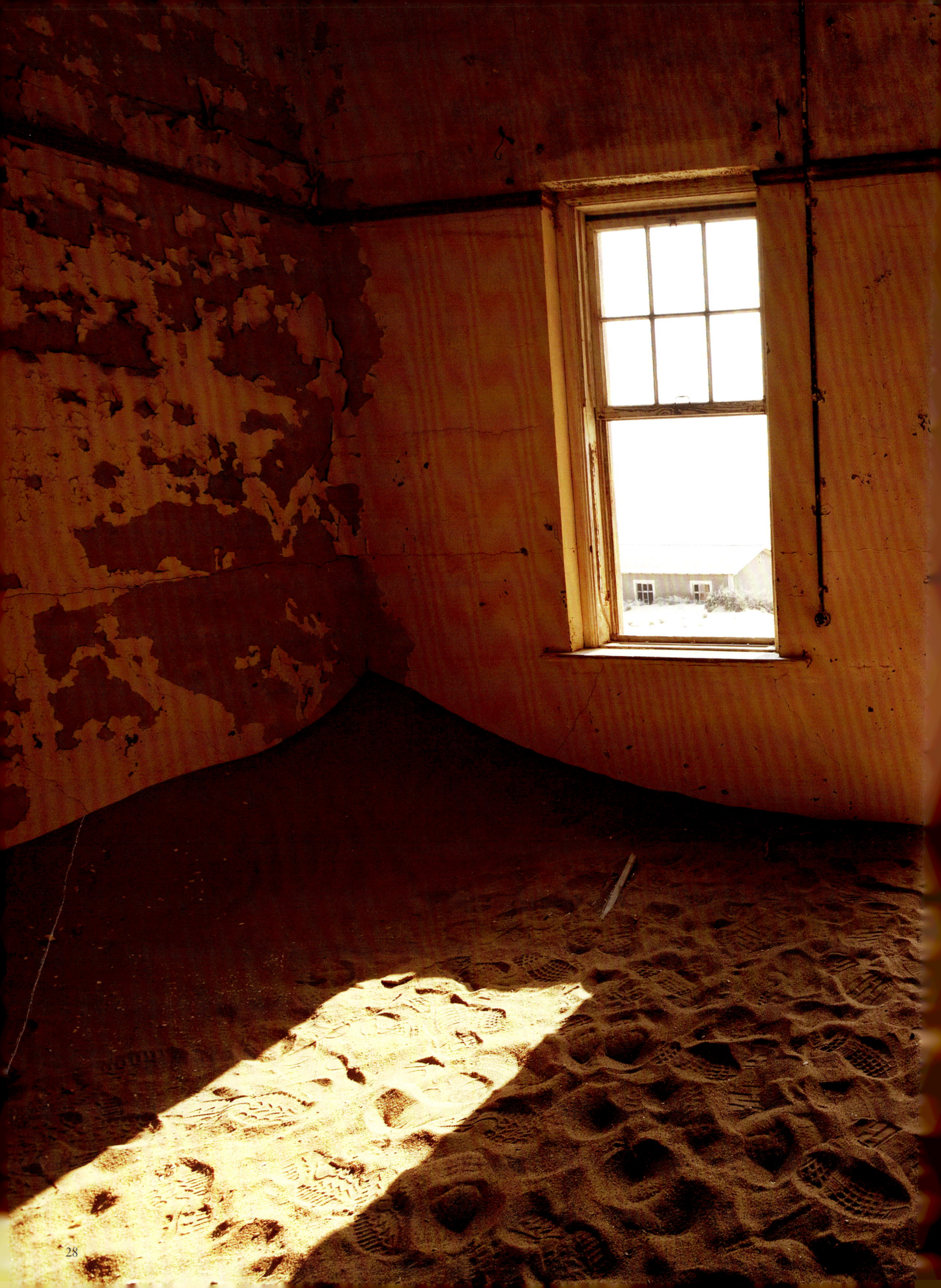

Kolmanskop, Namibia
Where was the first X-ray station in the southern hemisphere? Or the first tram in Africa? The answer: in the town of Kolmanskop in the Namib Desert. Located 6 miles (10km) from the then German colonial port of Lüderitz, Kolmanskop sprang up after diamonds were discovered there in 1908. The settlers soon built a German-style town, complete with theatre, casino and ice factory, but after World War I the diamond field gradually became exhausted. The town was finally abandoned in 1954.

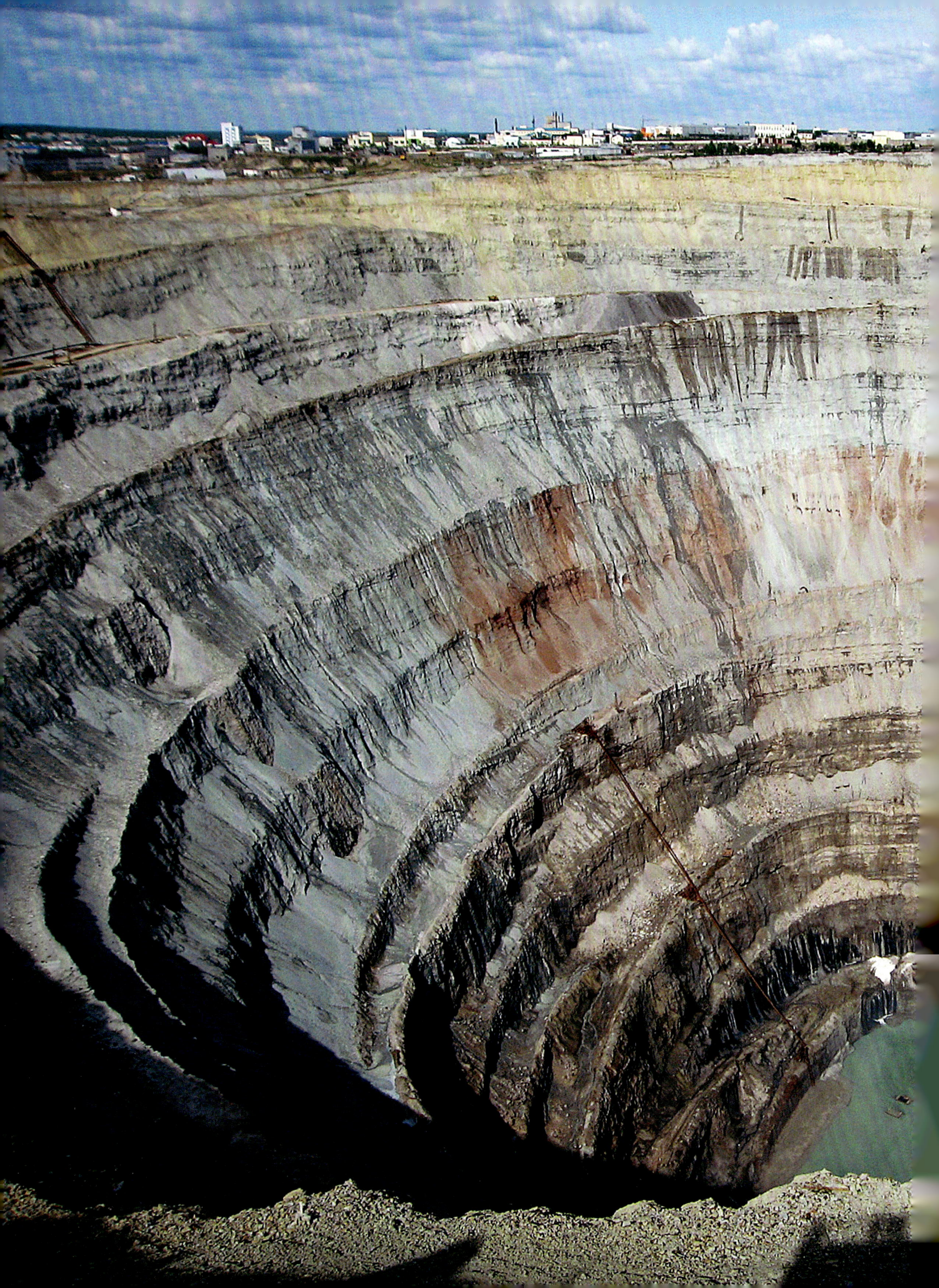

LEFT:
Mirny Diamond Mine, Eastern Siberia, Russia
The second largest excavated hole in the world (after the Bingham Canyon Mine in Utah), the Mirny opencast mine is 525m (1,722ft) deep and has a diameter of 1,200m (3,900ft). With the ground frozen for seven months of the year, construction of the mine and the town for its workers was difficult: car tyres would burst, oil would freeze and jet engines were needed to thaw the permafrost. Opened in 1957, the opencast mine closed in 2004 due to declining yields and safety concerns. Underground mining, however, continues at Mirny.

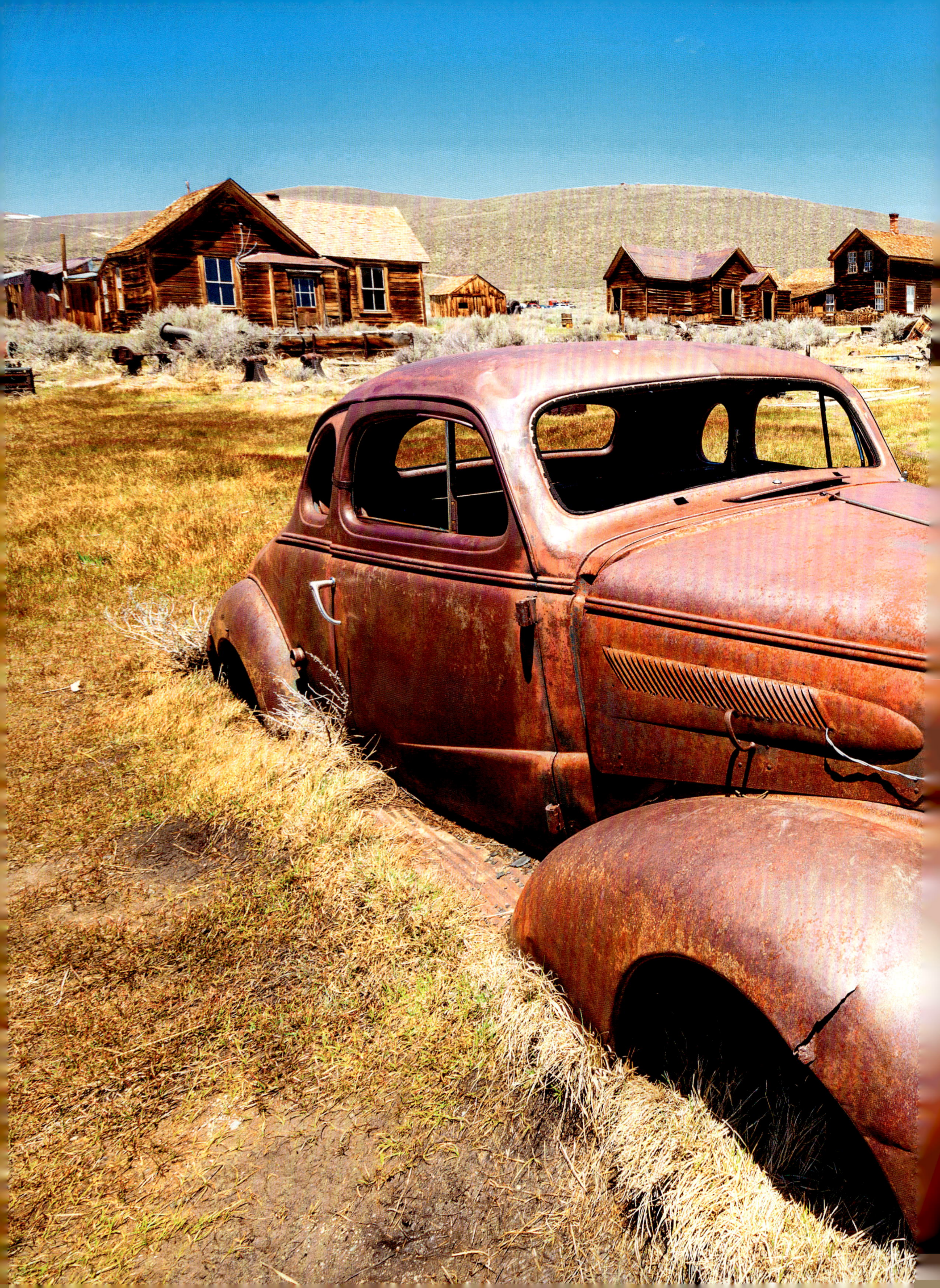

Bodie, Mono County, California, USA
After the California Gold Rush of 1848–55 had peaked, gold was discovered by a group of prospectors at Bodie, just east of the Sierra Nevada, in 1859. Initial expectations were, however, at first unfulfilled, with at least two businesses failing, before in 1876 a richer deposit of gold-bearing ore was found.

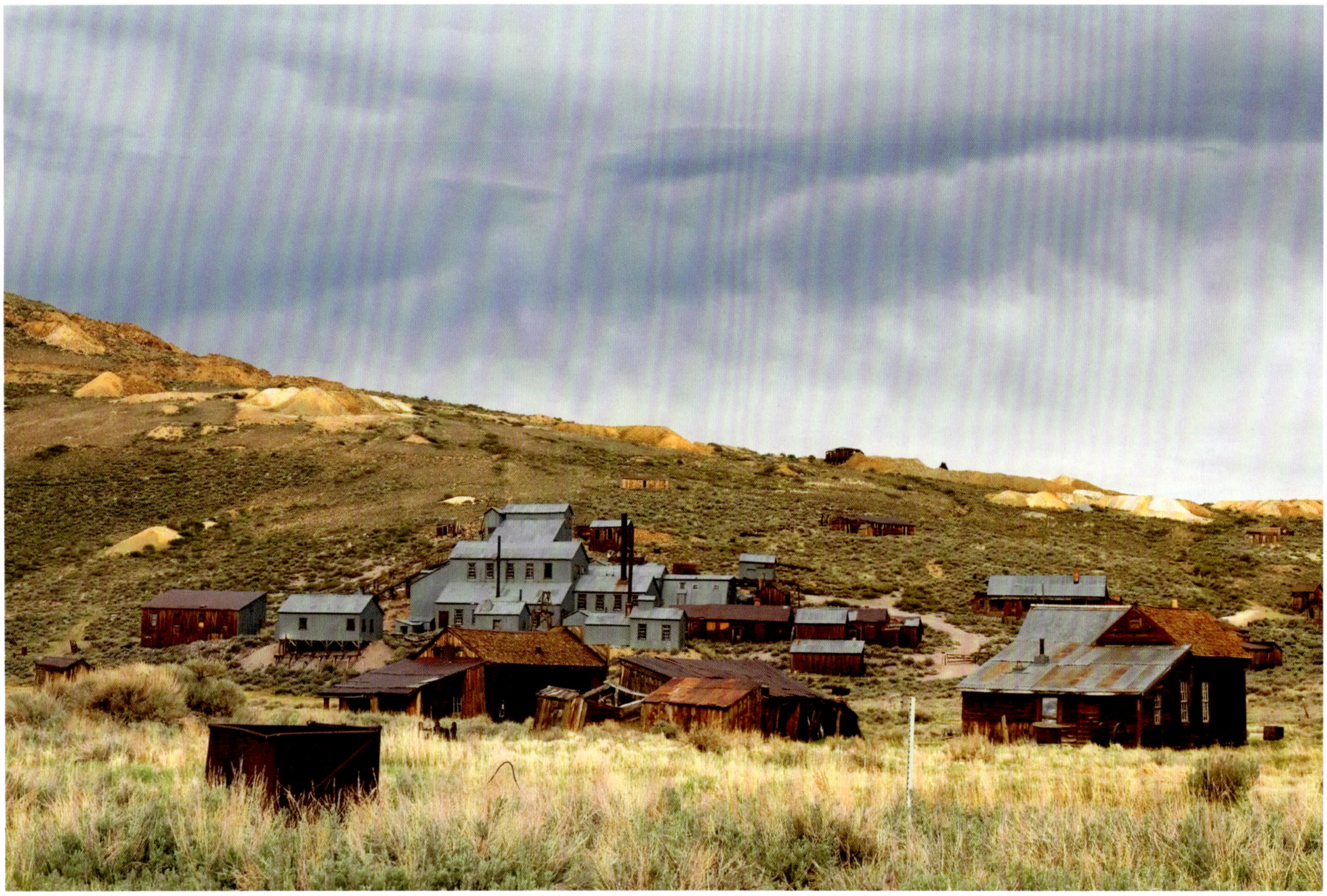

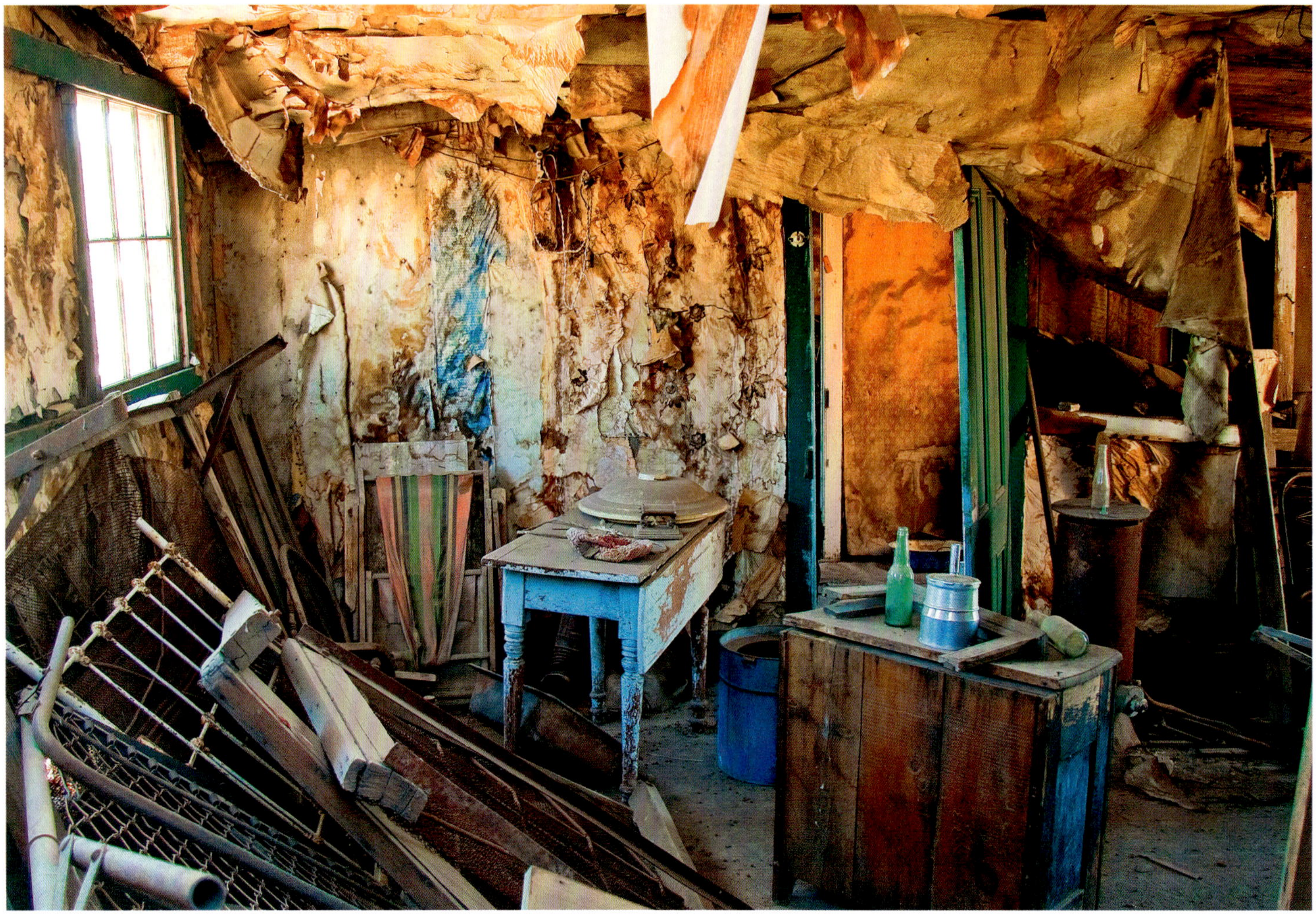

ALL PHOTOGRAPHS:
Bodie, Mono County, California, USA
Quickly Bodie went from mining camp to boomtown, and, by 1879, it had 2,000 buildings housing between 5,000 and 7,000 people, with a bank, a railway and several daily newspapers.

The following year, however, word spread of new boomtowns in Tombstone, Arizona, and Butte, Montana, and Bodie's decline began. With single men being the quickest to move, the population fell to around 2,700, leaving mainly families behind to attend the newly built Roman Catholic and Methodist churches in the town – and, for the sizeable Chinese community, a Taoist temple. With mining profits falling, the Standard Consolidated Mine closed in 1913, and four years later the Bodie Railway was abandoned. By 1940 the population was down to 40. The last mine closed in 1942, following a war order that all non-essential gold mines in the United States be shut down. Designated a National Historic Landmark in 1961, today Bodie is maintained in a state of arrested decay as a visitor attraction.

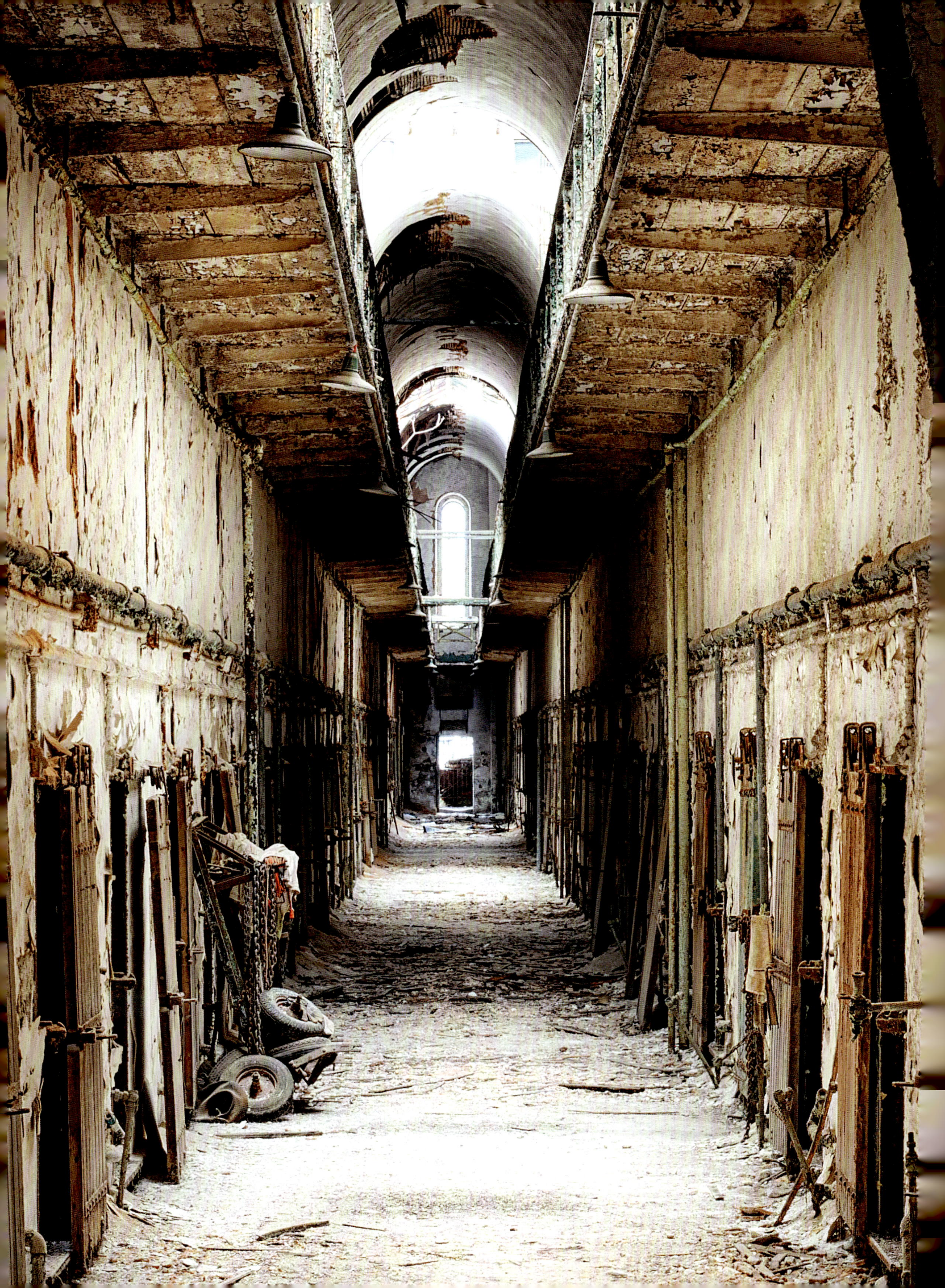

Public Buildings

High in the Cambodian jungle at the Bokor Hill Station stands the Bokor Palace Hotel. Built by settlers to escape the heat of the capital Phnom Penh, it is a relic of the French colonial era. The settlers are now long gone, having left after Cambodia gained independence in 1953, but the grand Bokor Palace has remained to witness the changing tides of history. By the 1970s, the Khmer Rouge had taken it over, but, later, when they'd fallen from power, the Palace's remote location served them as one of their final strongholds. Like many of the public buildings included here – whether a Communist monument in Bulgaria, a Protestant church in Poland or a palace in Afghanistan – the Bokor Palace would have originally reflected the society that made it. But, almost a century later, its story is much more than that. It is the story of all the history that has happened around it. If only walls could talk…

Similarly, in the isolated smallpox hospitals, imposing prisons and neo-Gothic mental asylums in these pages, we can understand a little of how theories towards health and punishment have developed from the 19th century to the present day.

In all, whether hotels or hospitals, through these buildings we see the passage of history.

LEFT:
Eastern State Penitentiary, Philadelphia, Pennsylvania, USA
When it was built in 1829, the Eastern State Penitentiary was the largest and most expensive public structure ever erected. With a radial floor plan and a cell for each inmate, it is considered the world's first true penitentiary – a place where prisoners would reflect in solitary on their crimes and, it was hoped, come to show penance. Its design quickly became a model for more than 300 prisons worldwide. It closed in 1971.

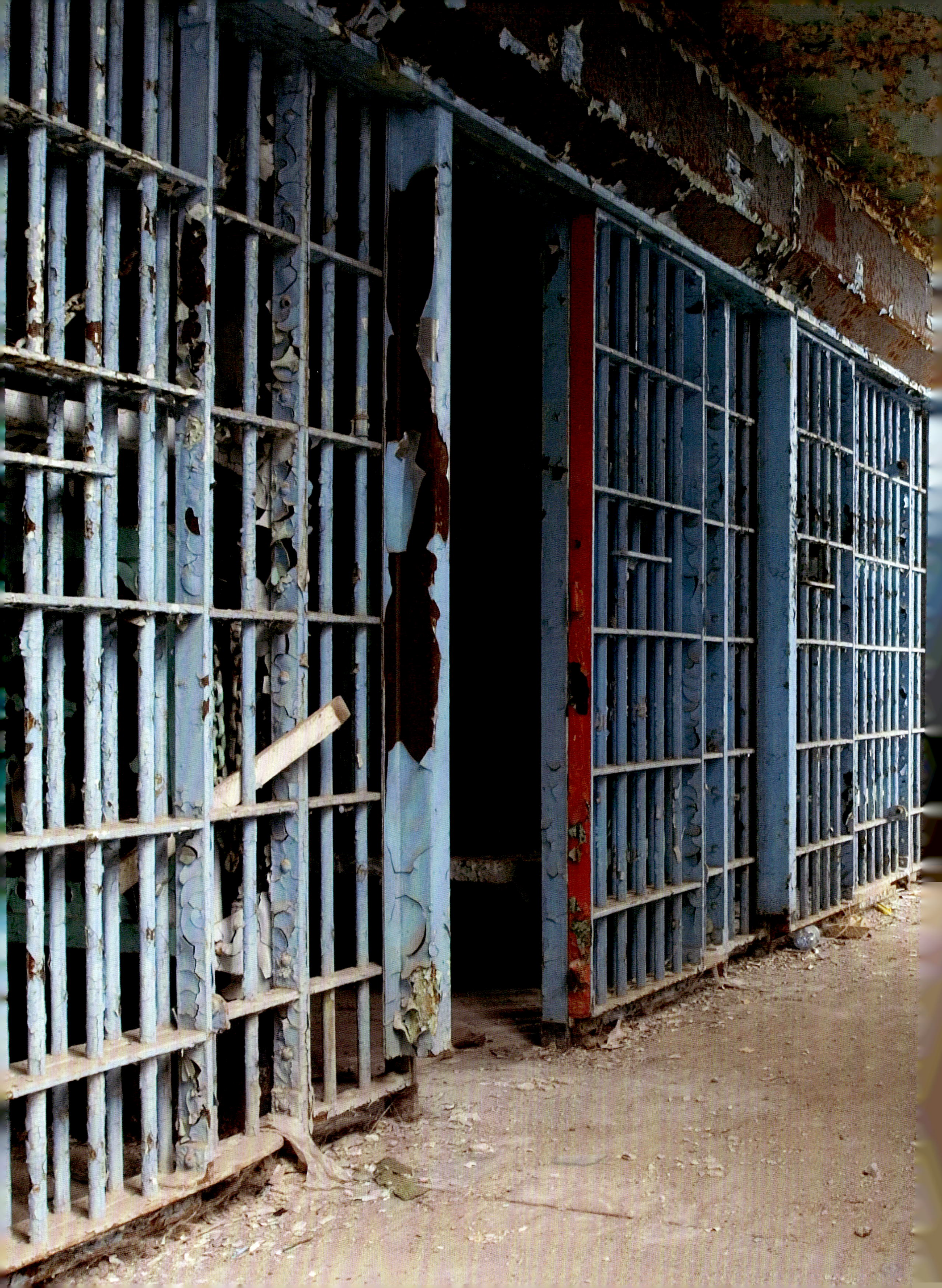

LEFT:

Nebraska Reformatory, Lincoln, Nebraska, USA
The state reformatory for young offenders was opened in 1921 and closed in 1979. Inmates, aged 16–30, would do farming work and gardening, as well as making car number plates and road signs. Photographed in 2008, the unsound building has since been torn down.

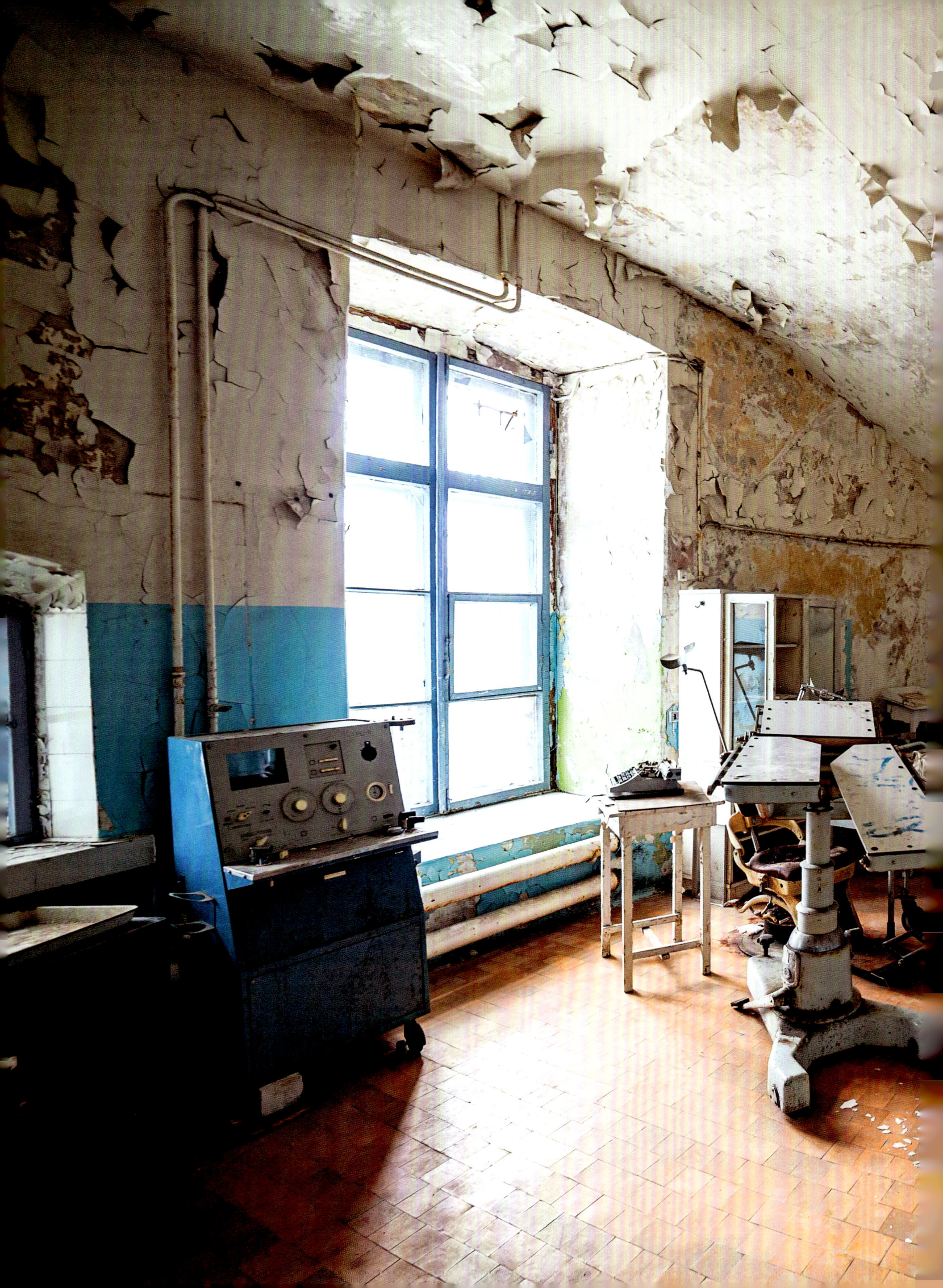

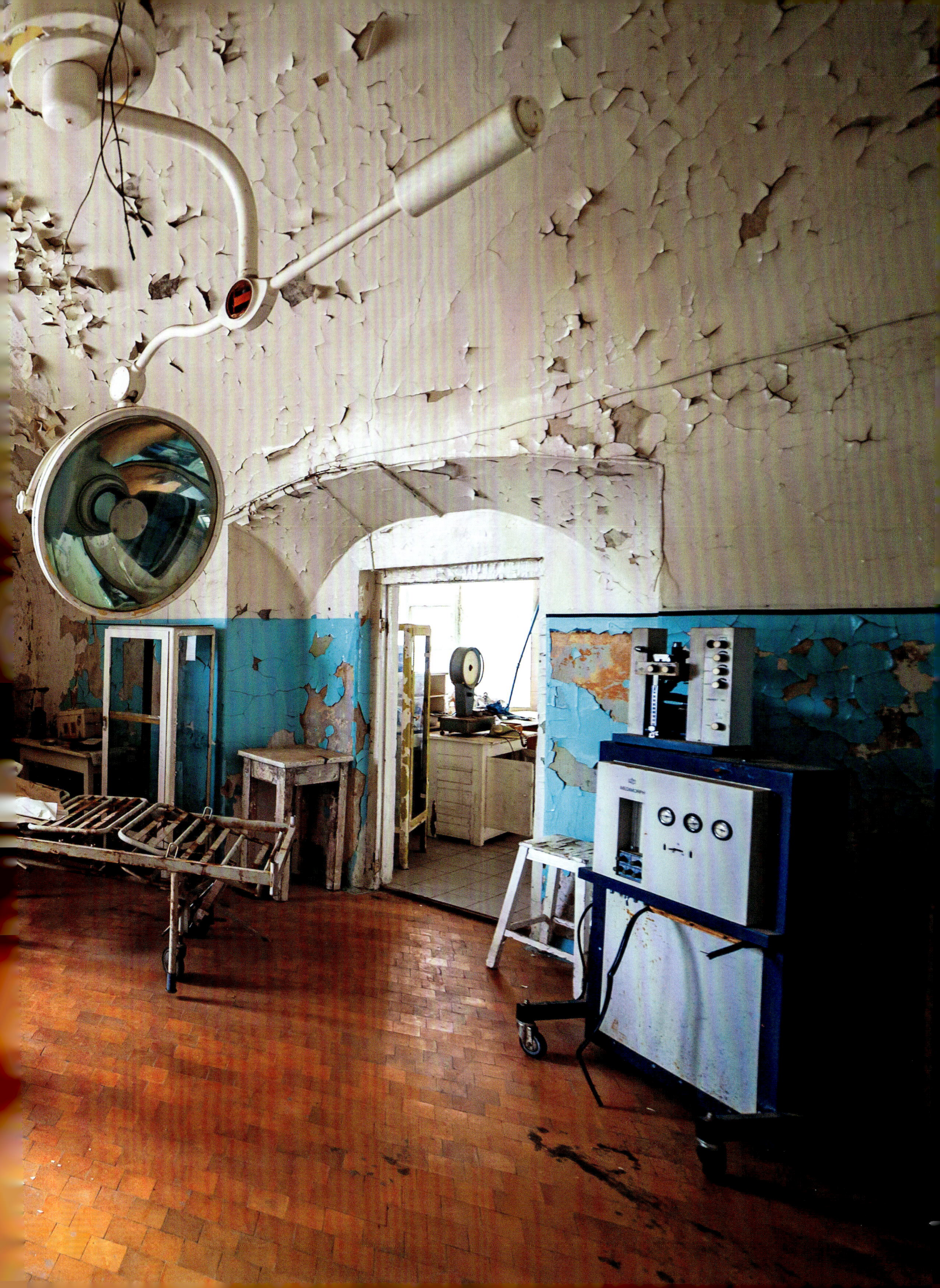

PREVIOUS PAGE:
Operating room, Patarei Prison, Tallinn, Estonia
Originally built as a sea fortress in 1840, Patarei Prison housed inmates from 1919 until 2004. During the Soviet era it was also used for KGB interrogations. Now open to the public, the cells, bunk beds and prisoners' books and magazines remain as they were left when the building was closed.

RIGHT:
Beelitz-Heilstätten Hospital, Brandenburg, Germany
Near Potsdam and not far from Berlin, Beelitz-Heilstätten was used as a military hospital during World War I. After World War II it served Soviet troops based in East Germany, many of its wings being abandoned after the Russian army left in 1994.

OVERLEAF:
Beelitz-Heilstätten Hospital, Brandenburg, Germany
Adolf Hitler was a patient here after being wounded in the leg at the Battle of the Somme during World War I. Three-quarters of a century later another patient, Erich Honecker, was admitted in December 1990, weeks after he'd been forced to resign as the head of the East German government.

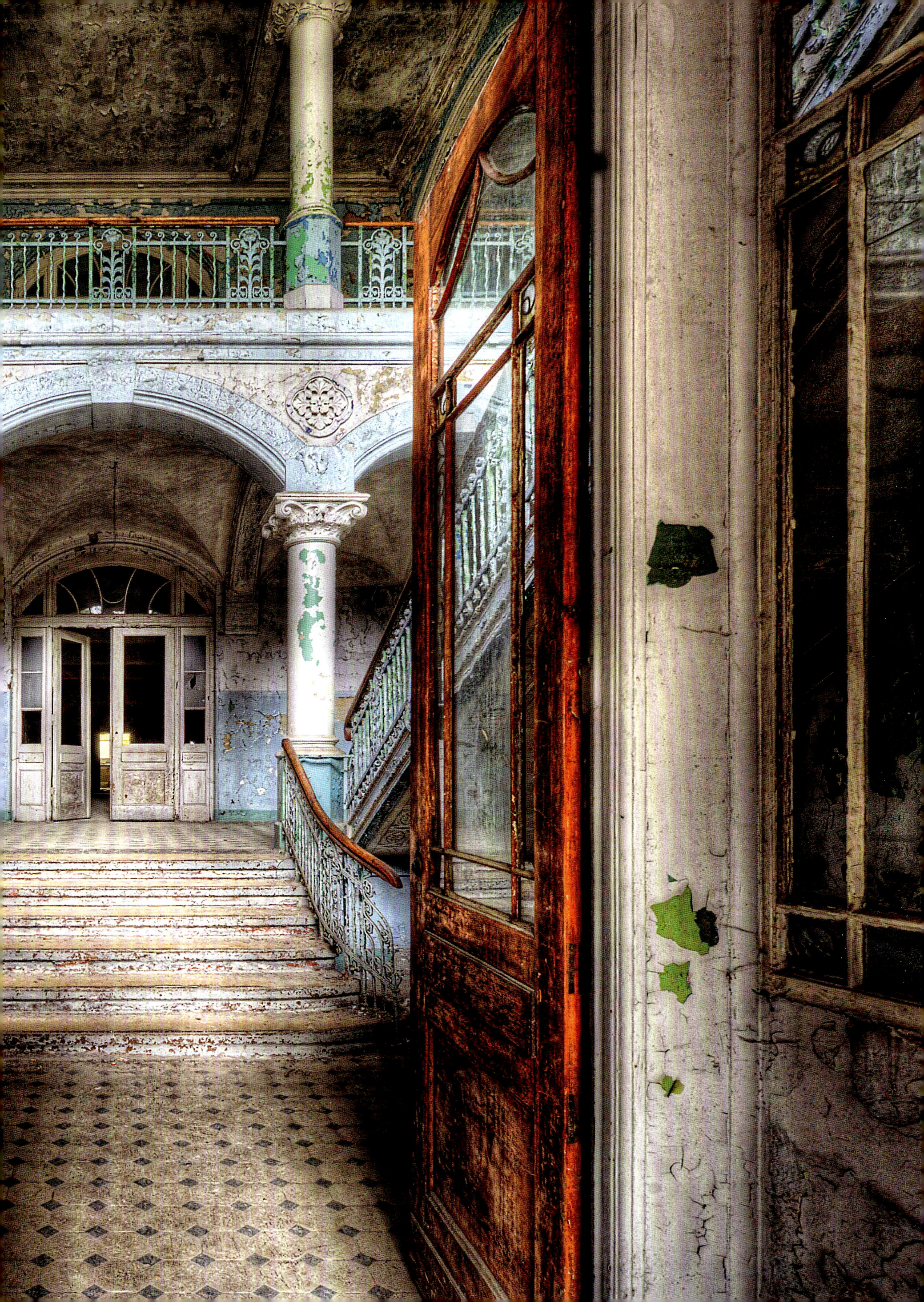

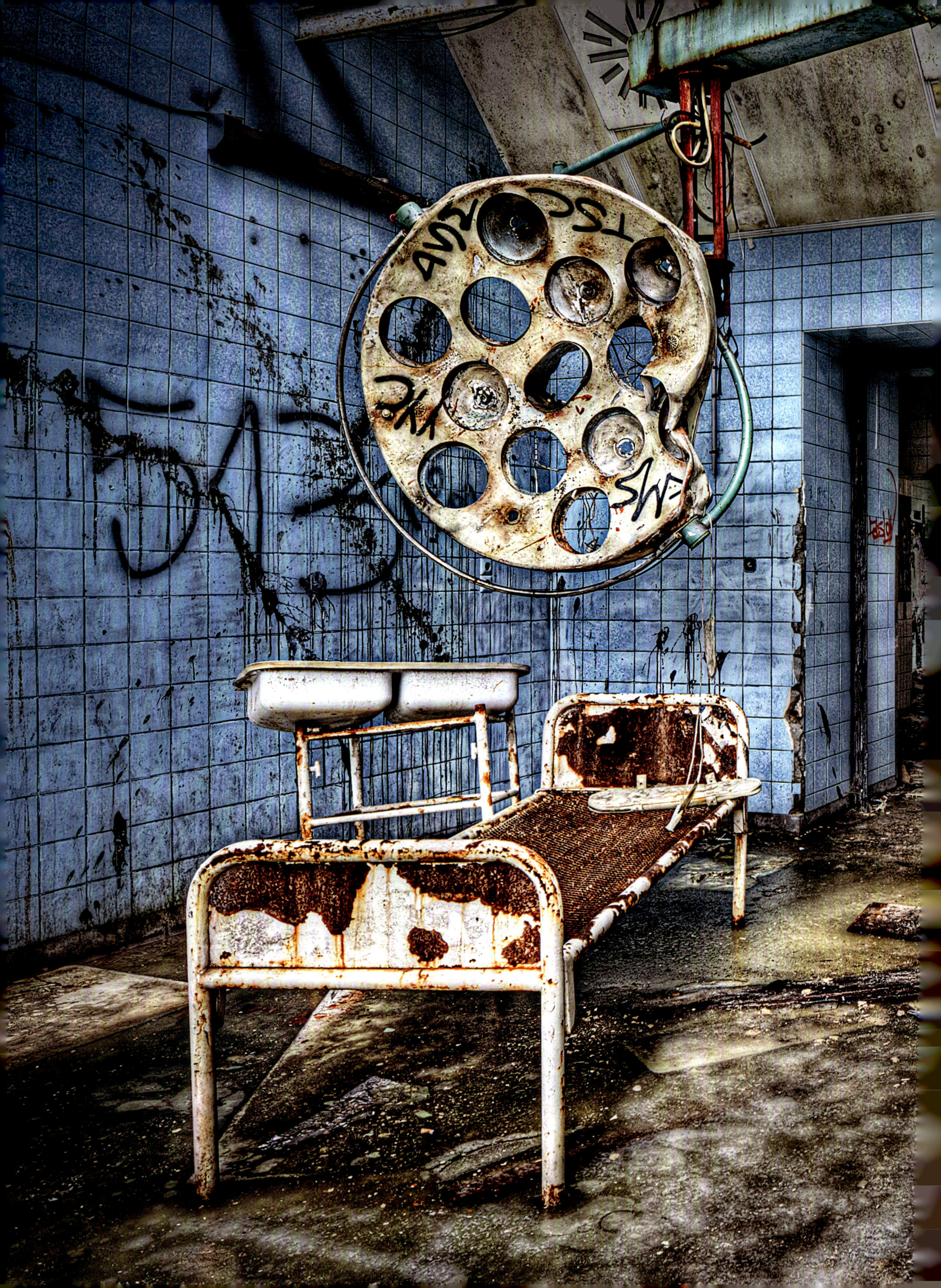

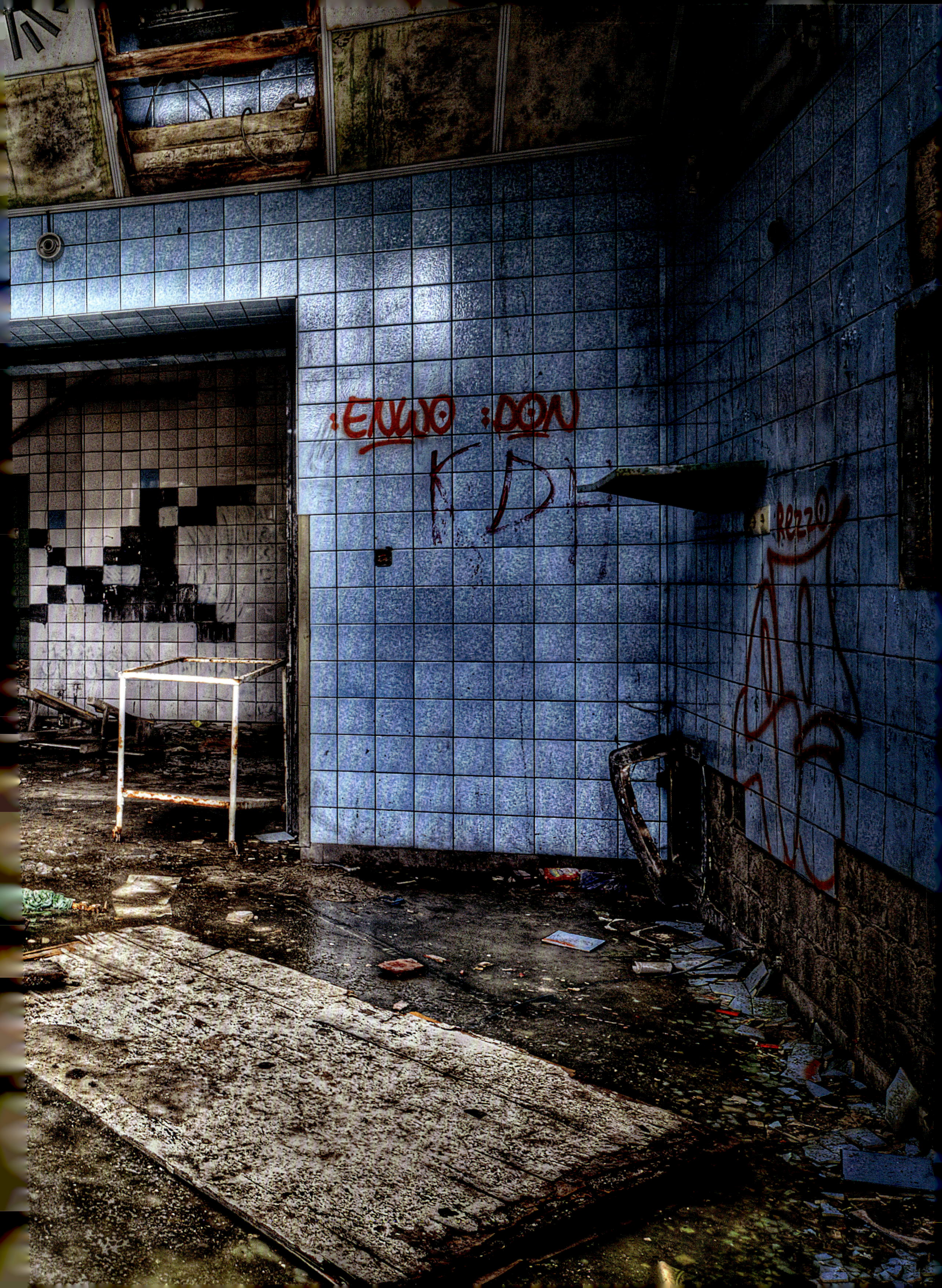

Beelitz-Heilstätten Hospital, Brandenburg, Germany
In the late 1990s, Beelitz's faded grandeur made it a popular location for photographers and film-makers. The piano and armchair are presumably props left behind from a photo or film shoot.

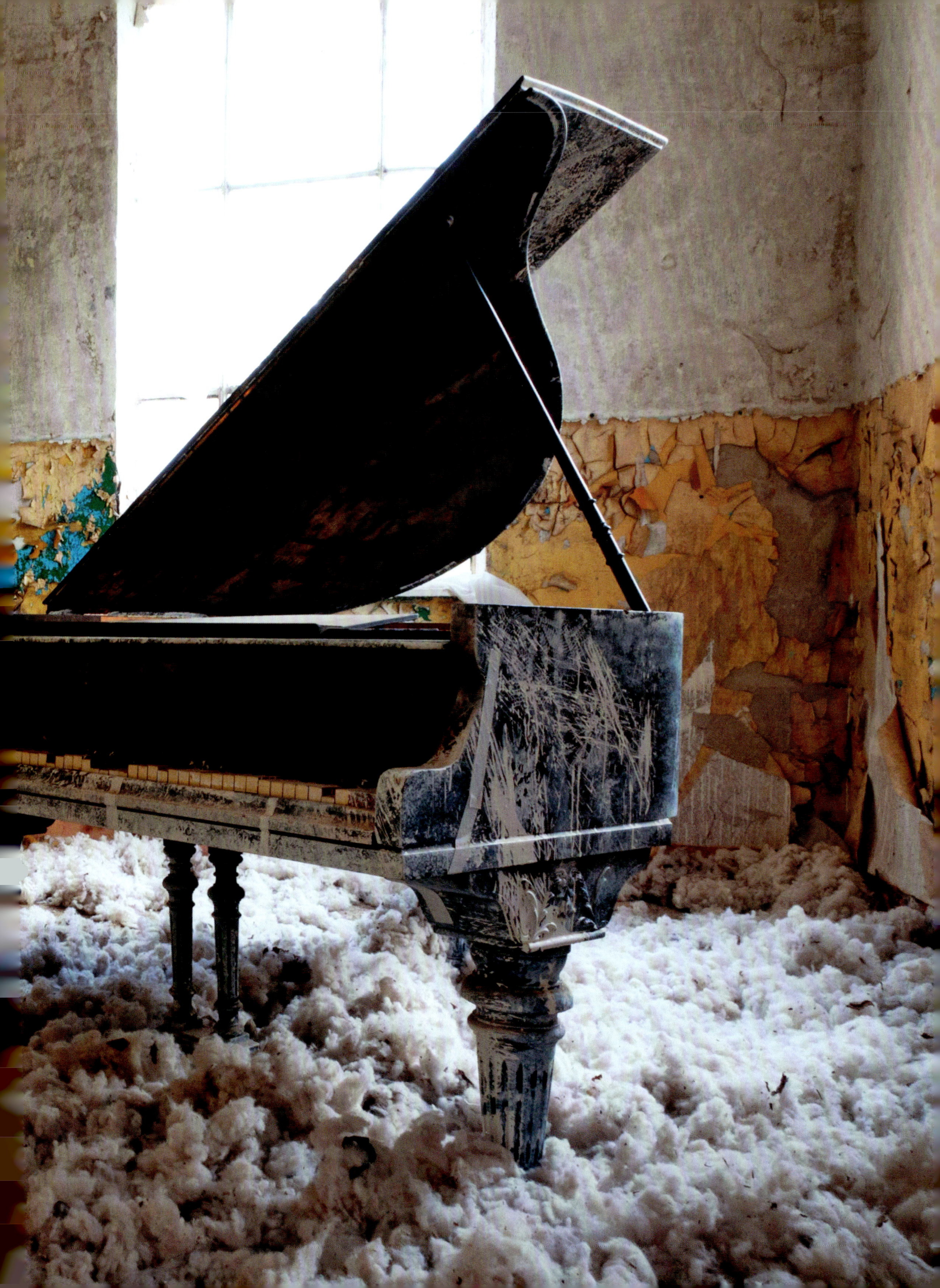

ALL PHOTOGRAPHS AND OVERLEAF:
Trans-Allegheny Lunatic Asylum, Weston, West Virginia, USA
Built between 1858 and 1881, the Trans-Allegheny, later renamed the Weston State Hospital, is the largest hand-cut stone masonry building in North America. It was designed following the Kirkbride Plan, a system devised for treating mental illness, it being hoped that the building itself would have a curative effect on its psychiatric patients. To achieve this, long rambling wings were arranged in a staggered formation, ensuring that each of the connecting structures received plenty of sunlight and fresh air. At its overcrowded peak in the 1950s, the hospital housed 2,600 patients, but these numbers declined when changes in the treatment of mental illness meant fewer patients were institutionalized.

The hospital was closed in 1994. It is now a National Historic Landmark and parts of it are open for tours.

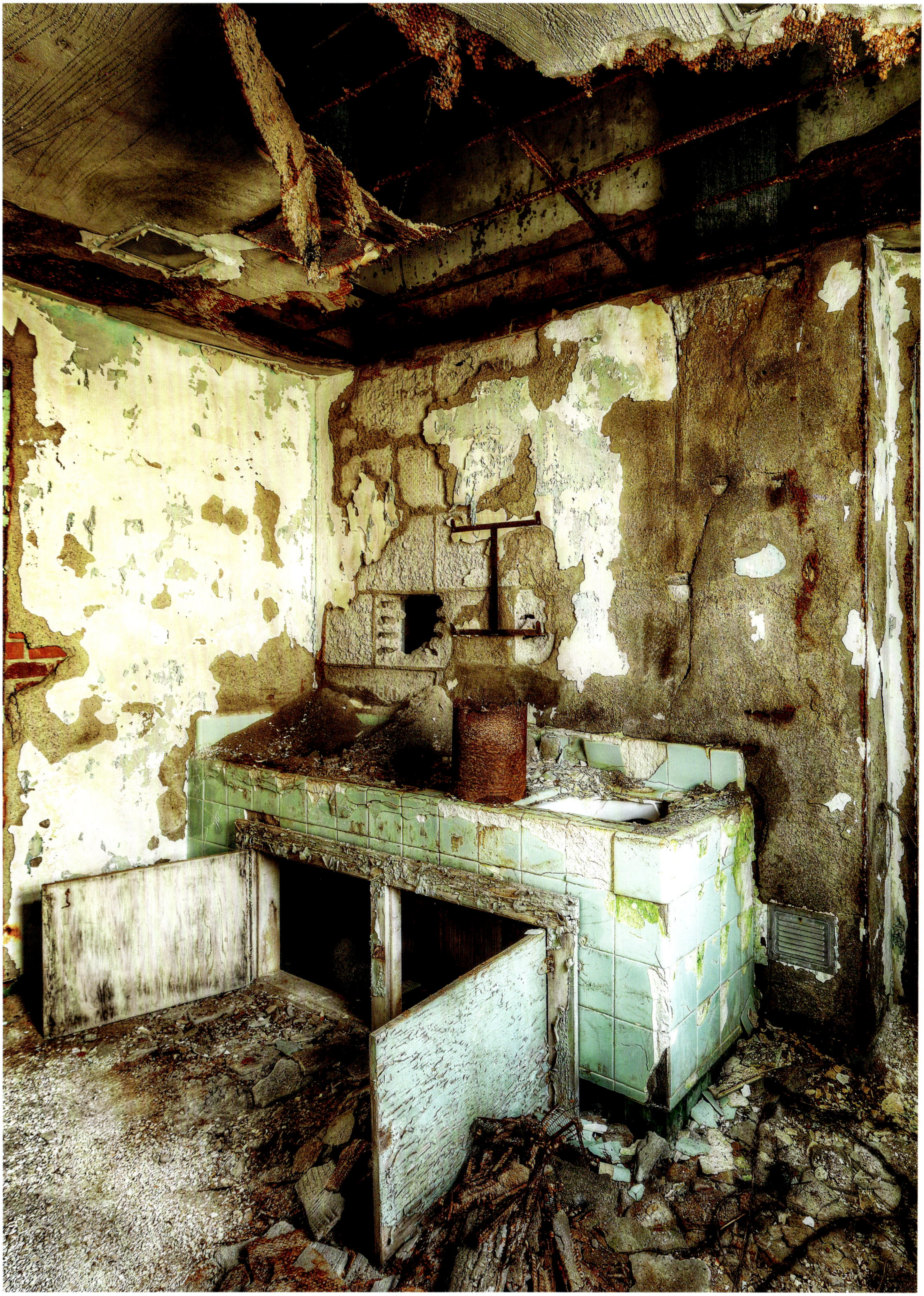

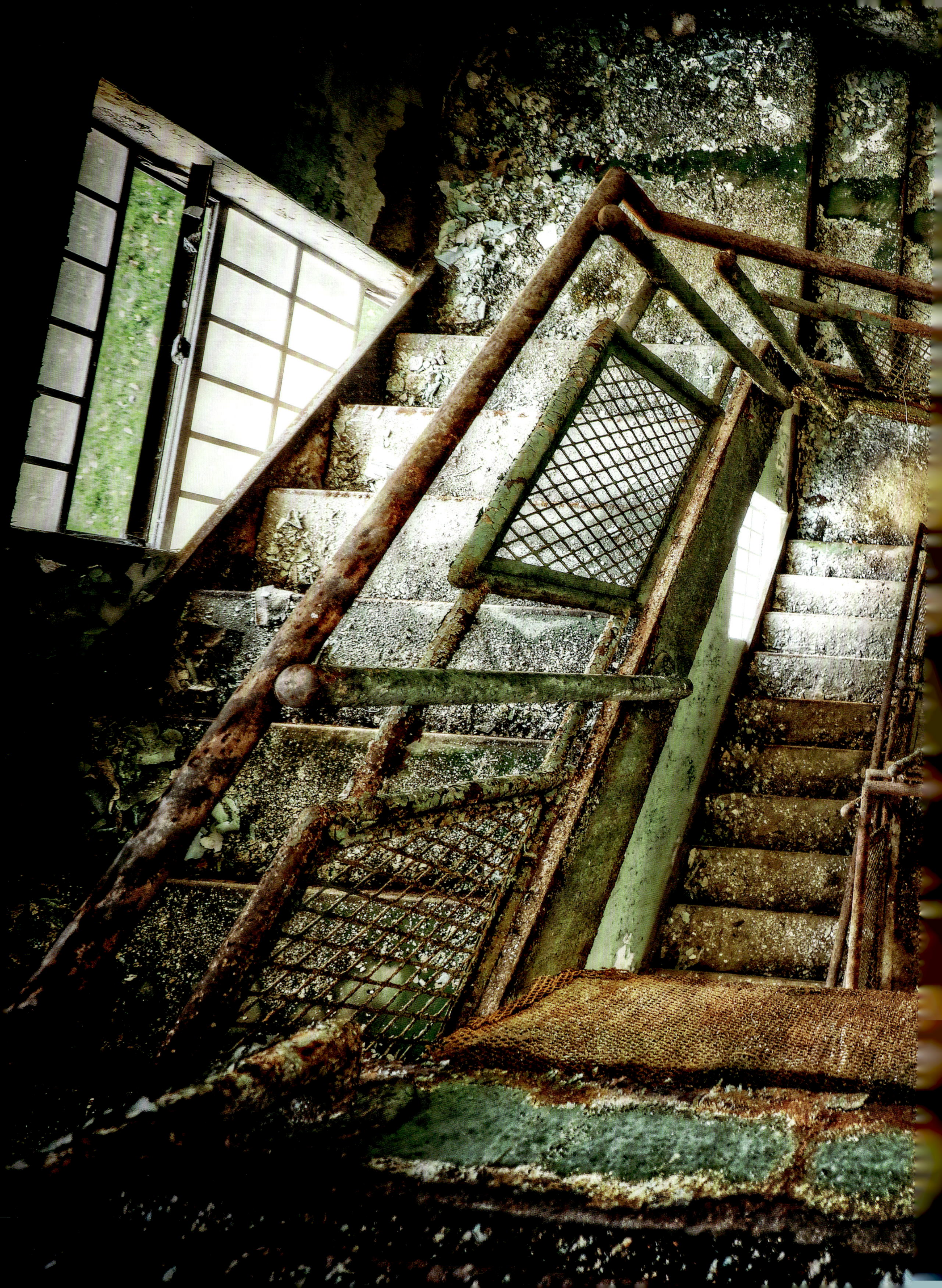

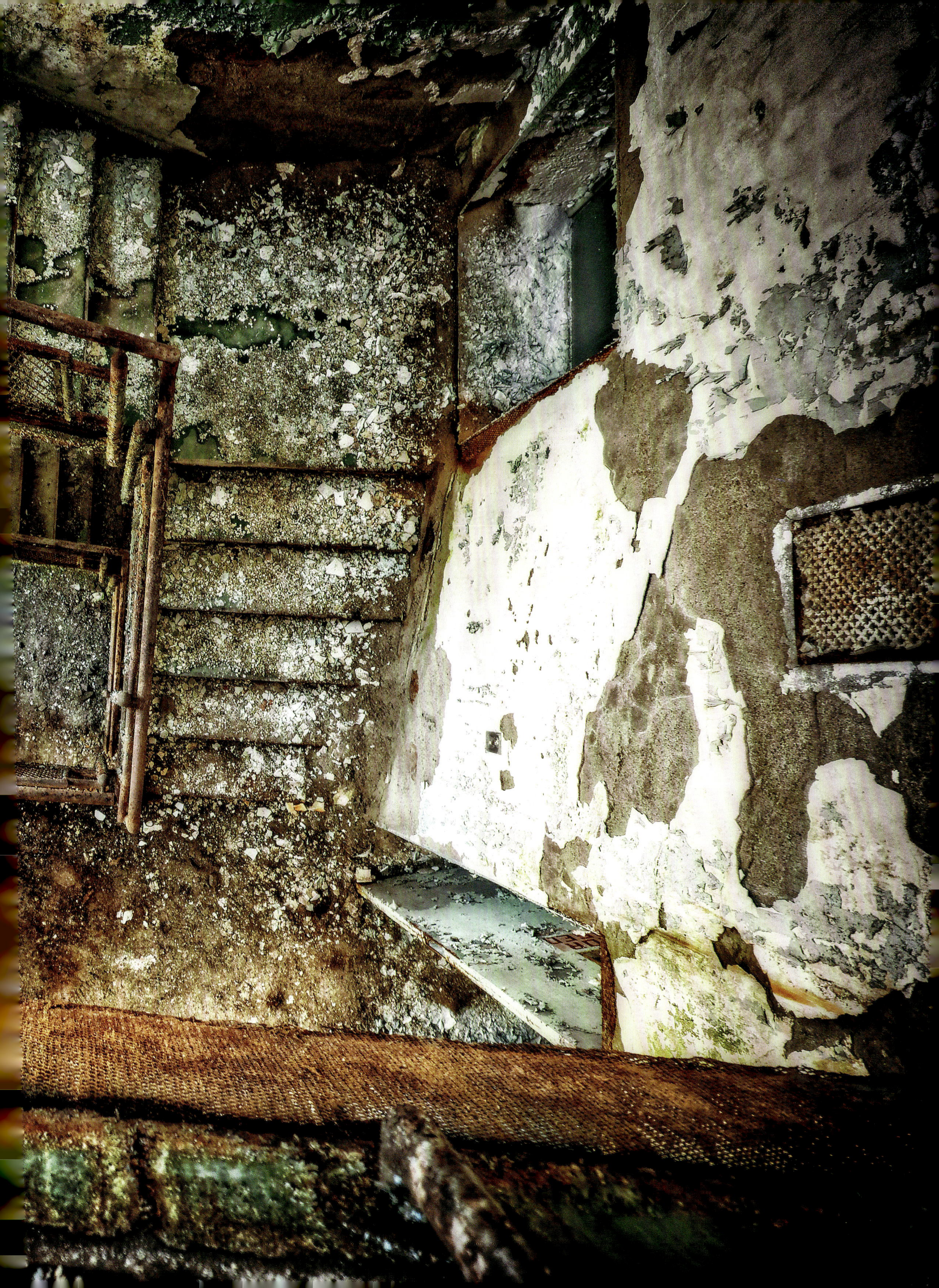

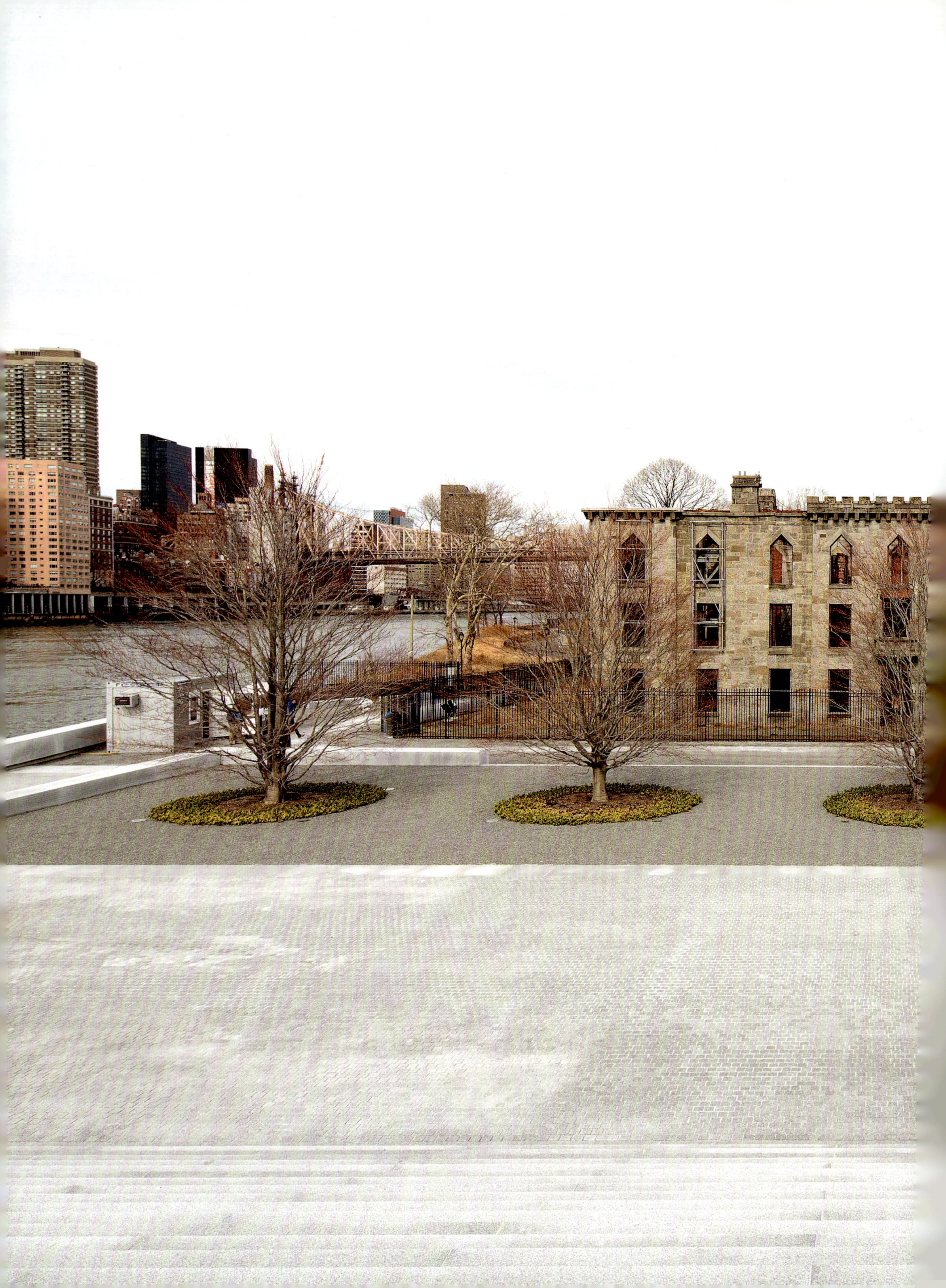

Renwick Smallpox Hospital, Manhattan, New York City, USA
Positioned at the remote southern tip of Roosevelt Island in an effort to quarantine its patients, the 100-bed smallpox hospital was opened in 1856. Twenty years later it became a nursing school. When that closed in the 1950s, the building fell into disrepair, and in 1972 the hospital was added to the National Register of Historic Places, making it New York City's 'only landmarked ruin'. Although the interior walls and floors have collapsed, the exterior shell is now being renovated.

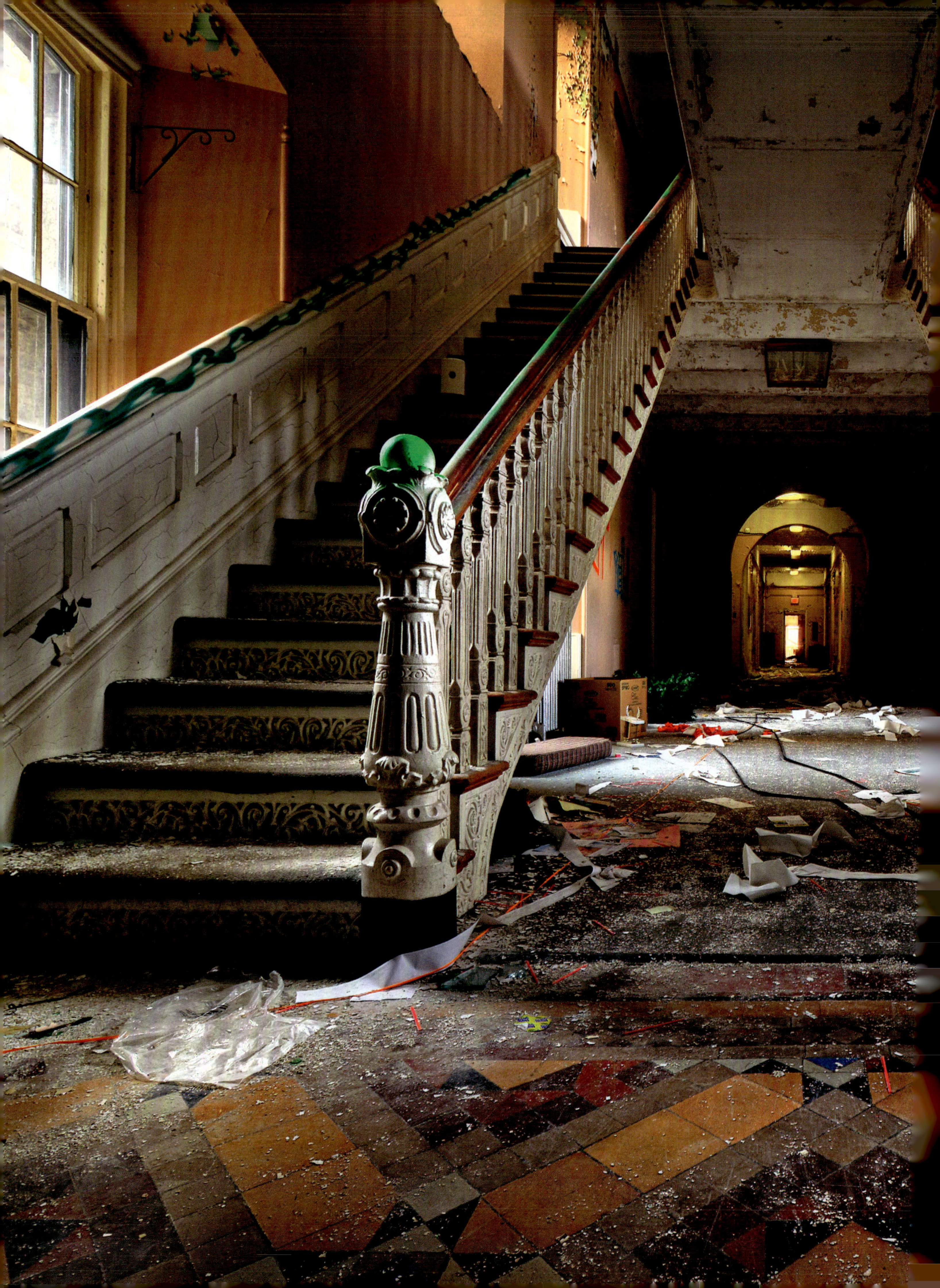

Main Building, Greystone Psychiatric Hospital, New Jersey, USA
Built in 1876, Greystone once housed 7,700 patients, before overcrowding and deteriorating conditions eventually led to it being shut down and replaced by a modern hospital. Despite public opposition, the main building was demolished in 2015.

НА КРАК
О ПАРИИ ПРЕЗРЕНИ
НА КРАК О РОБИ НА ТРУДА!
ПОТИСНАТИ И УНИЖЕНИ
СТАВАЙТЕ СРЕЩУ ВРАГА!
НЕКА БЕЗ МИЛОСТ Е ЛОШАТ
НЕМ...

LEFT:

Buzludzha Monument, Buzludzha, Bulgaria
Built to commemorate Bulgarian Communism, the Buzludzha Monument is situated high in the Balkan Mountains, in the area where socialists first assembled in 1891 to form an organized political movement. Opened in 1981, any efforts to maintain the monument were abandoned when Communism fell in 1989.

OVERLEAF:

Buzludzha Monument, Buzludzha, Bulgaria
This may look like a hovering UFO, but actually it is the ceiling of the Buzludzha Monument. Stripped by thieves of its roof tiles, the monument has been left open to the elements – snow can be seen covering the floor in this photograph.

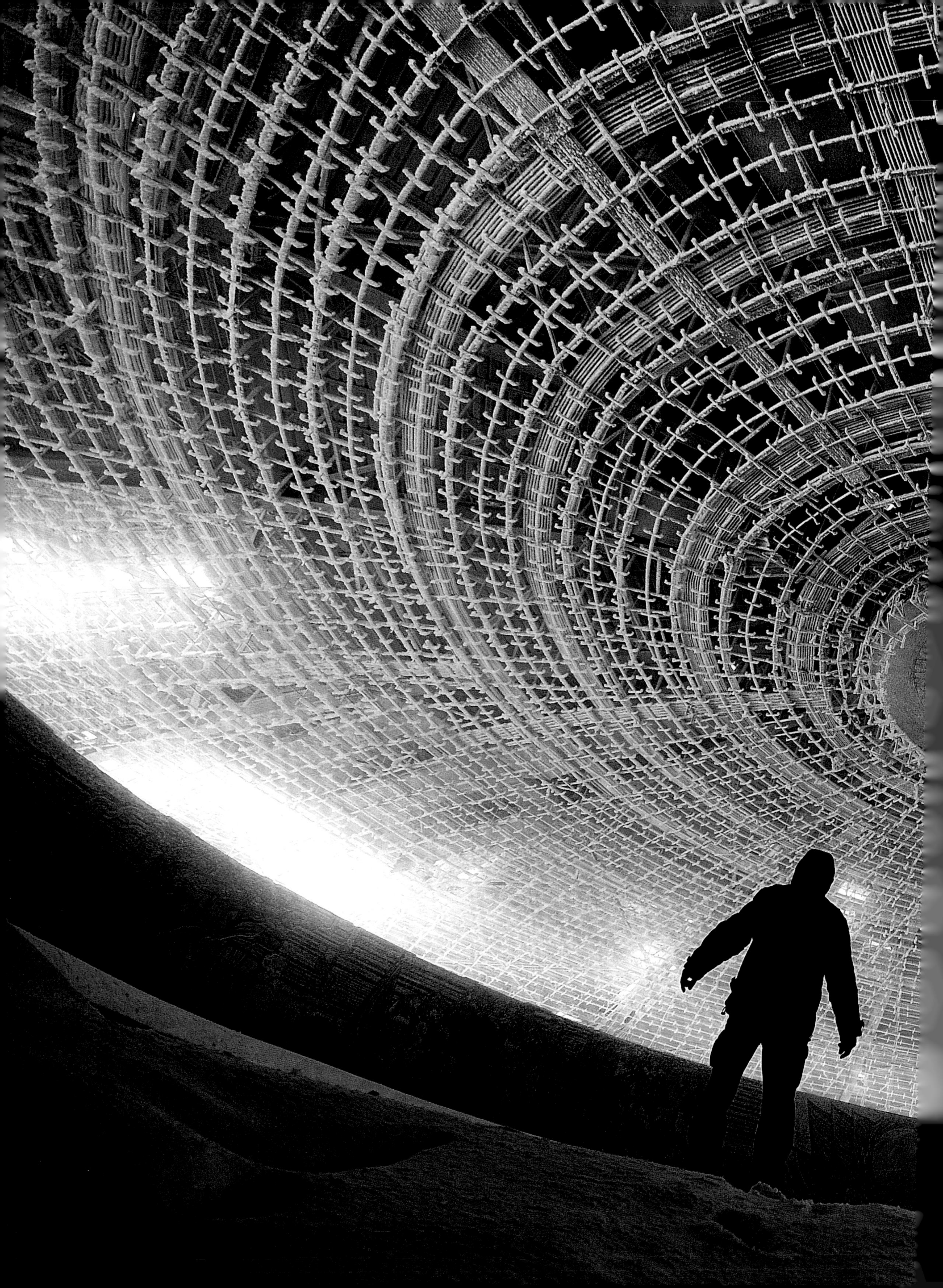

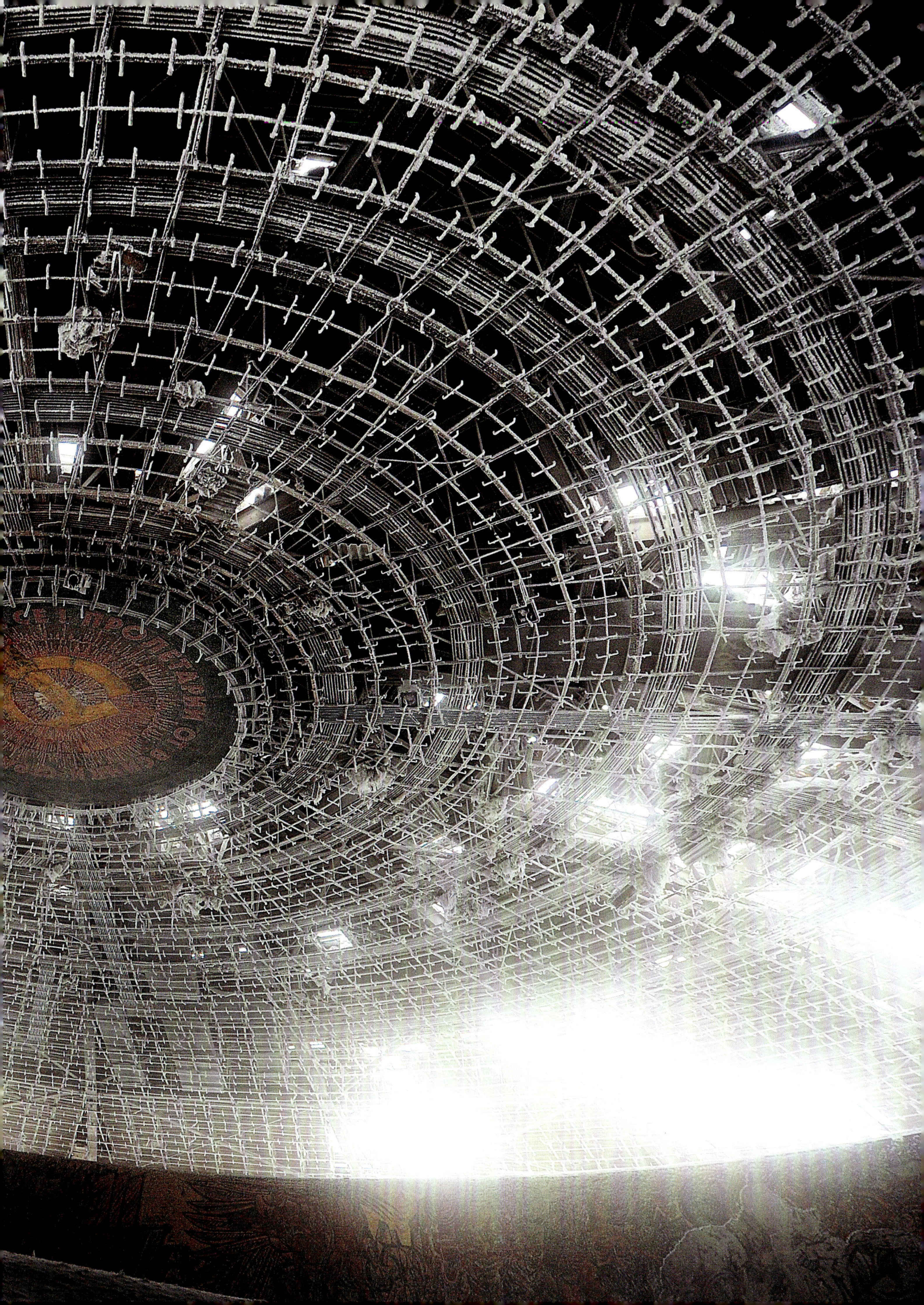

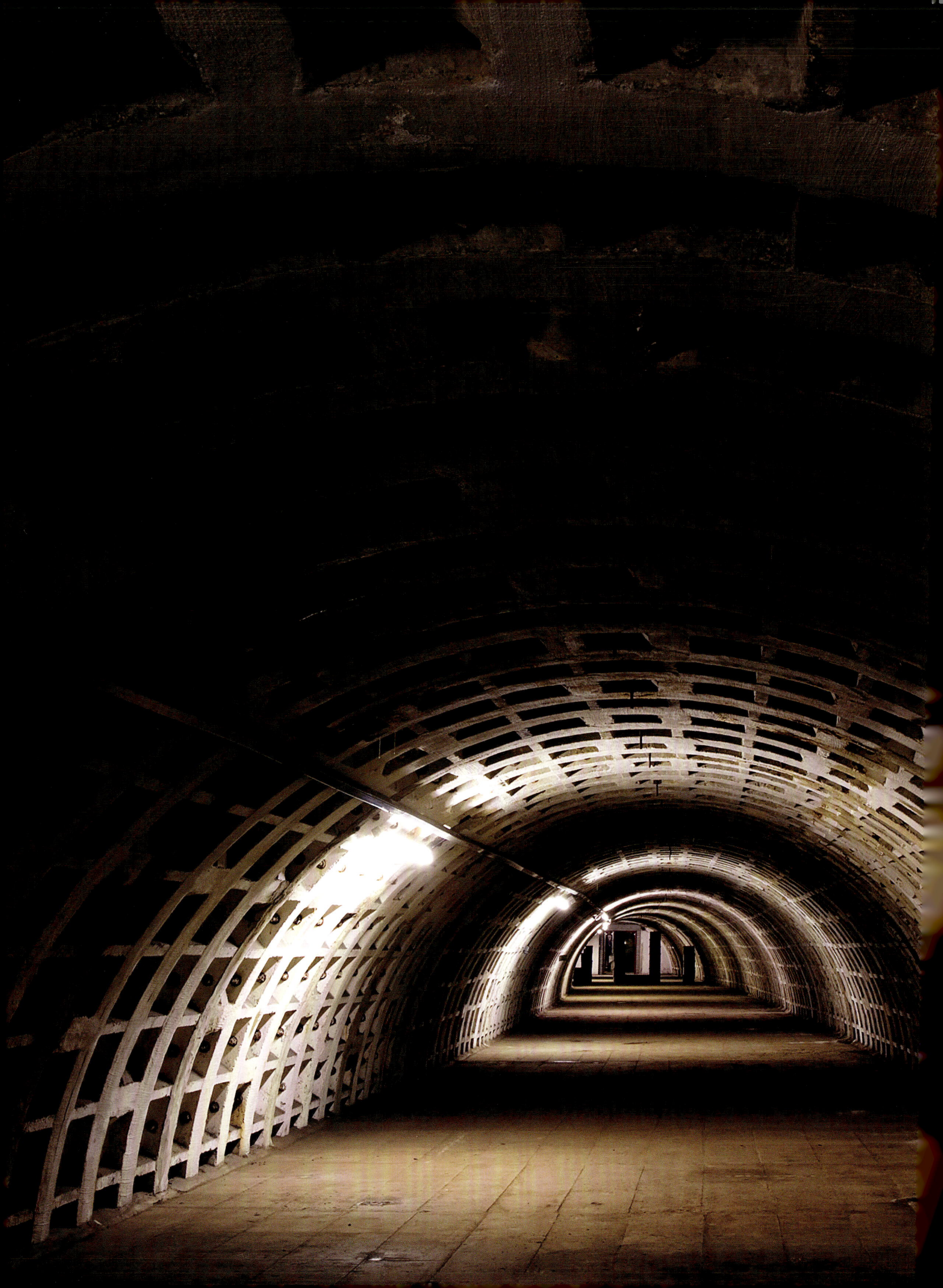

LEFT:

Clapham North deep-level air-raid shelter, London, England
During World War II, eight deep-level air-raid shelters were constructed beneath London Underground tunnels. Able to accommodate 8,000 people each, the shelters had bunk beds, canteens, toilets and medical aid posts. After the war the shelters were used for archive storage or, even, as temporary hostels. Since 2012, Clapham North shelter has been used as an urban farm, growing herbs and salad leaves.

Ryugyong Hotel, Pyongyang, North Korea
At 105 storeys tall, the Ryugyong Hotel is certainly striking, but, almost 30 years after construction began, it is still unfinished. Halted first in 1992 during North Korea's economic crisis following the collapse of the Soviet Union, construction resumed in 2008, only for it to be suspended again in 2012.

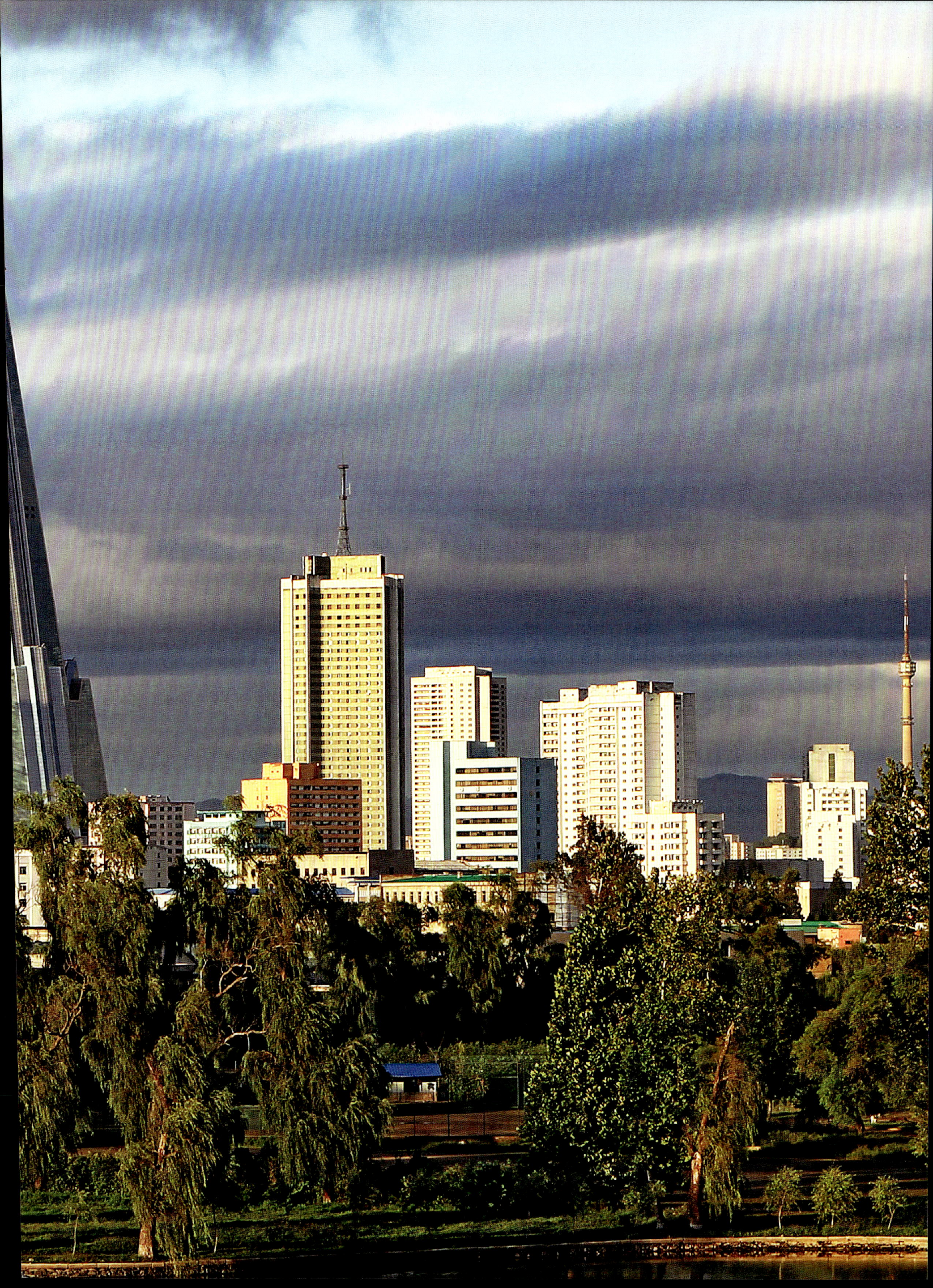

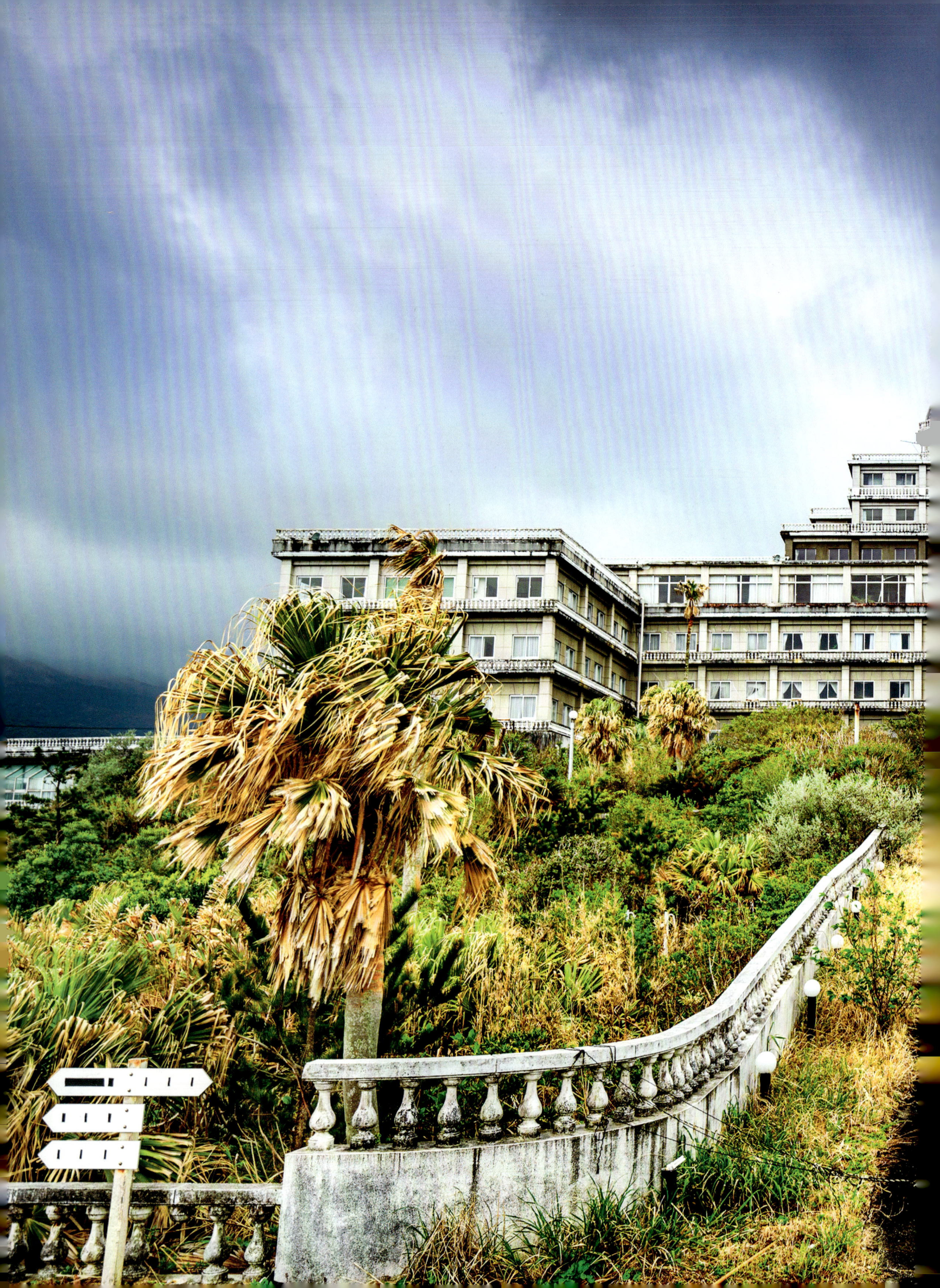

Hachijo Royal Hotel, Hachijojima, Japan
This is what happens to a hotel when there are no guests and apparently no gardeners. The Hachijo Royal opened in 1963 when Hachijojima, a volcanic island 178 miles (287km) off the coast of Japan, was being promoted as the 'Hawaii of Japan'. The hotel closed in 2003.

Abandoned motel, near Perry, Florida, USA
Where indoors and outdoors blend: mirroring the painting of palm trees on a wall, a fern grows on the floor of a motel room.

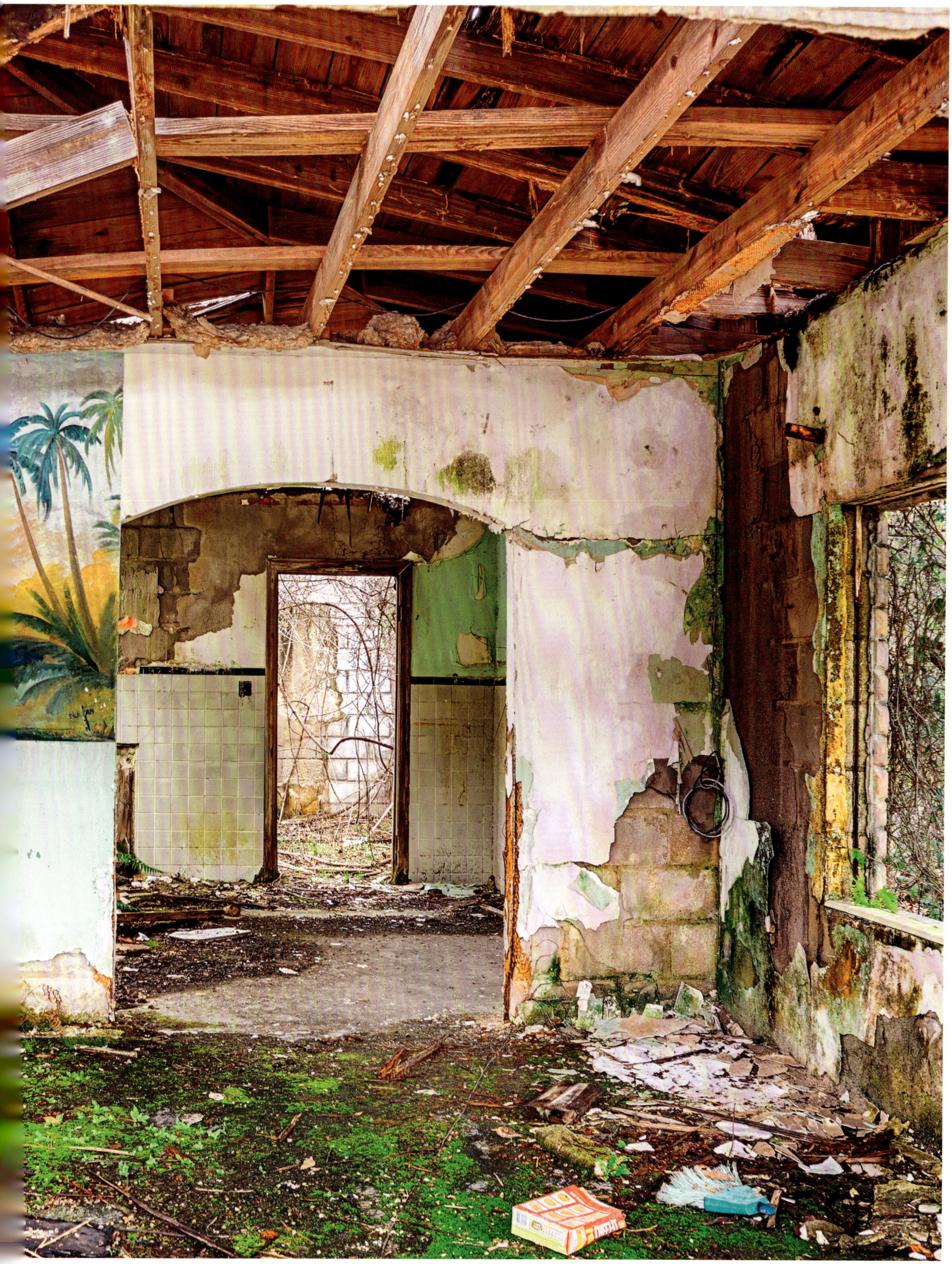

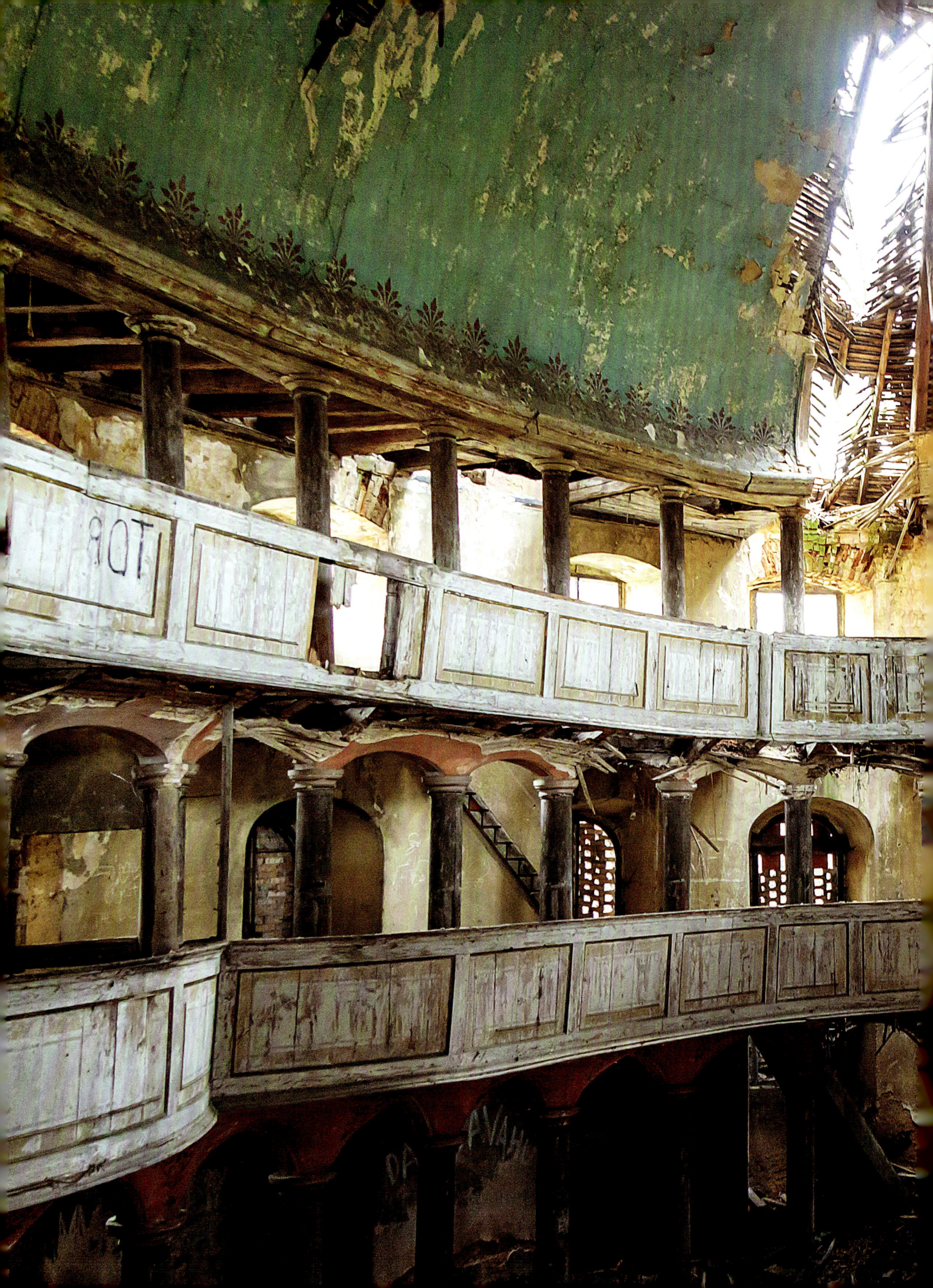

Zeliszów Protestant Church, Lower Silesia, Poland
Today this Protestant church is in western Poland, but until 1945 it was in eastern Germany. The church didn't move, but, at the end of World War II, Poland's borders were moved westwards. With that came the resettlement of millions of people, meaning that the local German Protestant congregation had to abandon their church. It was designed in 1796 by Carl Gotthard Langhans, who also designed Berlin's Brandenburg Gate.

Bokor Palace Hotel, Kampot Province, Cambodia
A vestige of colonialism, the Bokor Hill Station was built by French settlers in the 1920s as an escape from the heat of Phnom Penh. Alongside a church, shops and a post office, the Bokor Palace Hotel was the centrepiece. The hill station was abandoned by the French in the late 1940s during the First Indochina War.

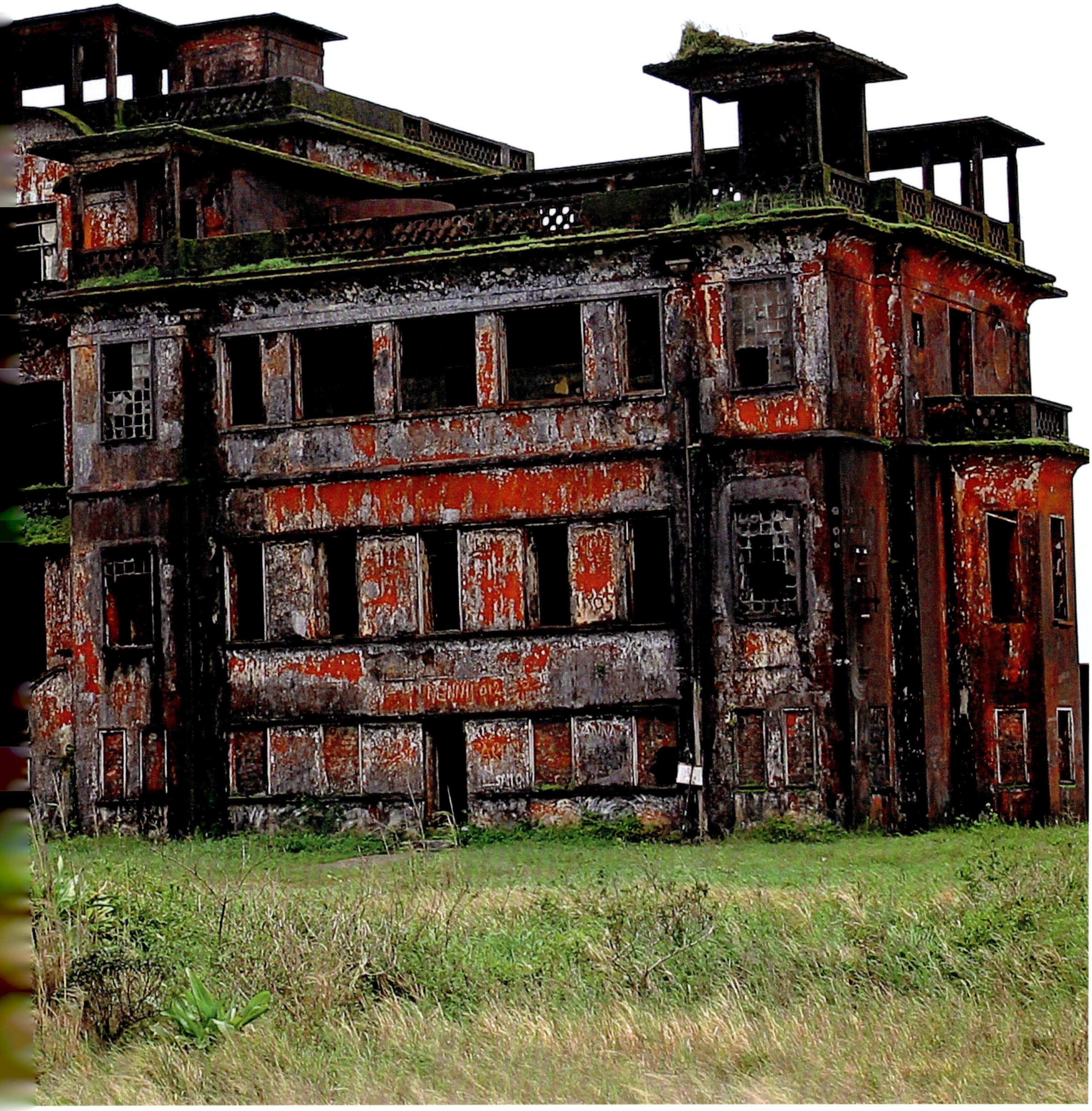

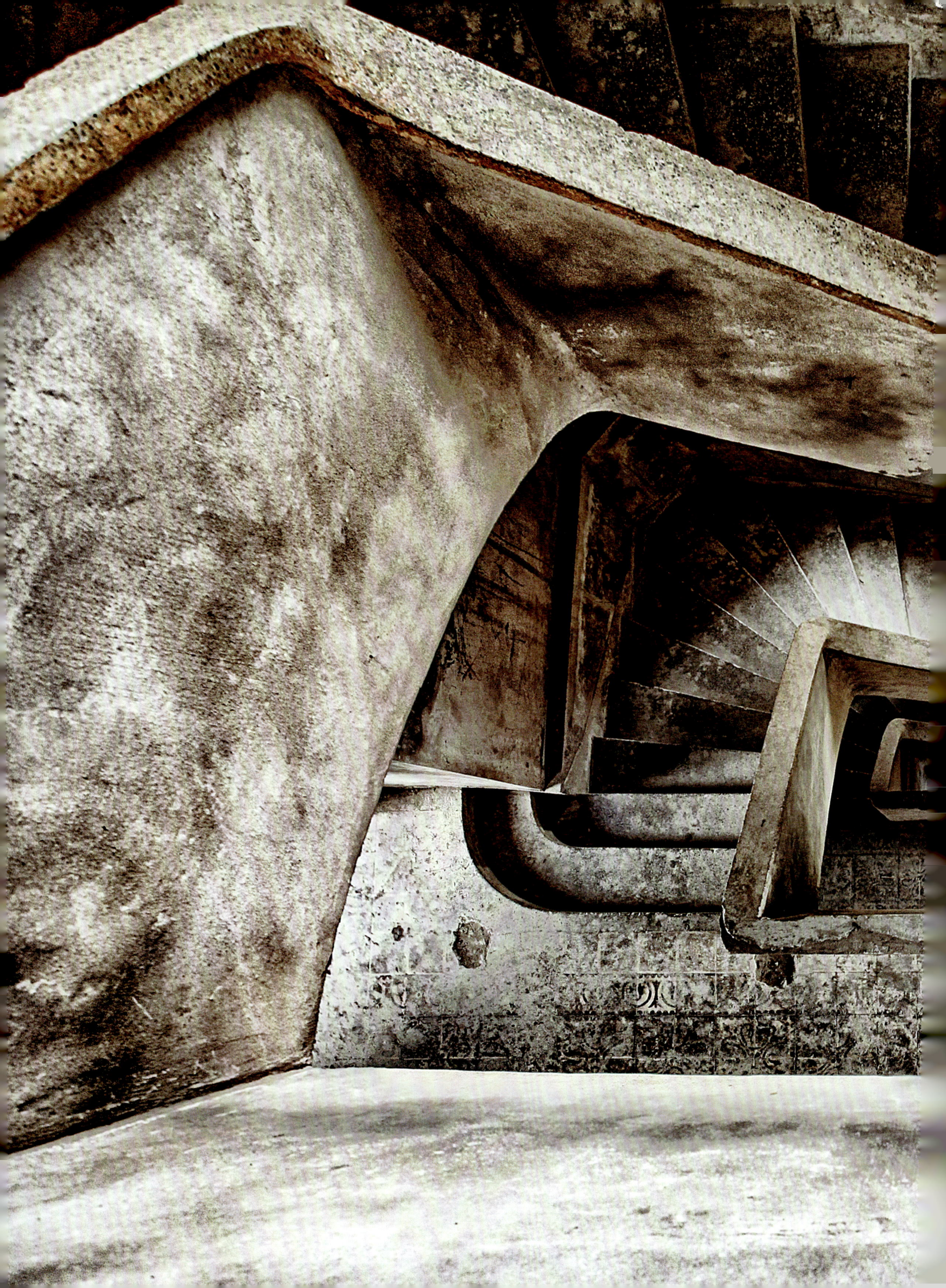

Bokor Palace Hotel, Kampot Province, Cambodia
In the 1970s, the Khmer Rouge took over the abandoned Bokor Hill Station. When Vietnam invaded Cambodia in 1979, the Khmer Rouge managed to hold on to the mountainous and remote area for several years.

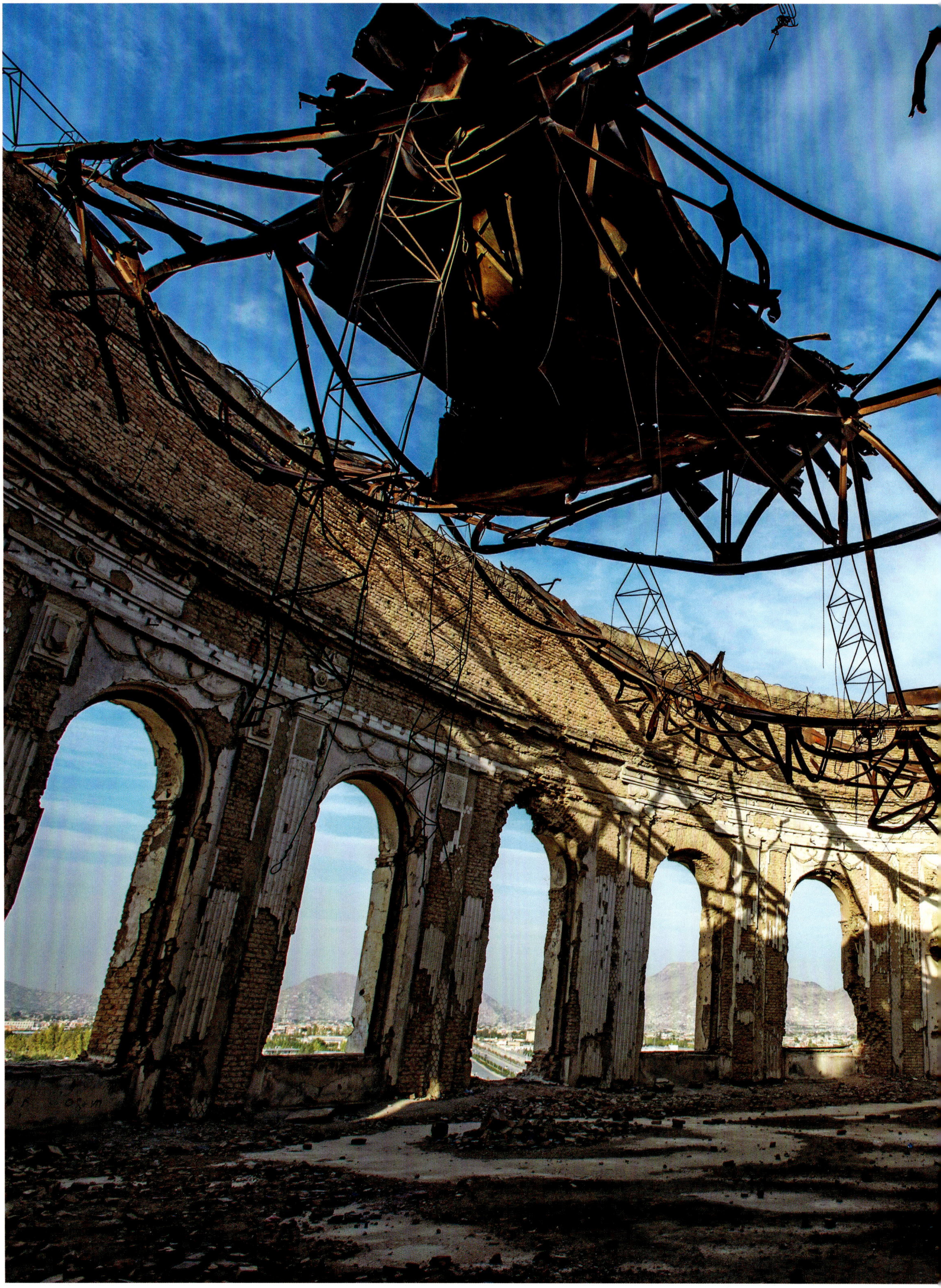

LEFT:

Darul Aman Palace, near Kabul, Afghanistan
Ruined as rival Mujahideen factions fought for control of Kabul in the early 1990s, Darul Aman Palace had been built in the 1920s in an effort by King Amanullah Khan to modernize Afghanistan. However, it then lay unused for many years after the king was forced from power. The palace was attacked again and further ruined by the Taliban in 2012.

Unfinished hotel, near Fengdu Ghost City, China

Fengdu isn't called a ghost city because it's an abandoned place, but because its complex of shrines, temples and monasteries are all dedicated to the afterlife in Chinese mythology and Buddhism. The Ghost King is one of the world's largest stone sculptures; the carving of his body covers the rest of the mountainside. However, the hotel that was to be built behind his head was never completed when financing fell through.

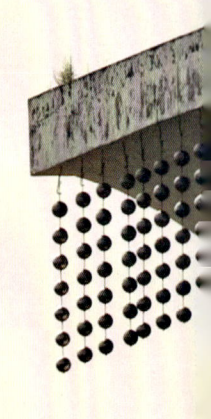

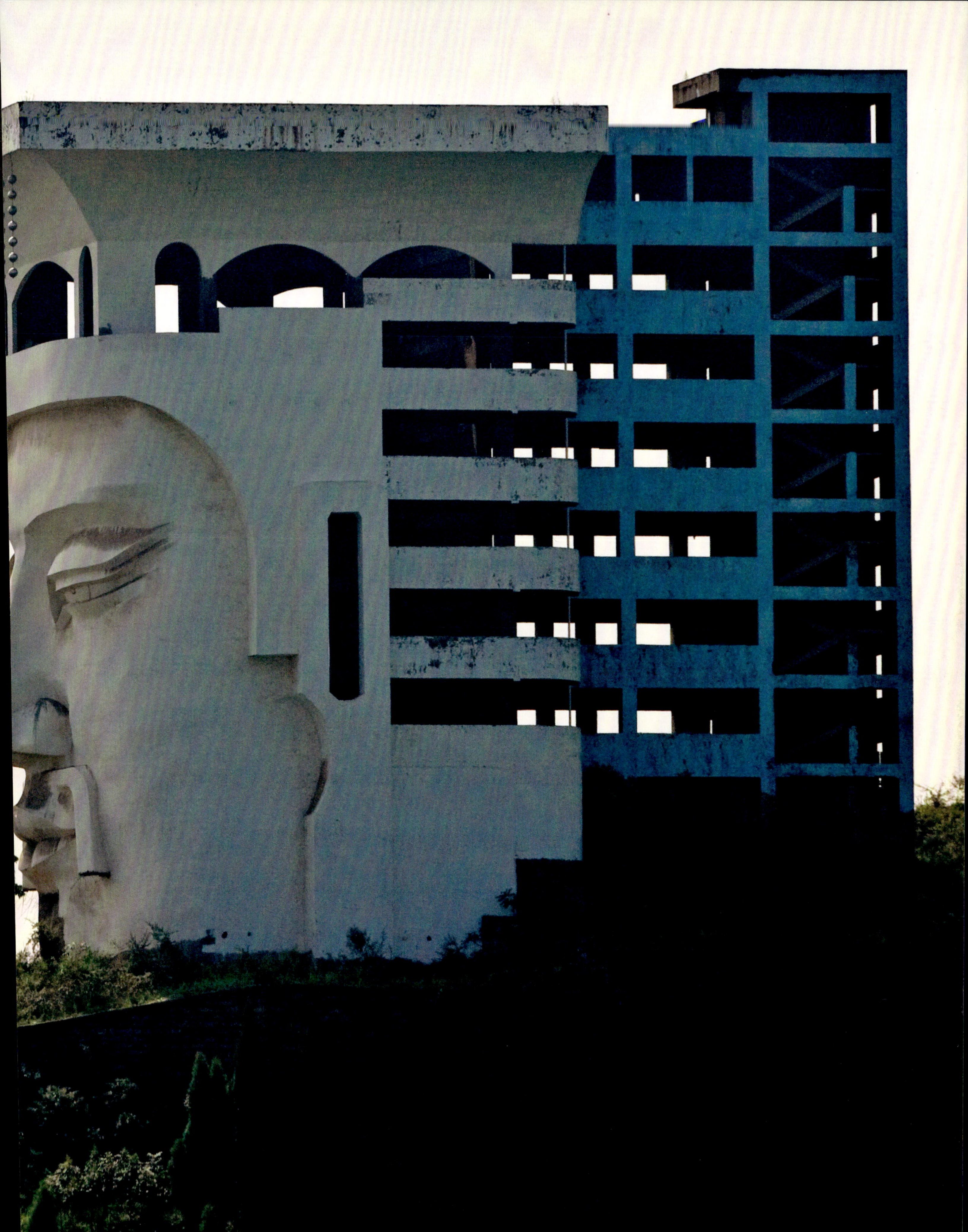

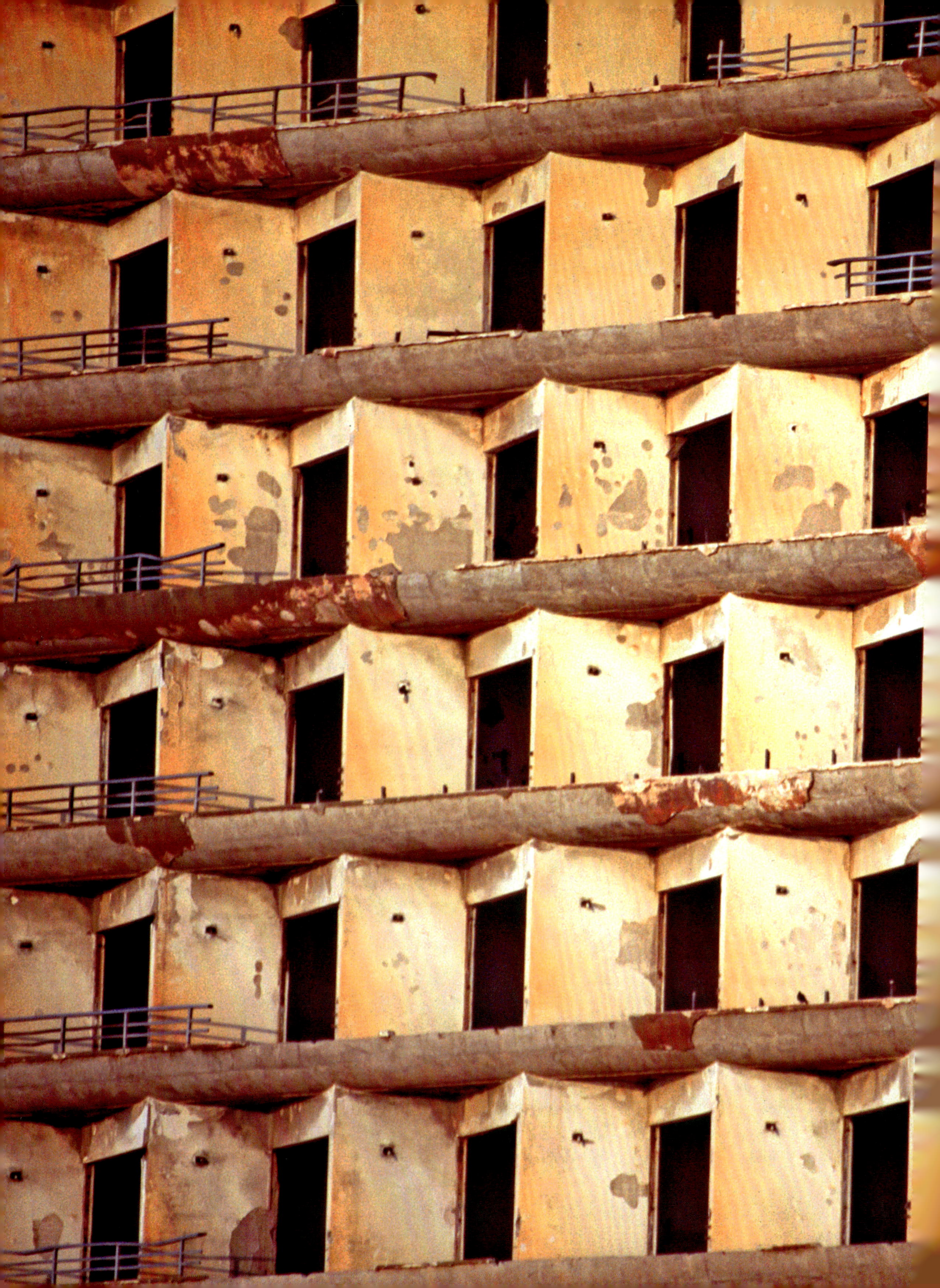

Ghost Towns & Cities

An empty wilderness is beautiful, a busy city can be tiring or energizing, but an empty city is simply unnerving – as shown in the many movies which imagine life after an apocalypse. Cities aren't supposed to be quiet, we shouldn't be able to walk down the middle of main roads, and there should always be someone, however unwelcome, in sight. Which perhaps explains our fascination with ghost towns. Whether through war, natural disasters, economic collapse or, in the case of Pripyat and the towns around Fukushima, nuclear meltdown, deserted towns offer us a larger look at worlds as they shouldn't be and worlds as they once were. As towns they shouldn't be silent, the roads should be clean, the weeds kept in check. But in that silence, we can gain more than just a glimpse of how things used to be. In the shop windows of ghost towns, we can see the mannequins wearing long-forgotten fashions, while in the car showrooms the 'latest' models are on sale. And, in the absence of humankind, nature has been allowed to run wild. Trees grow through pavements or floors, moss grows over roads, and animals repopulate the urban environment. But, we may wonder, what would have changed these places more: being left to nature or humankind's 'modernizing' hands?

LEFT:
Varosha, Famagusta, Northern Cyprus
No man's land. Varosha was first abandoned by its Greek Cypriot population after Turkey invaded the island in 1974. Fenced off by the Turks since then, its buildings now crumble and the plants grow wild… but the political stand-off remains unchanged.

Argentiera, Sardinia, Italy
Silver was mined in Argentiera from Roman times, and the town was still thriving in the 1940s. After World War II, however, production fell as the ore reserves began to run out and the mine was closed in 1963. It is now an attraction as a ghost town.

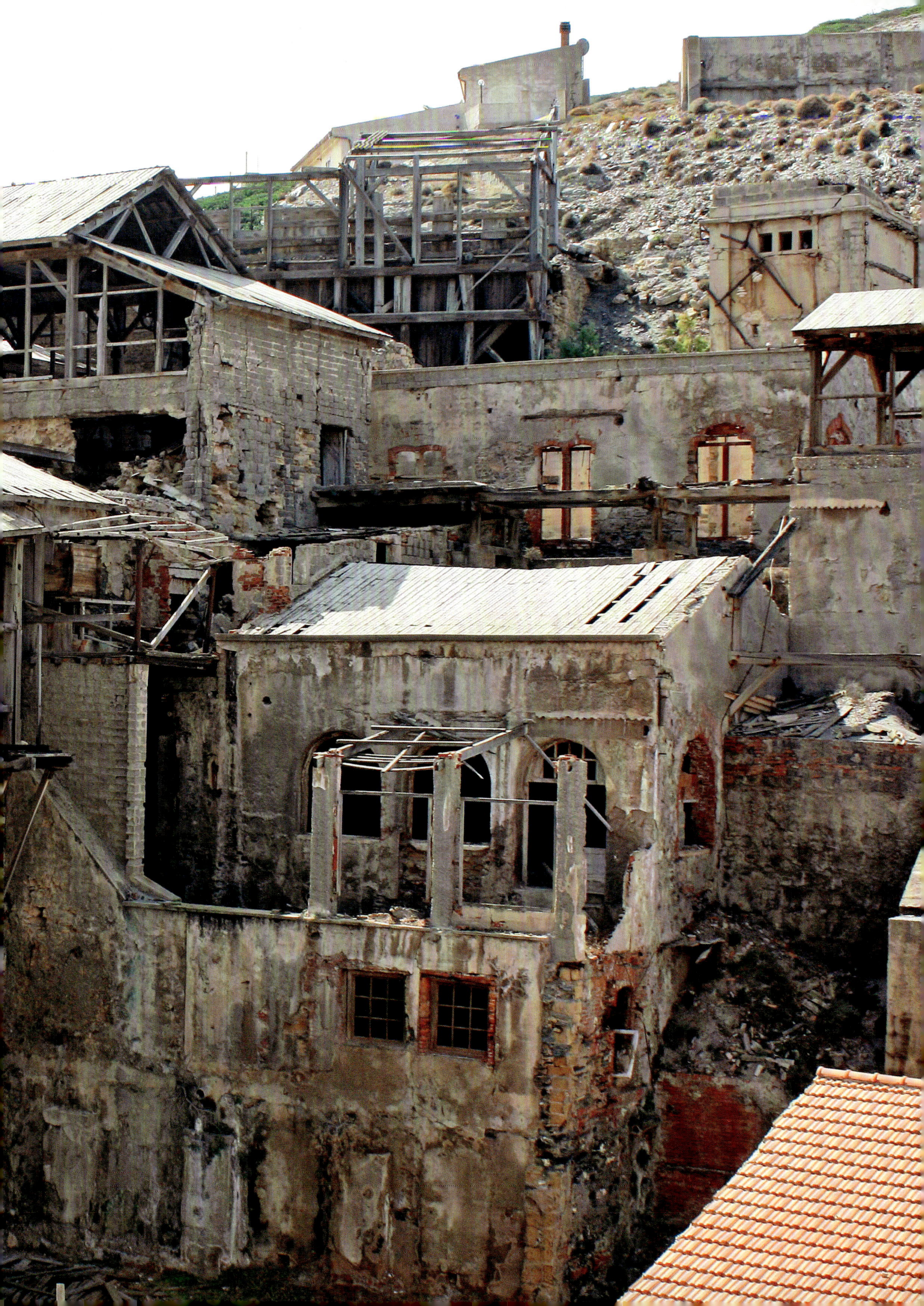

Church of St. Martin of Tours, Belchite, Province of Zaragoza, Spain

The town of Belchite was destroyed in August–September 1937 in a battle in the Spanish Civil War. After the war, General Franco ordered that the ruins be left untouched as a 'living' monument of war. A new town and church were built nearby.

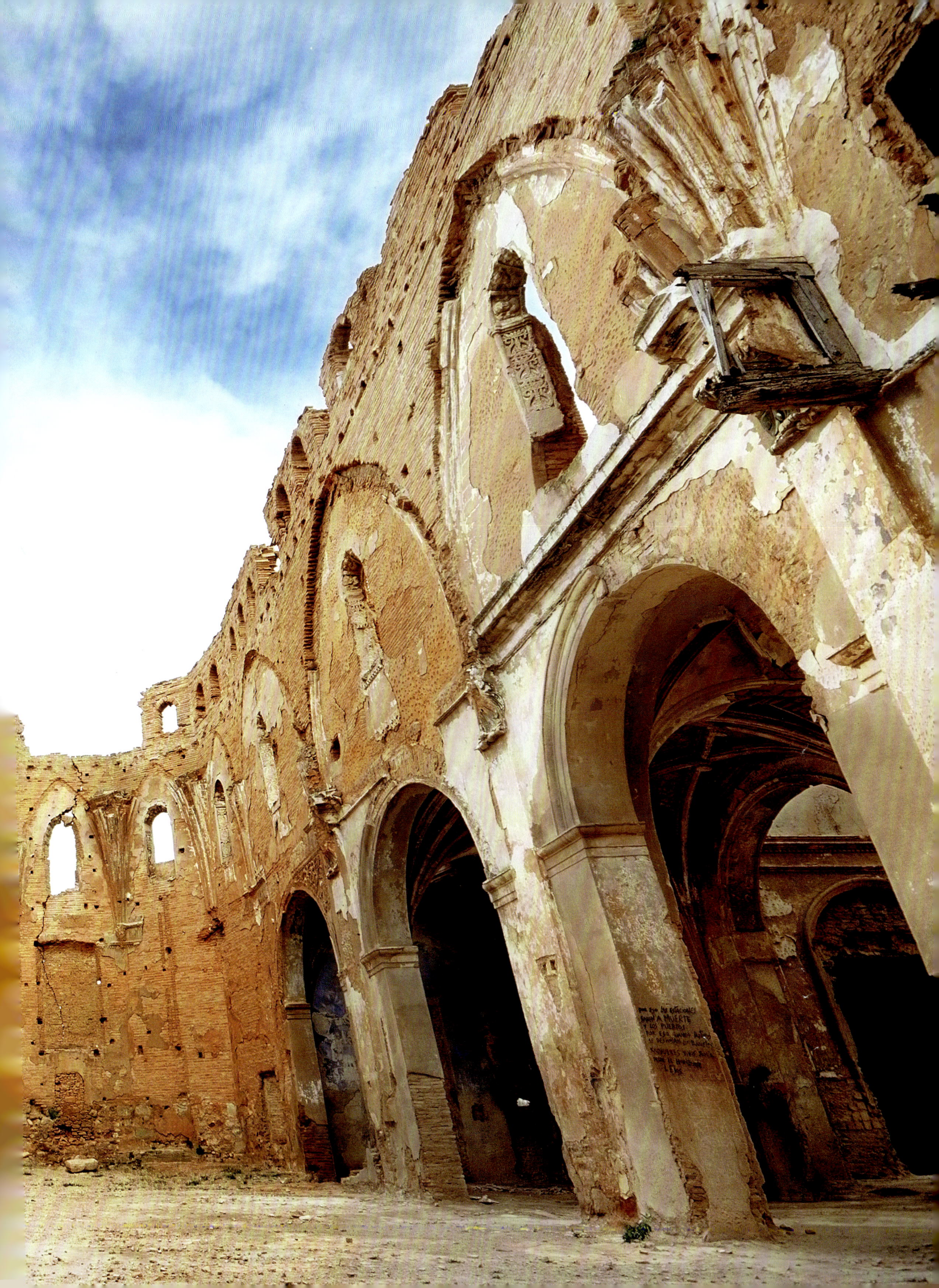

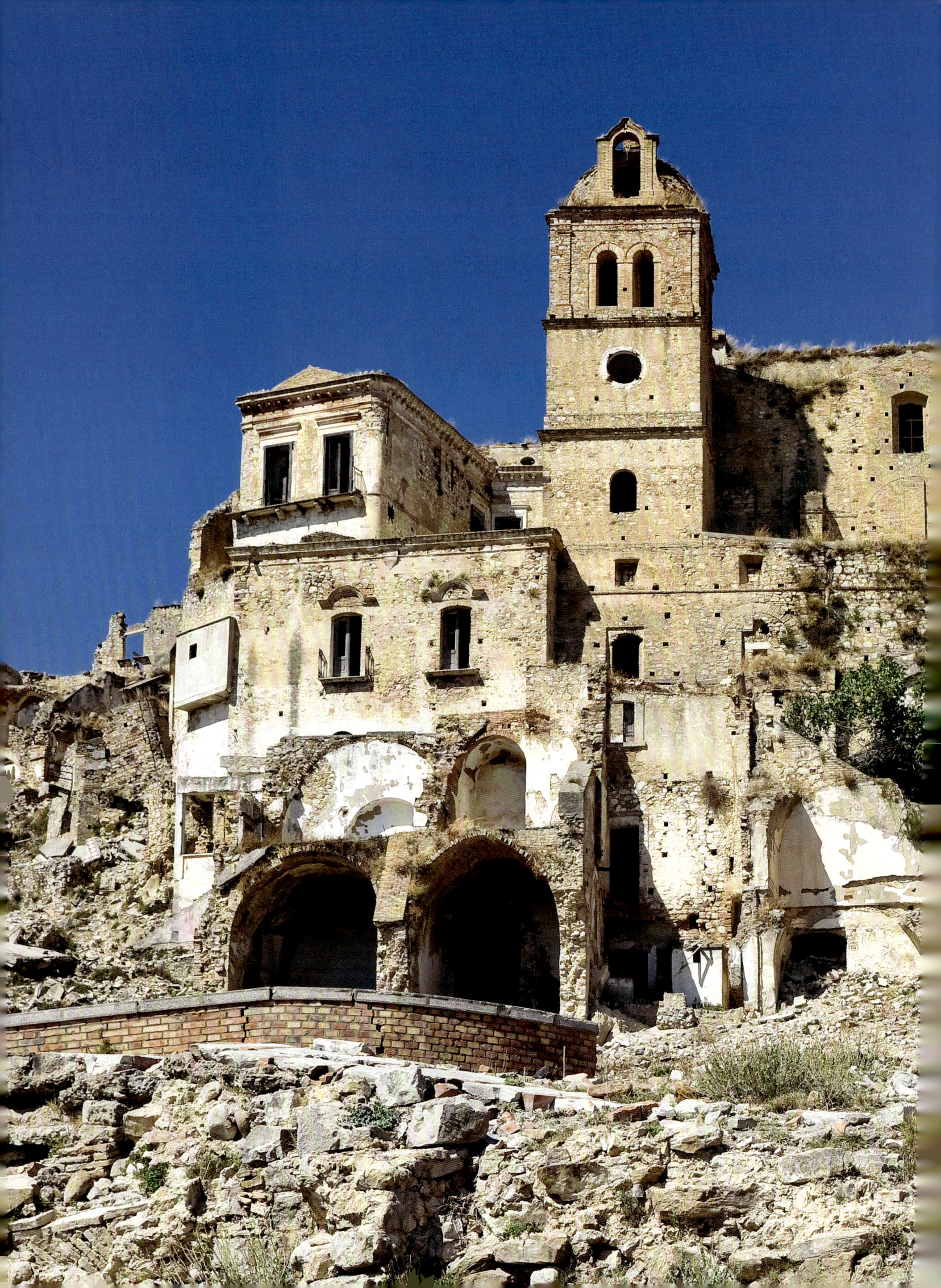

Craco, Basilicata, Italy
Environmental carelessness and geological factors have probably combined to cause Craco to be abandoned. When a landslide in 1963 – possibly caused by sanitation works – made part of the town unsafe, some residents had to be resettled nearby. Then, following the 1980 Irpinia earthquake, the final inhabitants were moved from their homes.

Chaitén, Chile
The Chaitén volcano had been dormant since at least 1640 – and possibly for thousands of years before that. Then, on 2 May 2008, it entered an eruptive phase. The 4,200 inhabitants of the town of Chaitén, just 6 miles (10km) away, were forced to leave that day as volcanic ash covered the town and a mudflow caused the Blanco River to burst its banks. The town remains deserted.

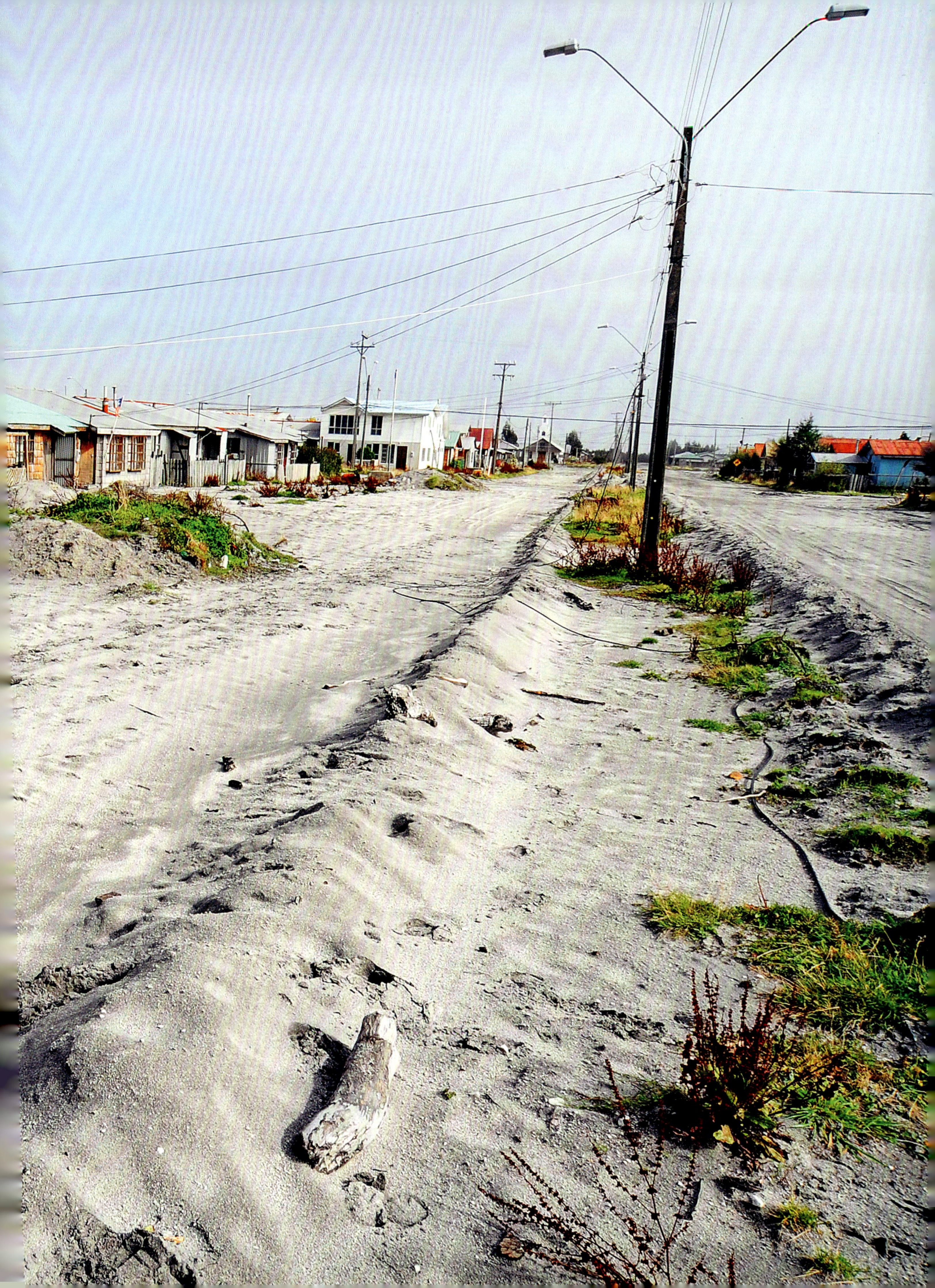

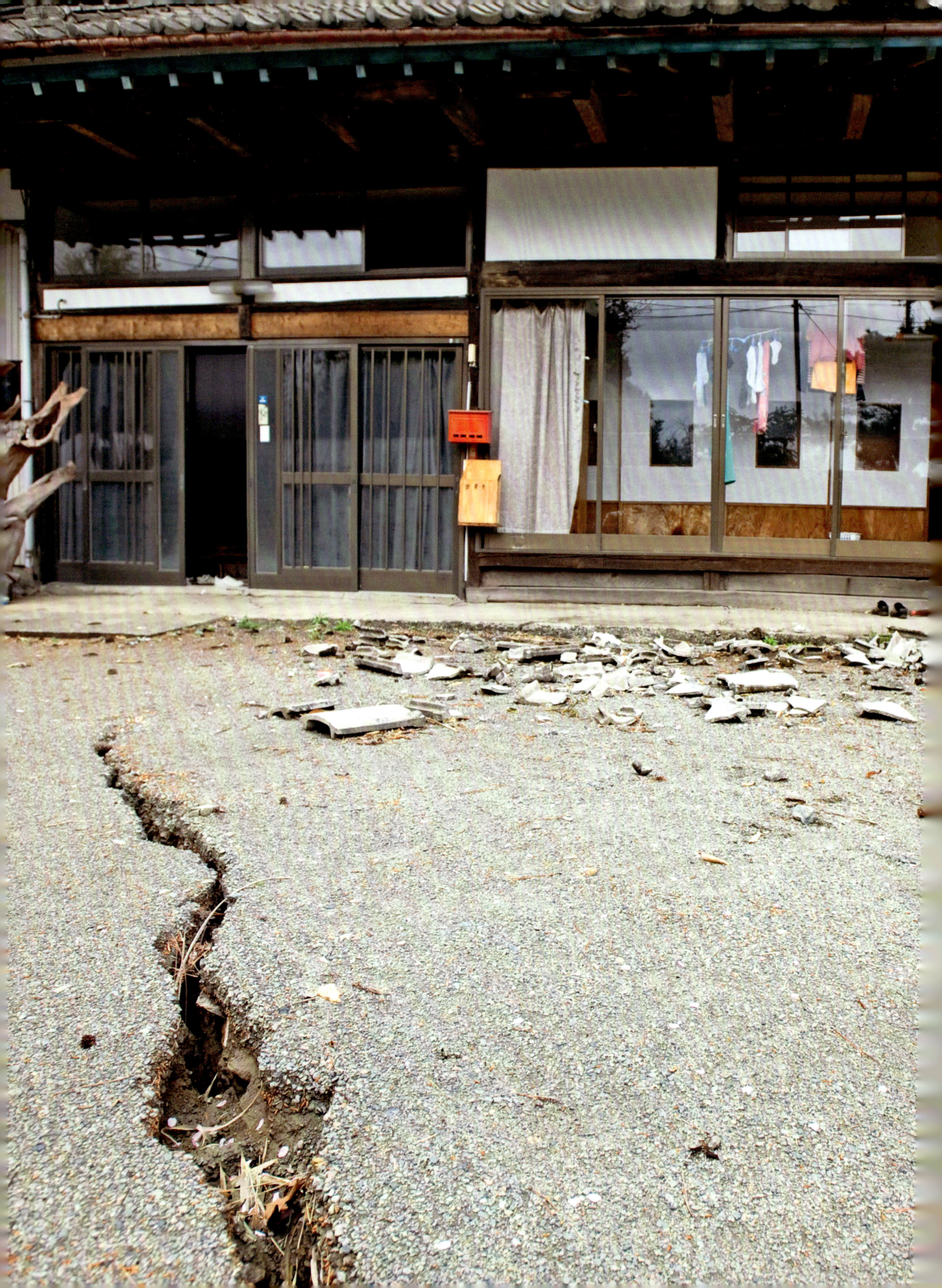

Naraha, Fukushima Prefecture, Japan
A crack in the surface of a deserted street. This is six weeks after the Tohoku tsunami hit the town of Naraha and caused the subsequent Fukushima nuclear power station meltdown of March 2011. The town remained evacuated due to radiation fall-out until September 2015, when, following clean-up efforts, residents were allowed to return home.

TOP LEFT:
Iitate Village, Fukushima Prefecture, Japan
An abandoned playground photographed almost a year after the Fukushima disaster.

BOTTOM LEFT:
Swimming pool, Namie, Fukushima Prefecture, Japan
The swimming pool of an elementary school in Namie in the Fukushima exclusion zone.

TOP RIGHT:
Tomioka, Fukushima Prefecture, Japan
A damaged house a month after the Fukushima disaster. The accident severity level was 7, the highest level on the International Nuclear Event Scale.

BOTTOM RIGHT:
Namie, Fukushima Prefecture, Japan
Rubble remains on the deserted streets nearly a year after the tsunami hit the now abandoned town. Six other towns and two villages also fell within the Fukushima exclusion zone.

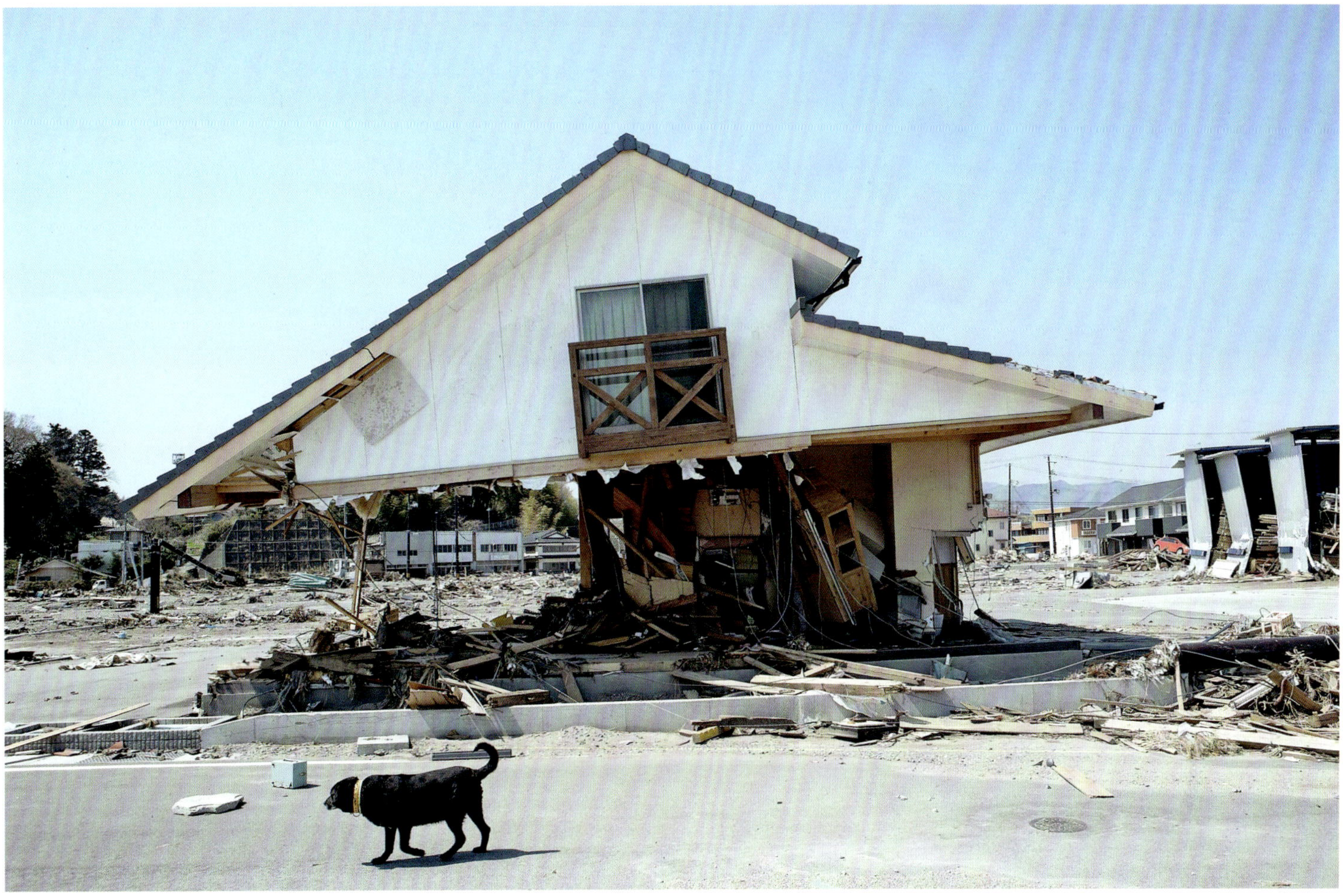

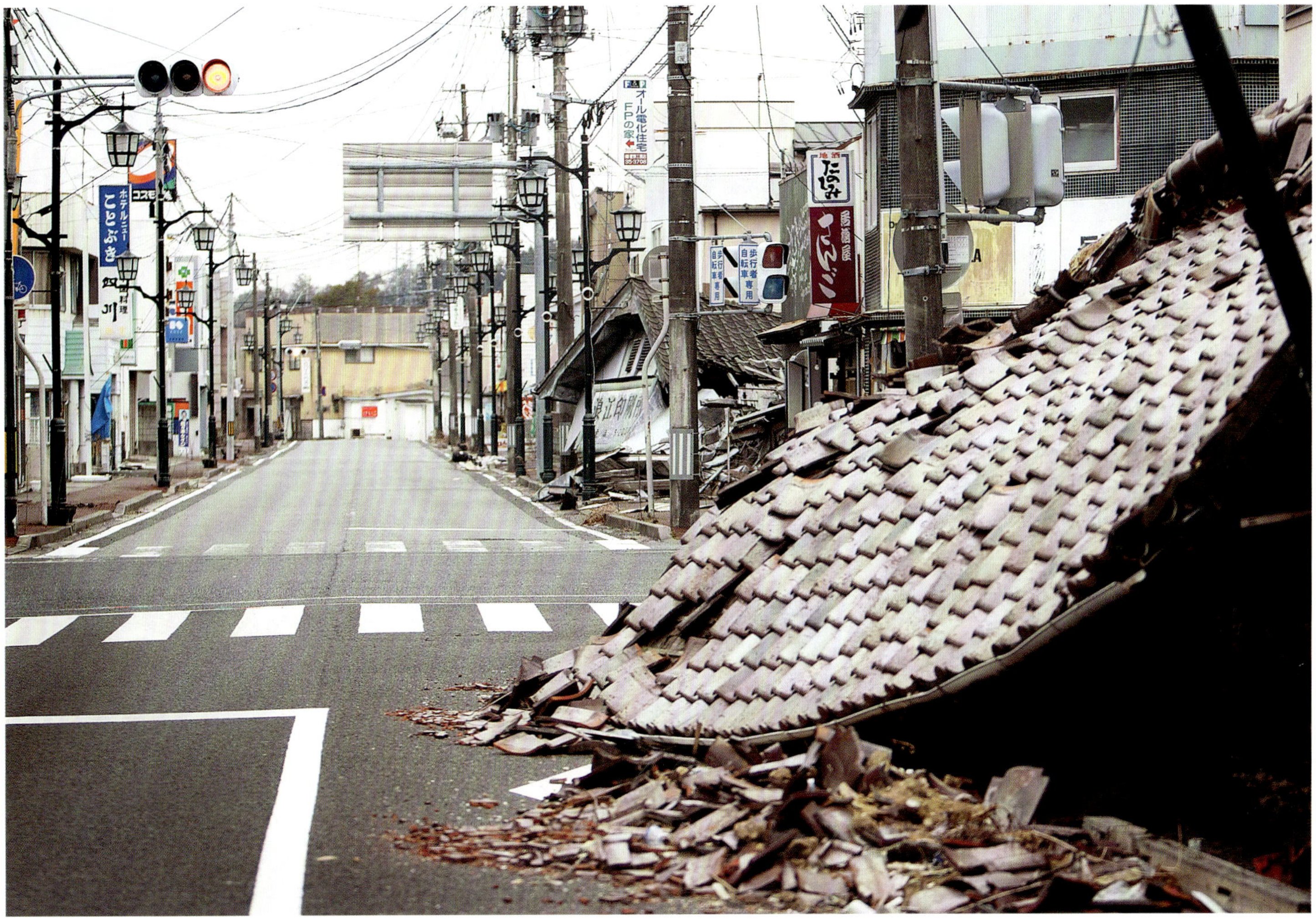

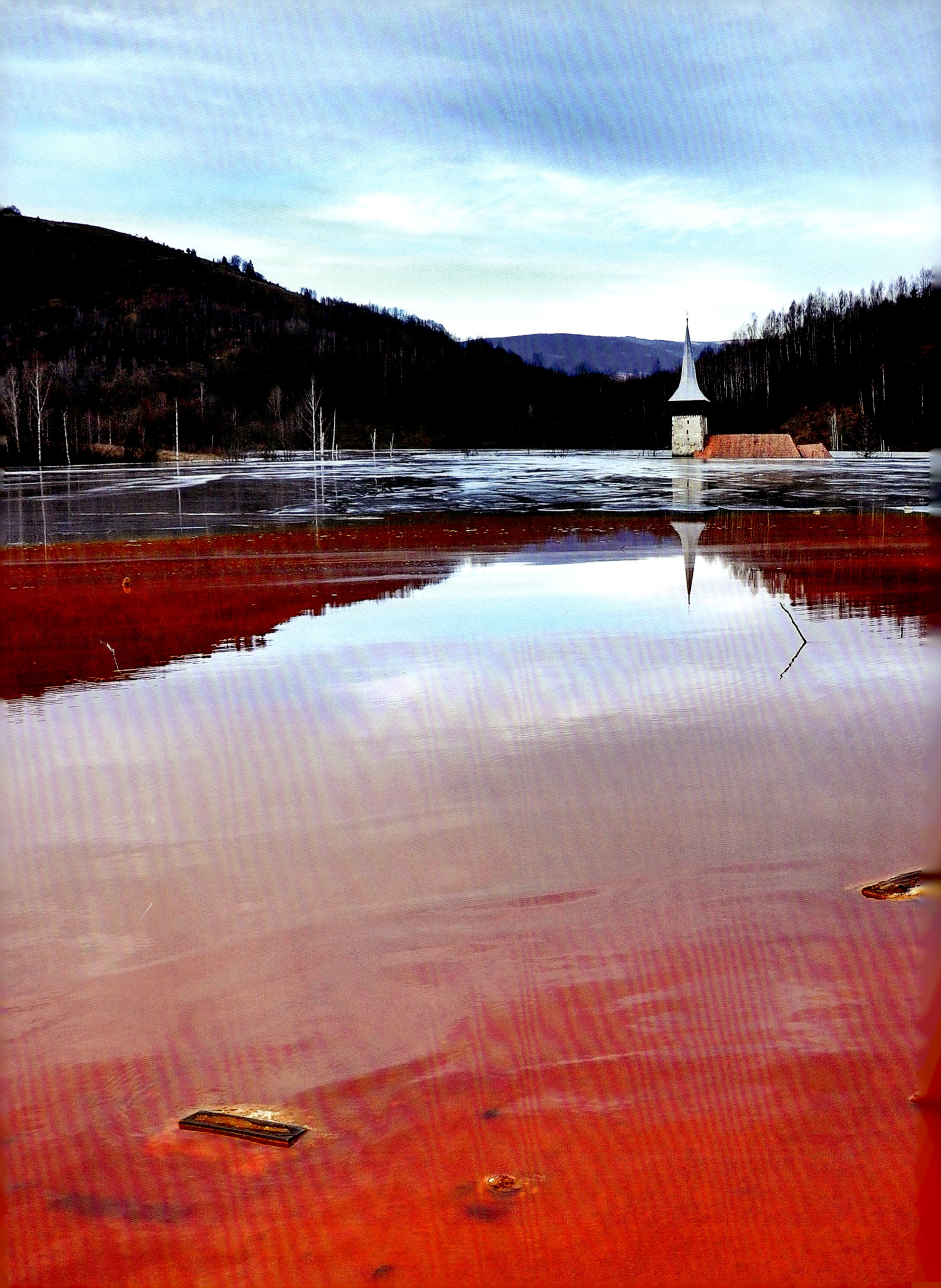

LEFT:

Geamana, Apuseni Mountains, Alba County, Romania
When copper was discovered in the hills above the village of Geamana in the 1970s, its residents probably didn't think that it would mean the destruction of their pretty valley. But, with the engineers needing somewhere to dump waste water from the new copper mine, dictator Nicolae Ceausescu ordered that Geamana's 400 families be resettled and the village flooded.

OVERLEAF:

Geamana, Apuseni Mountains, Alba County, Romania
All that can be seen of the village today is the church steeple and a few of the buildings on higher land, while the waste water isn't merely a copper-red colour but polluted with cyanide and other chemicals.

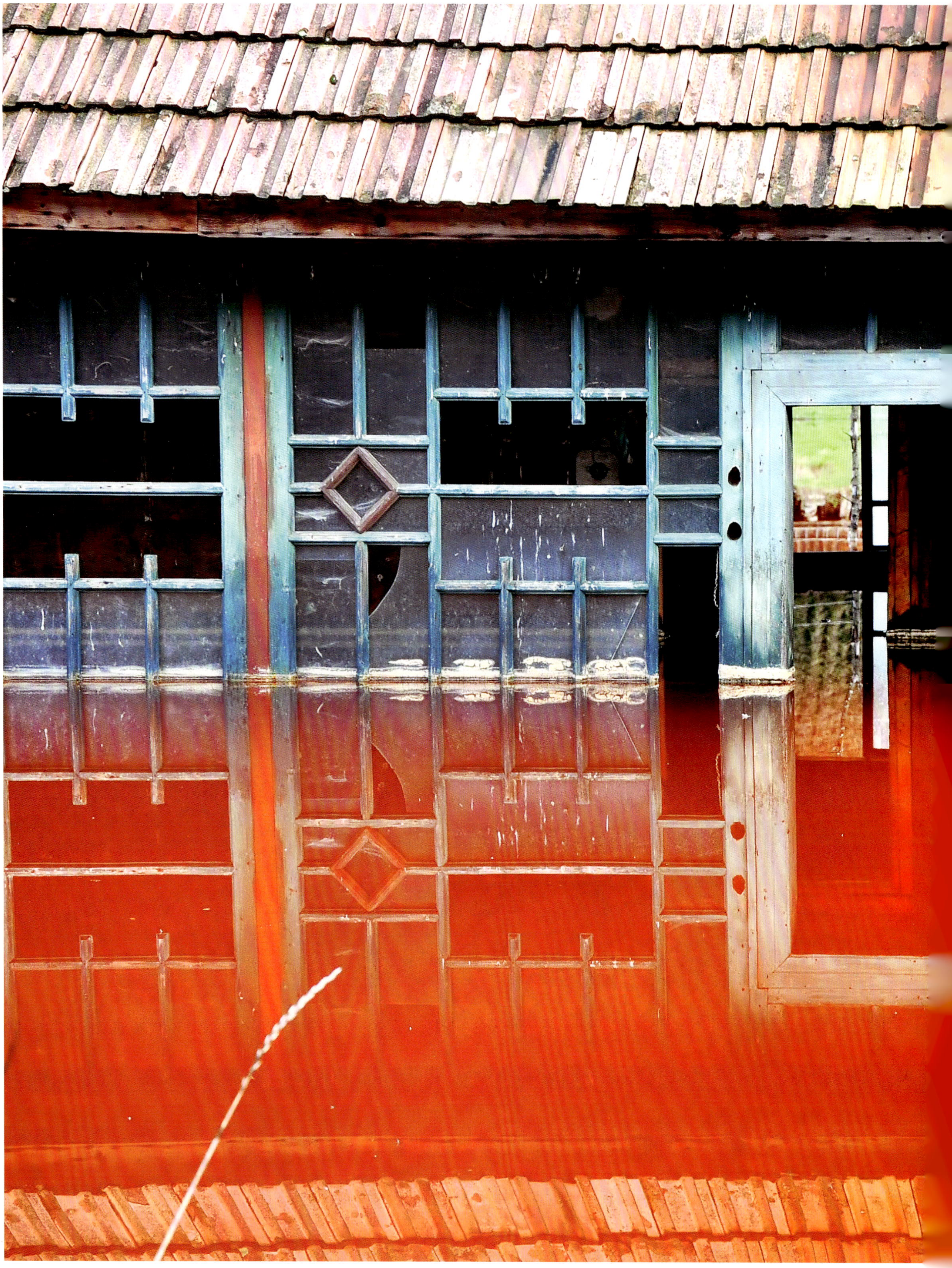

95

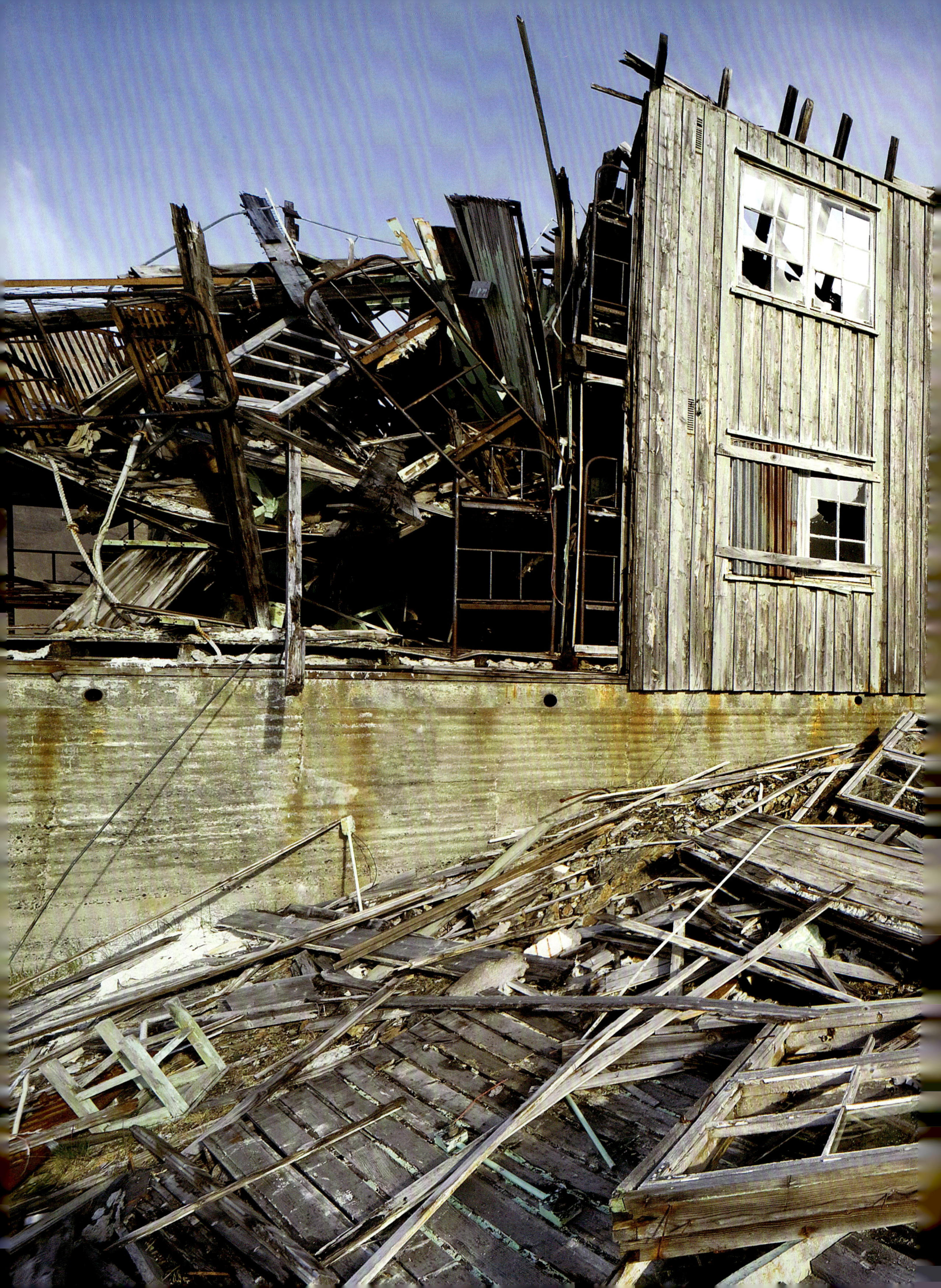

Leith Harbour Whaling Station, South Georgia, Atlantic Ocean
With its own hospital, library, cinema and narrow gauge railway, the British whaling station at Leith Harbour operated from 1909 to 1965. It is now off limits due to dangerous buildings and high levels of asbestos.

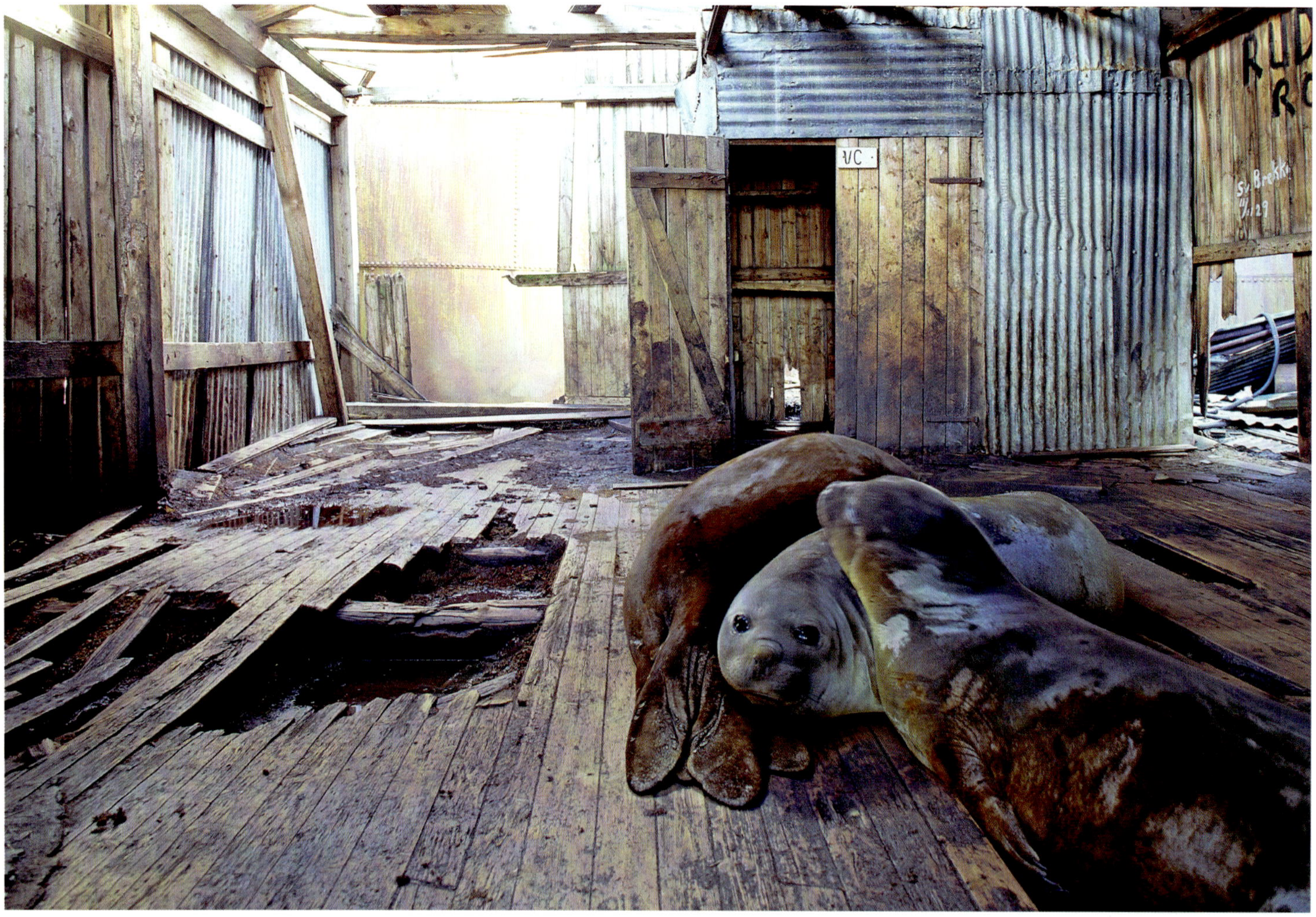
VC

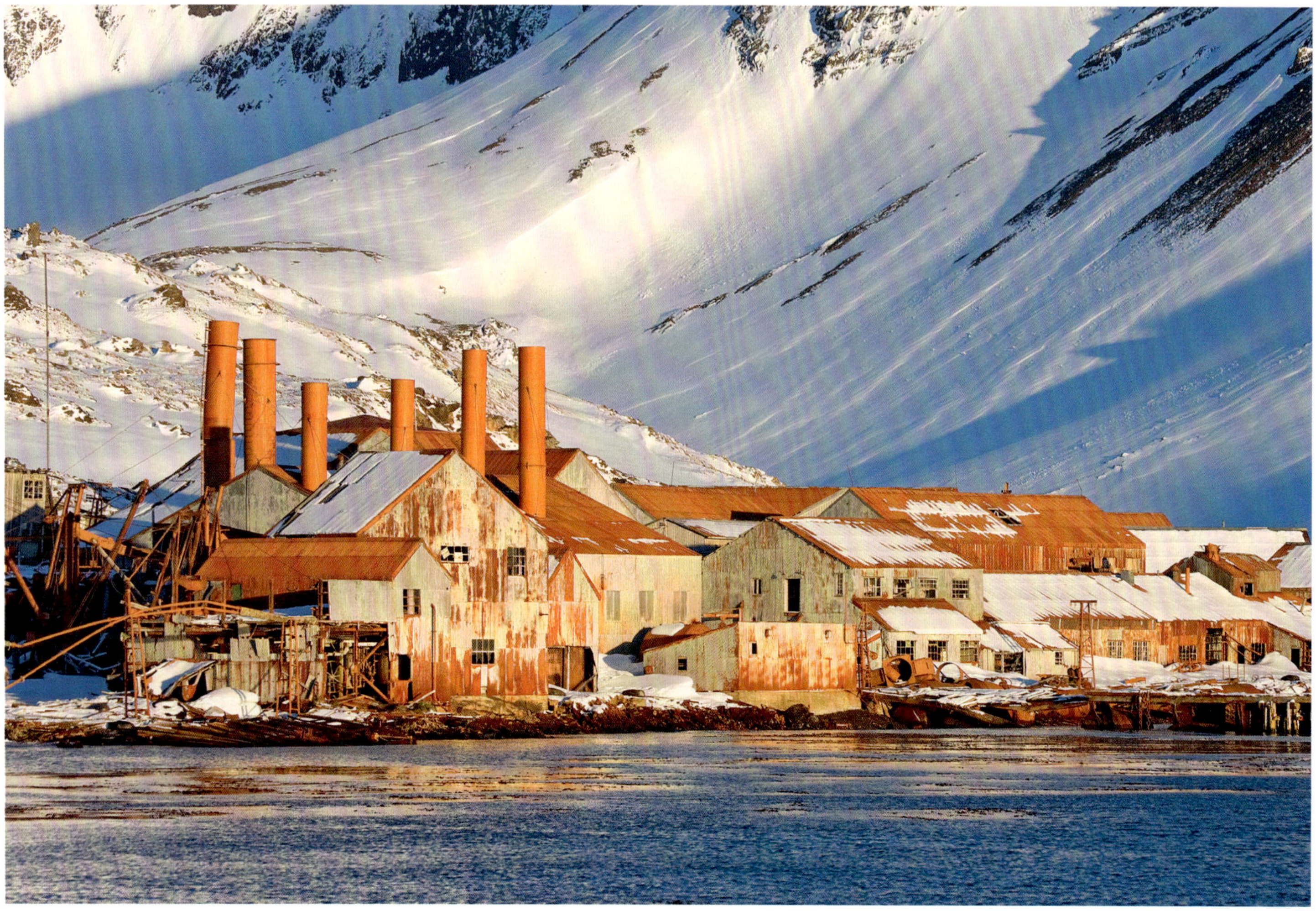

ALL PHOTOGRAPHS:

Leith Harbour Whaling Station, South Georgia, Atlantic Ocean
Having virtually eliminated the whale populations of the North Atlantic, at the beginning of the 20th century whalers looked south and made South Georgia the world's largest whaling centre. Five stations were built there, with Argentinian, Norwegian, British, South African and, later, Japanese companies operating under leases granted by the British government. Over the six decades of the South Atlantic whaling industry, about 1.6 million whales were killed to produce oil for use in the manufacture of soap and margarine. When substitutes such as kerosene and vegetable oils were developed, the industry fell into decline. Leith Harbour was the last of South Georgia's whaling stations to close.

Plymouth Courthouse Building, Montserrat, Caribbean
When the Soufrière Hills volcano erupted in July 1995, Montserrat's capital, Plymouth, was completely buried by ash. Following further eruptions, two-thirds of the population left as half of the island became uninhabitable. In theory, Plymouth is still the capital, giving it the unusual distinction of being the only ghost town that is also a capital city.

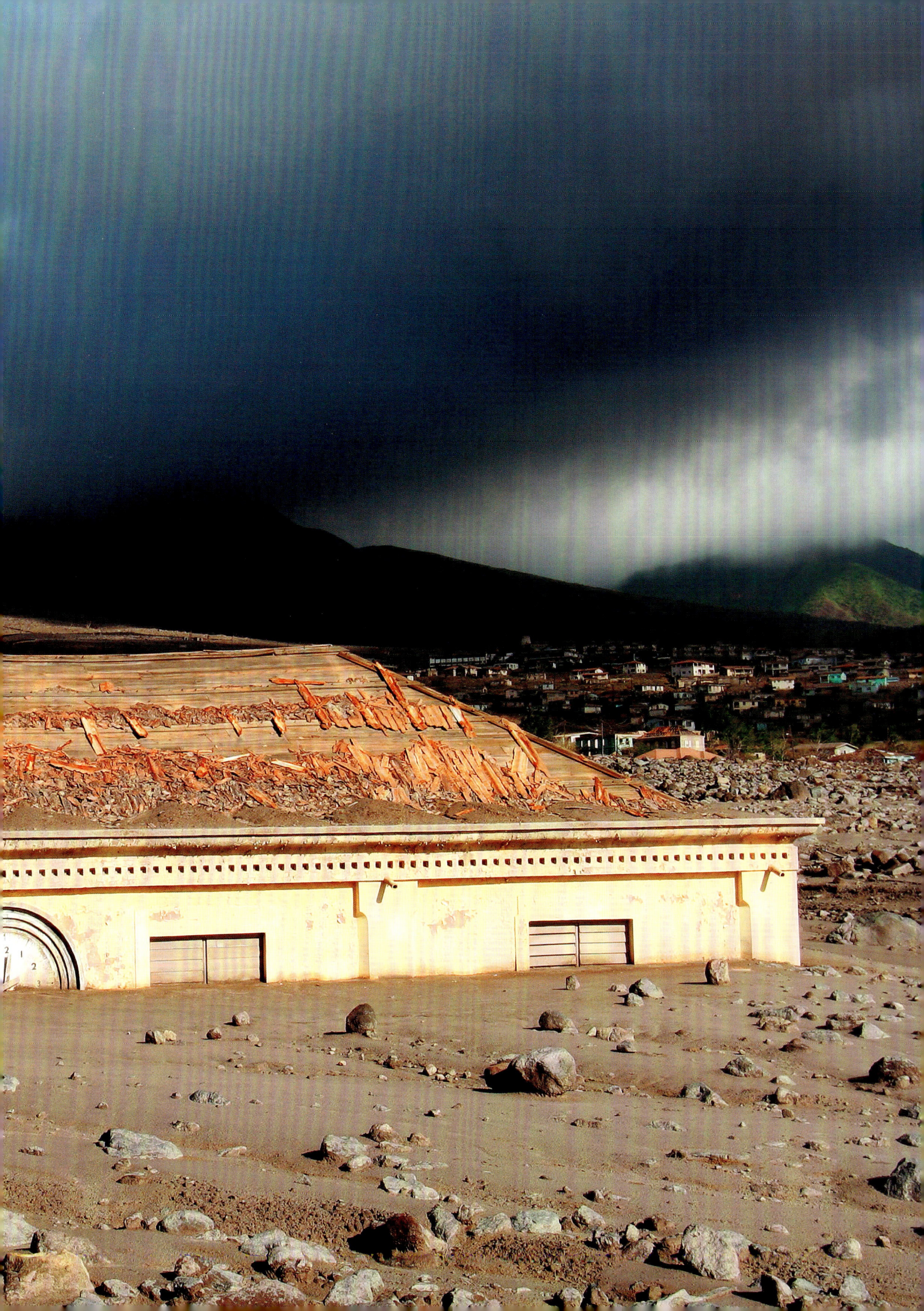

Poggioreale, Sicily, Italy
Destroyed by the Belice Valley earthquake in 1968, the 18th-century town of Poggioreale was eventually rebuilt in a safer place a few miles away. Almost all the residents escaped, other than for a small number who refused to leave their homes.

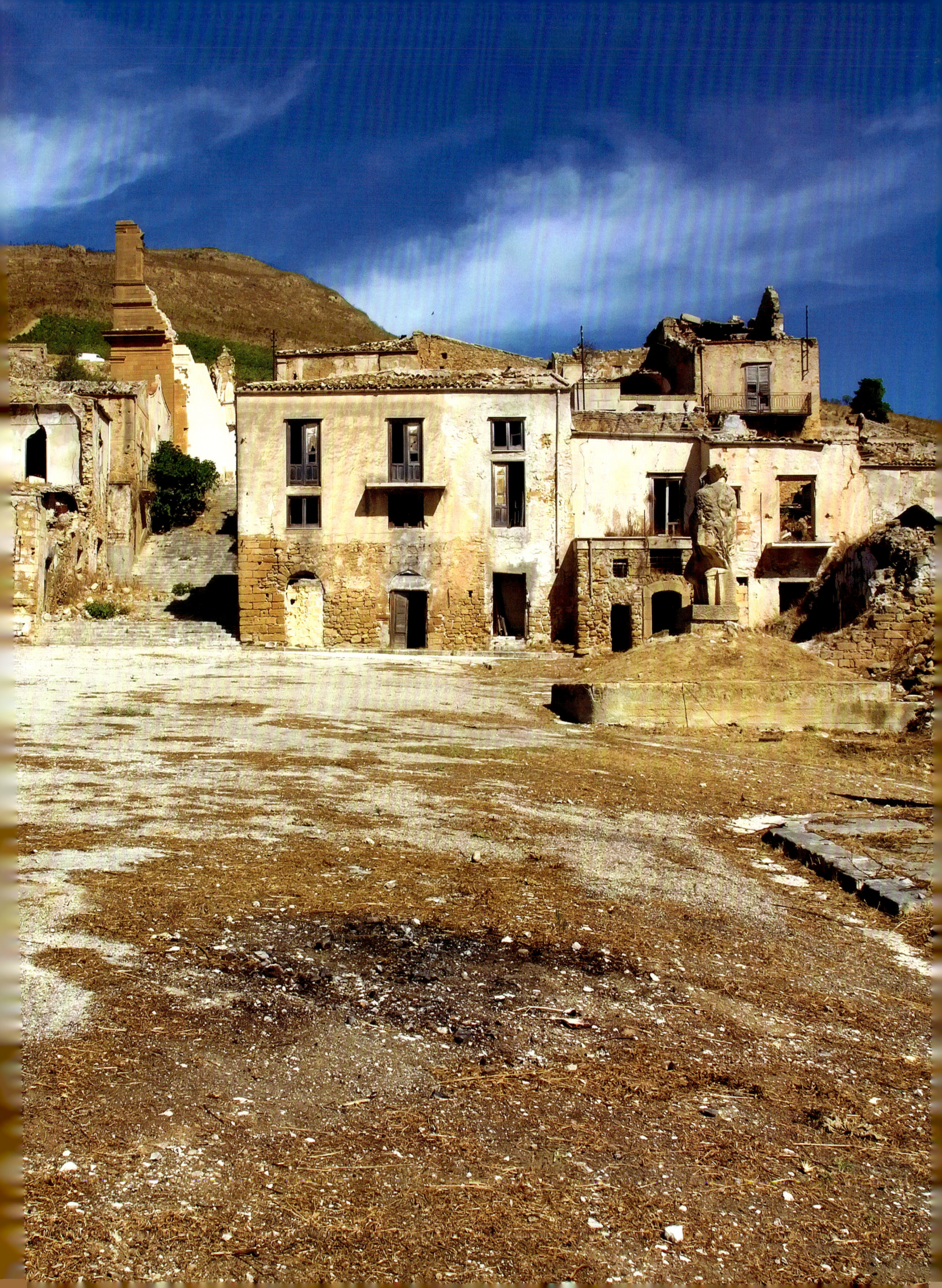

ALL PHOTOGRAPHS:
Mosque, Agdam, Nagorno-Karabakh, Azerbaijan
Following the 1993 conflict between Nagorno-Karabakh separatists and Azerbaijani forces, the town of Agdam was abandoned. While Azerbaijan is predominantly Muslim, Agdam is now in an area controlled by the Christian Armenian Nagorno-Karabakh Republic, whose army has destroyed and looted much of the town, thus discouraging Azerbaijanis from recapturing it. The town remains uninhabited, with only the derelict mosque surviving.

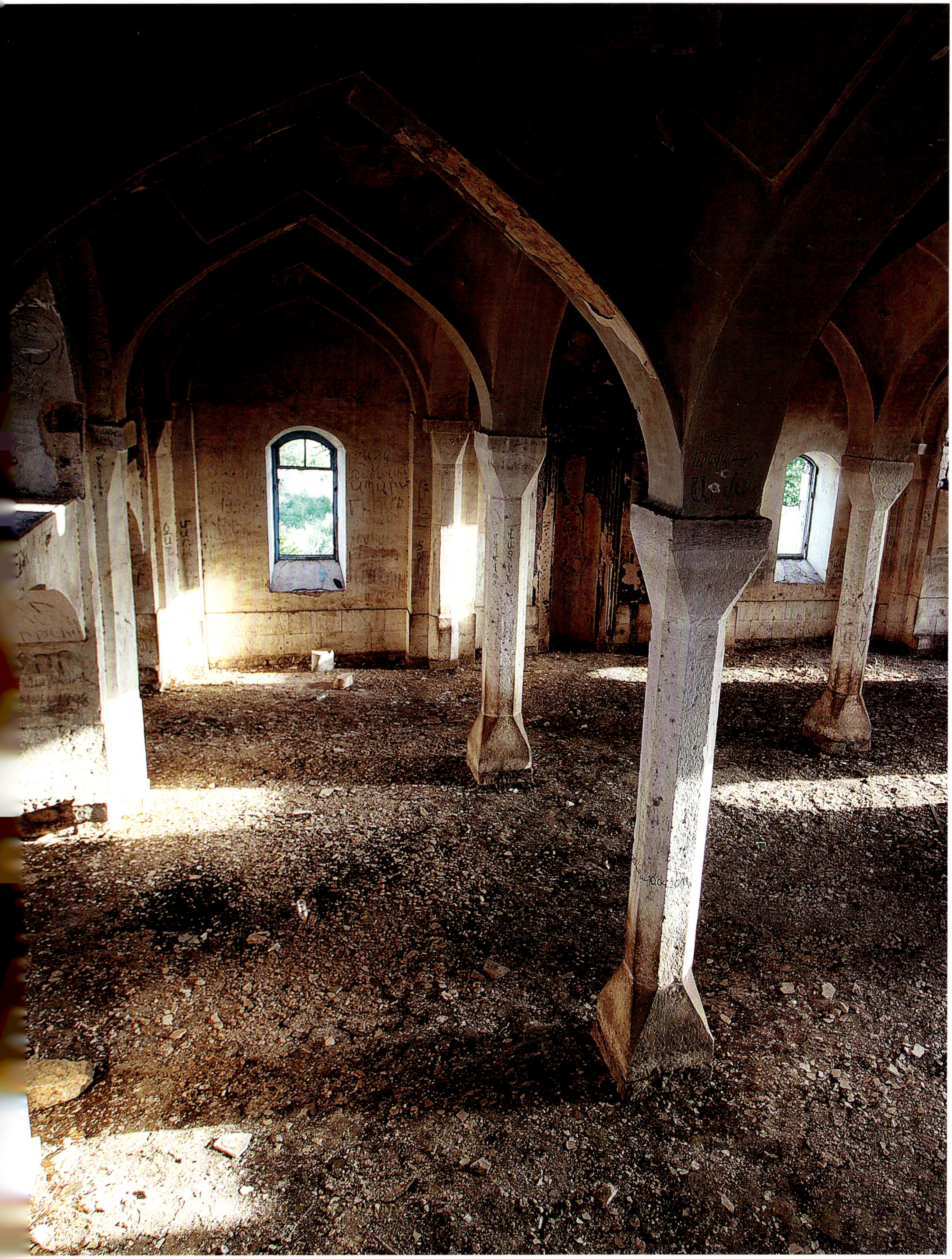

Rhyolite, Nevada, USA
The small town of Rhyolite sprang up in 1905 when gold was discovered there, but within three years the rush had already peaked. As many as 5,000 people lived there in 1908, before the richest ore was exhausted and production fell. In 1911, the mine closed.

107

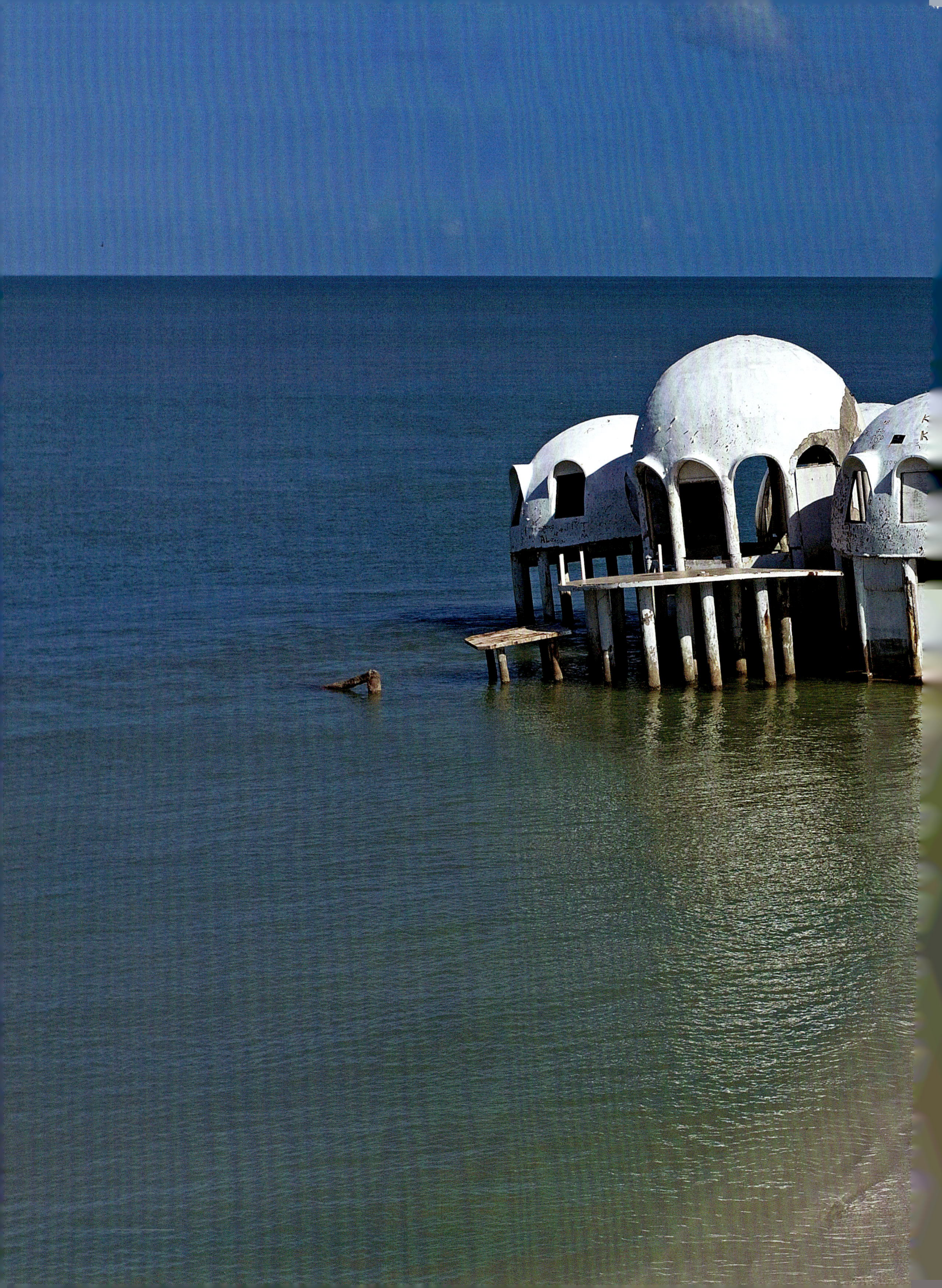

Cape Romano, Florida, USA
Built in the early 1980s, these solar-powered homes were occupied for ten years before 1992's Hurricane Andrew and 2005's Hurricane Wilma damaged the houses and tore away part of the coastline. Today, the houses can only be reached by boat.

Varosha, Famagusta, Northern Cyprus
At a glance this might just look like any out-of-season beach resort, but no tourists have visited Varosha for more than 40 years. A Greek Cypriot resort, Varosha was sealed off by Turkish forces after a brief war between the island's Turks and Greeks erupted in 1974 and divided the country. The Turks held on to Varosha, hoping to use it as a bargaining chip in negotiations with the Greeks, but the discussions never happened and today Varosha remains locked up, deserted and crumbling.

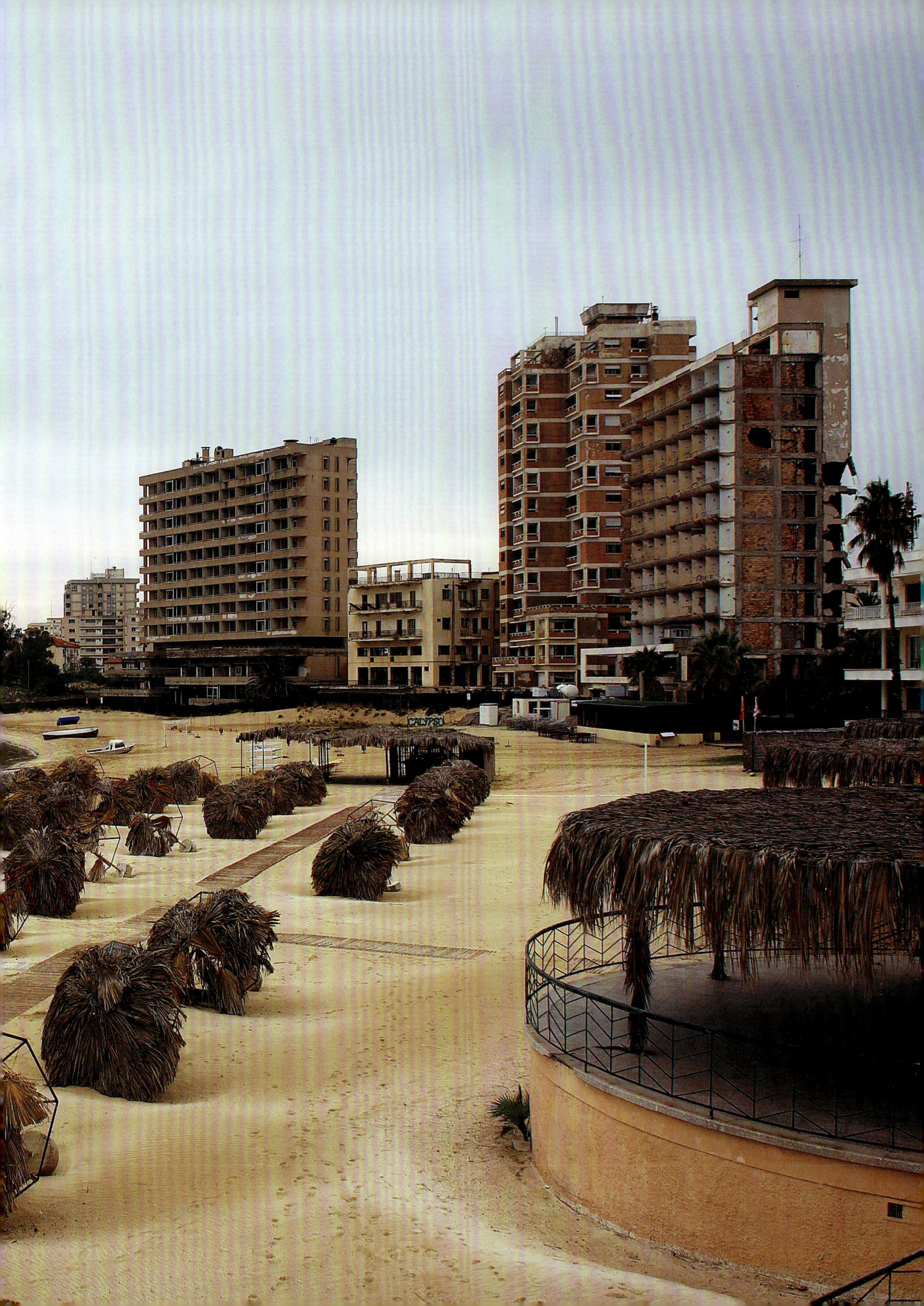
CALYPSO

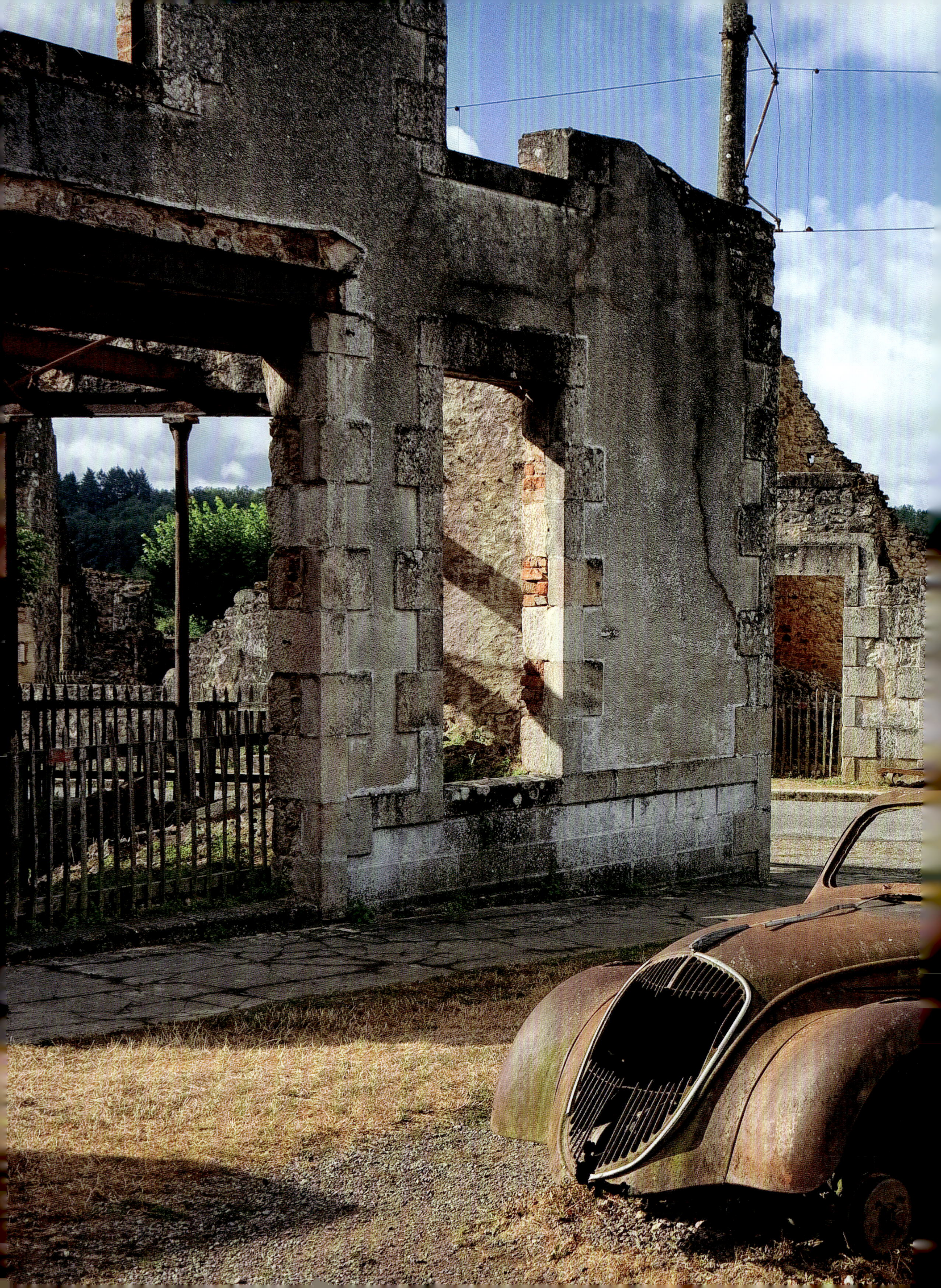

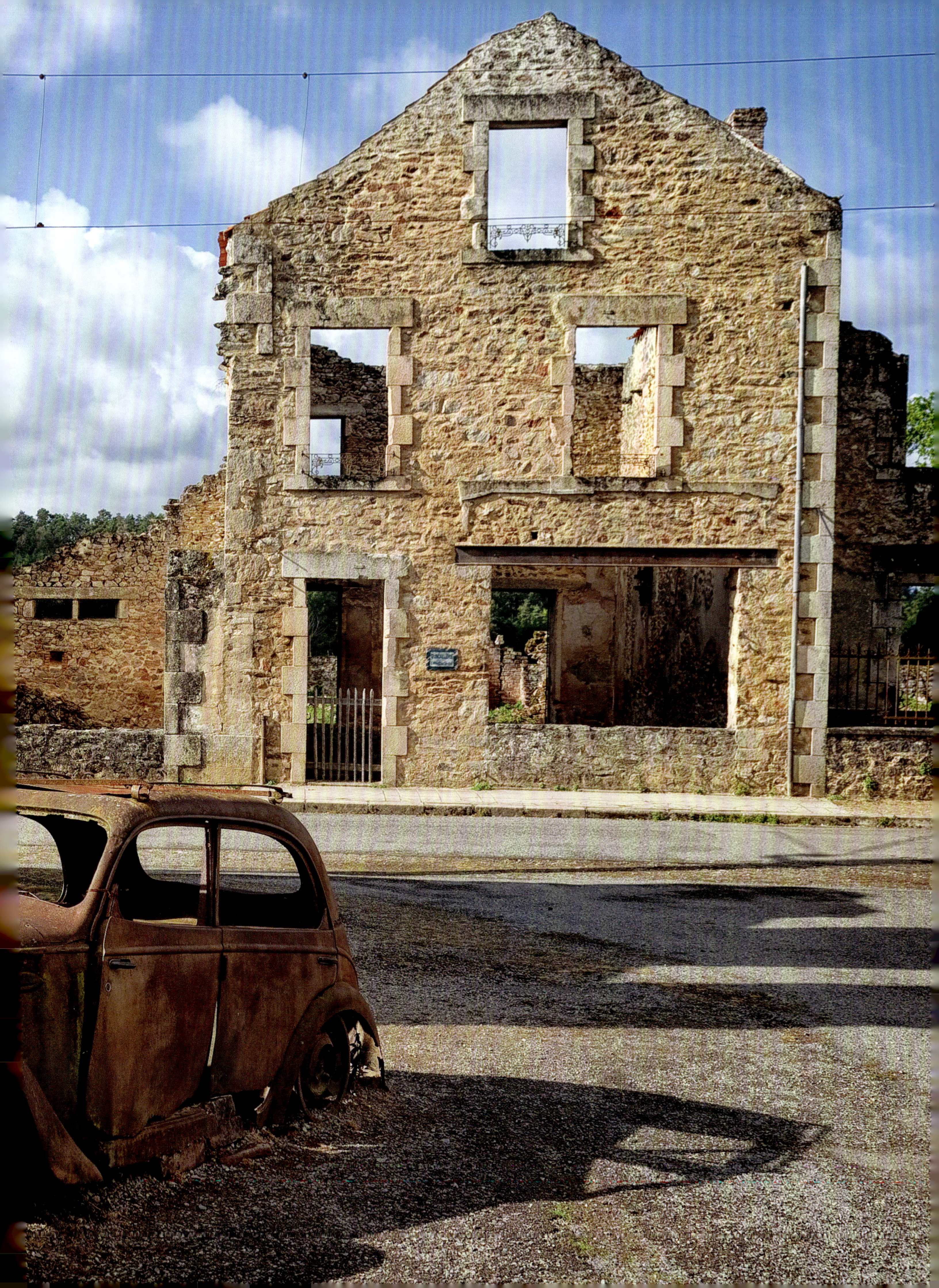

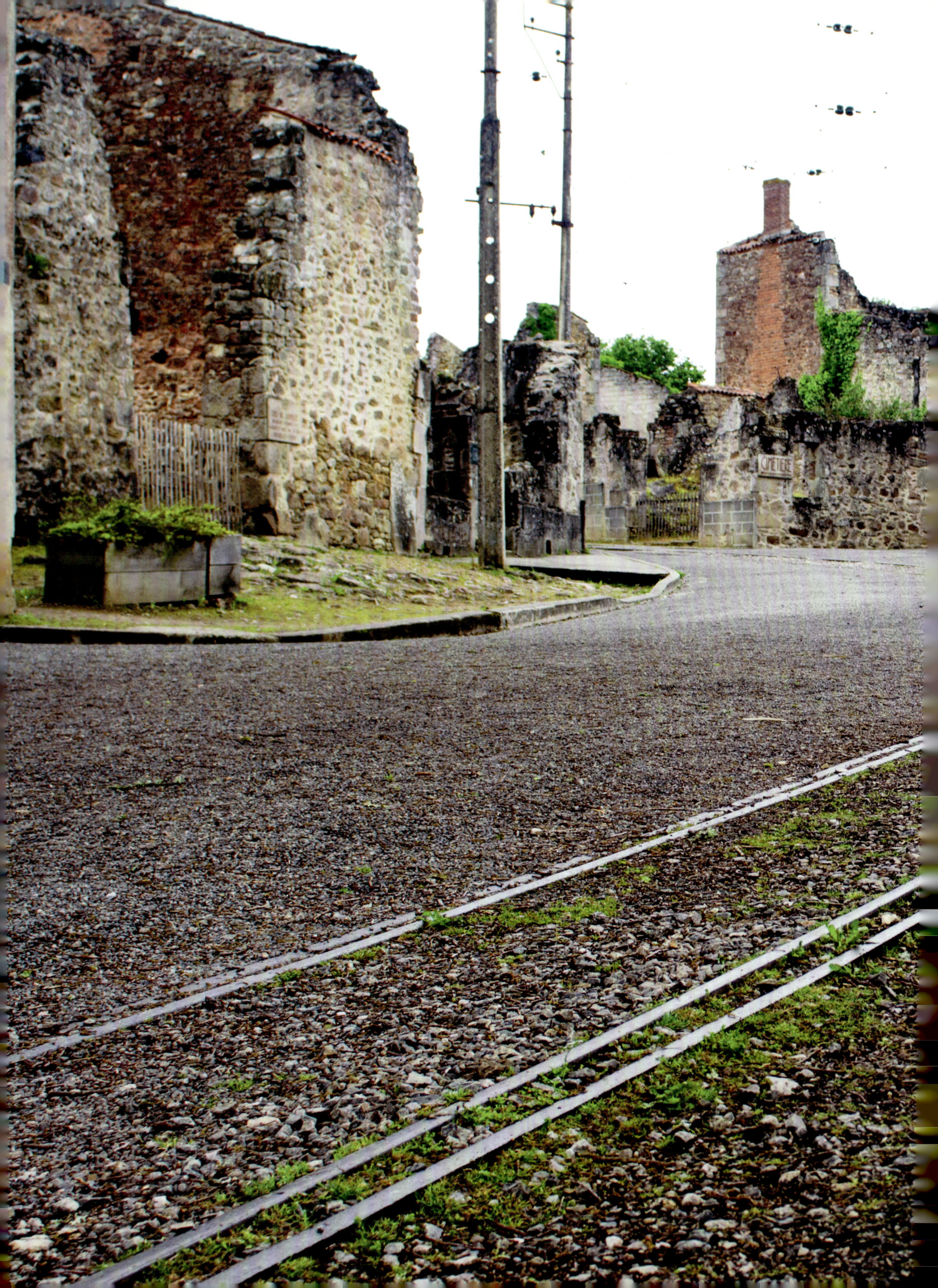

LEFT AND PREVIOUS PAGE:
Oradour-sur-Glane, Haute-Vienne, France
On 10 June 1944, 642 inhabitants of this village – men, women and children – were massacred by a Nazi Waffen-SS company. SS-Sturmbannführer Adolf Diekmann had been ordered to take 30 hostages to use in bargaining for the release of a Waffen-SS officer held by the French Resistance. Instead, he ordered that the whole village be rounded up and killed, claiming that it was in retaliation for local partisan activity.

When Diekmann's superiors heard of his actions, an investigation was begun, but he, and many of the 200 men involved, were killed in battle shortly after. Others came to trial after the war.

A new village with the same name was built nearby, but President Charles de Gaulle ordered the original be maintained as a memorial to the massacre.

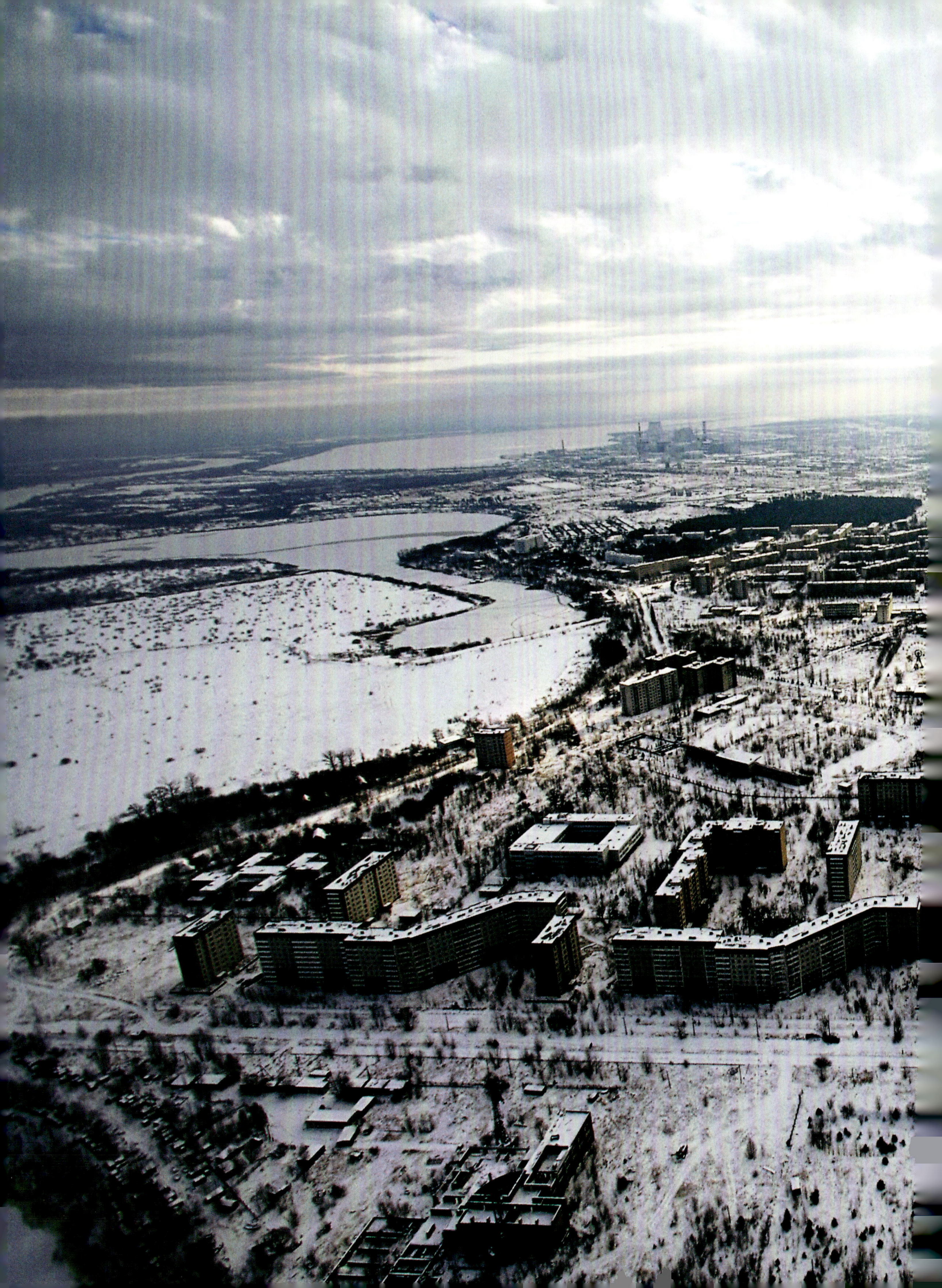

Pripyat, Ukraine
Momentarily it may look serene, but there are no cars, the roads haven't been snowploughed, and there are no lights anywhere. In fact, there isn't a soul to be seen. But then Pripyat has been void of residents since 27 April 1986, when its 50,000 inhabitants were evacuated on the day following the Chernobyl nuclear power station explosion. Chernobyl can be seen on the horizon towards the left.

ALL PHOTOGRAPHS:
Pripyat, Ukraine
Tall poplar trees now grow through Pripyat's pavements and into buildings, and the unused roads are covered with moss. While, in the short term, radiation levels caused wild animals in the area to be born with a greater number of genetic defects, in the absence of people the forests have expanded and become wilder: greater numbers of roe deer and wild boar have been joined by moose, lynx and wolves. Pripyat Amusement Park was to be officially opened on 1 May 1986, but, after the explosion, residents were allowed to use the fairground wheel for a couple of hours before the evacuation was ordered. Although Pripyat is still within the 19-mile (30km) safety exclusion zone, the radiation levels are now low enough that tourists can visit for short trips.

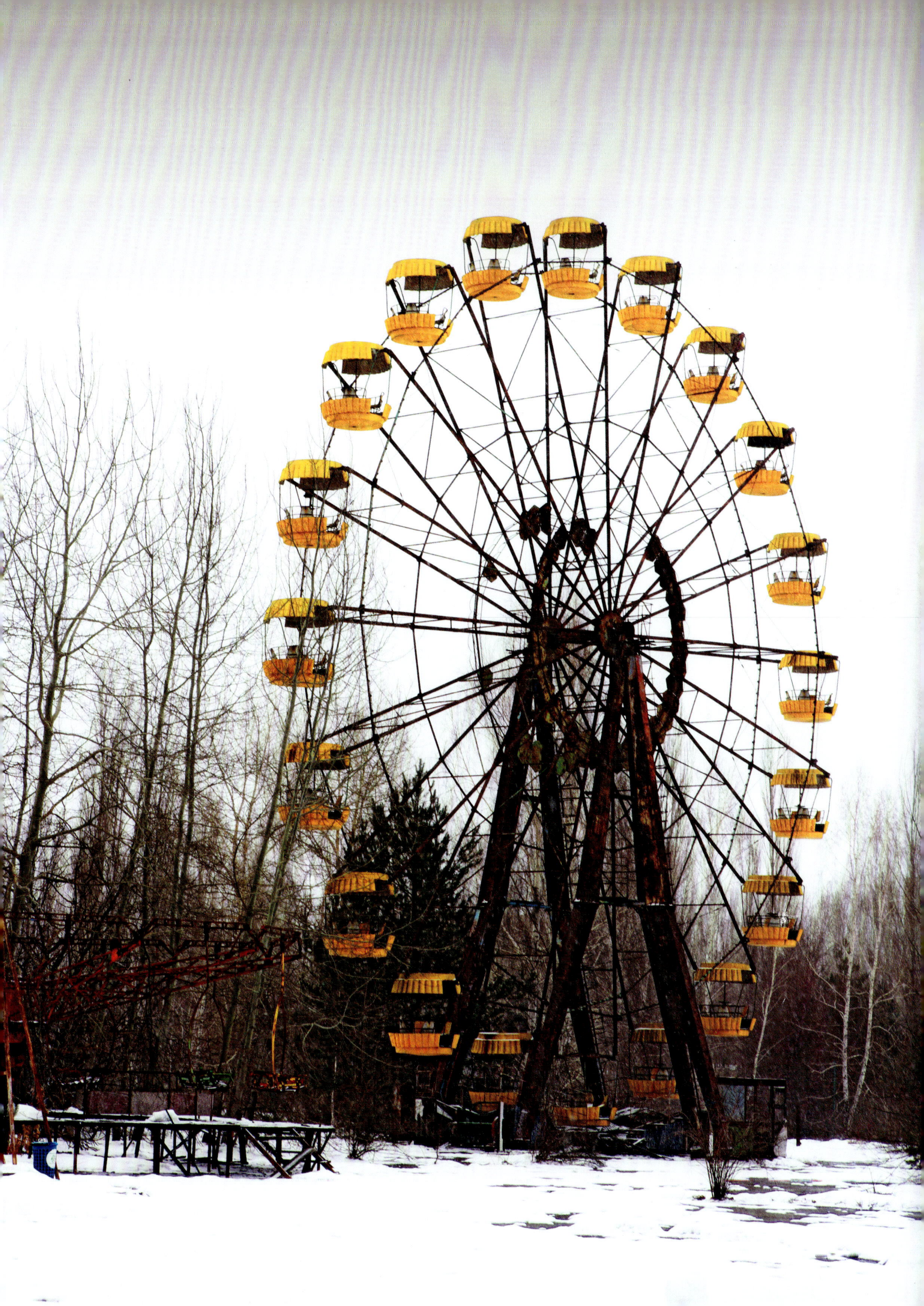

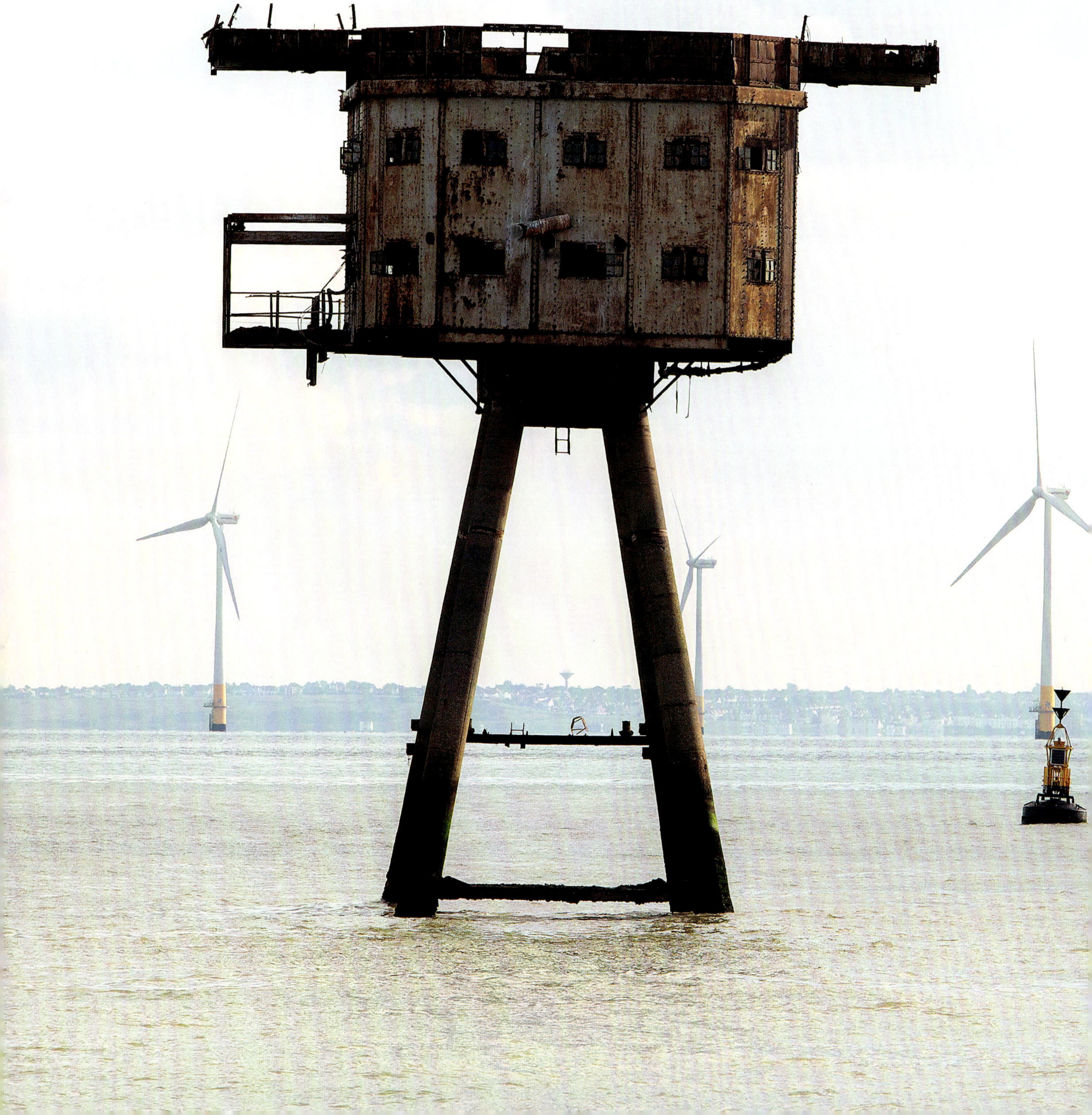

Military & Scientific Buildings

A hidden Soviet submarine base, a secret 1960s bunker and an Antarctic research station untouched for 50 years. Because of the Cold War, or just cold weather, these places have all been frozen in time. The military and scientific buildings included here take us into many highly specialized worlds, worlds that the general public didn't encounter, either because the buildings were so remote, or because very few people were ever even told about them. With the end of the Cold War, these bunkers and bases were first decommissioned and closed, before being made accessible to the public. Through them we don't only discover secrets about our recent past but we also open a door back through time on to the world as it was when these places were built. Most of us have probably forgotten, if we ever knew, why we say we 'dial' a phone number – until we see the old rotary dial phones in these Cold War bunkers.

Similarly, the Antarctic huts of Shackleton's early 20th century explorers or those of geologists in the 1950s were, quite literally, frozen in time. Abandoned but preserved by the climate, they still contain the tin cans, spare clothes, fuel and tools that their occupants depended upon.

LEFT:
Maunsell Fort, Shivering Sands, Thames Estuary, England
Looking like tripods from *The War of the Worlds*, the Maunsell Forts defended London from enemy aircraft during World War II. Situated 9 miles (14.5km) from land, they were decommissioned after the war and were abandoned in 1958.

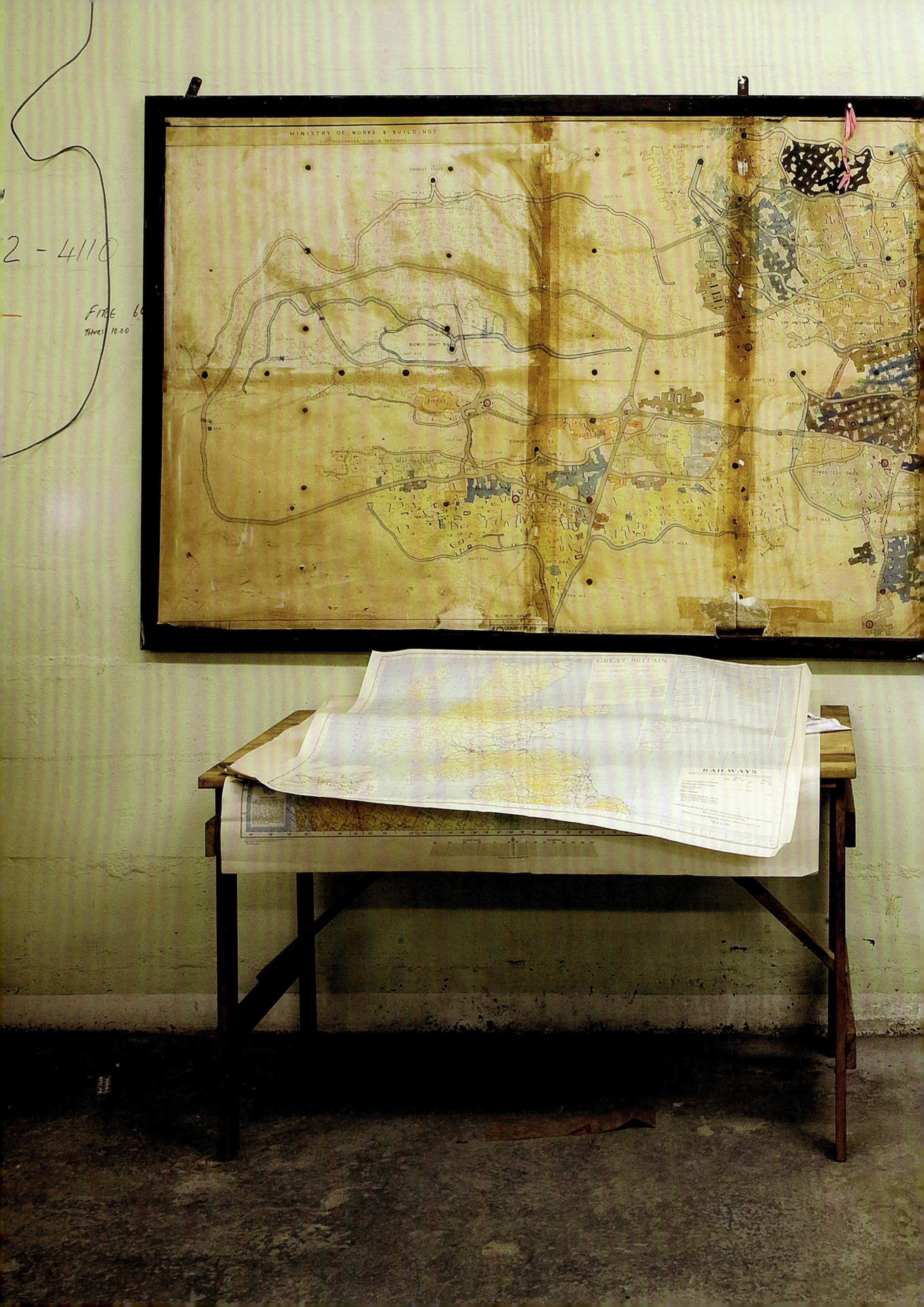
MINISTRY OF WORKS & BUILDINGS
GREAT BRITAIN
RAILWAYS

Burlington Bunker, Corsham, Wiltshire, England
Developed during the 1950s as a shelter from which the British government could operate in the event of a nuclear attack, the Burlington Bunker remained secret until it was decommissioned in 2004. Built in disused underground quarries, the bunker could accommodate 4,000 staff.

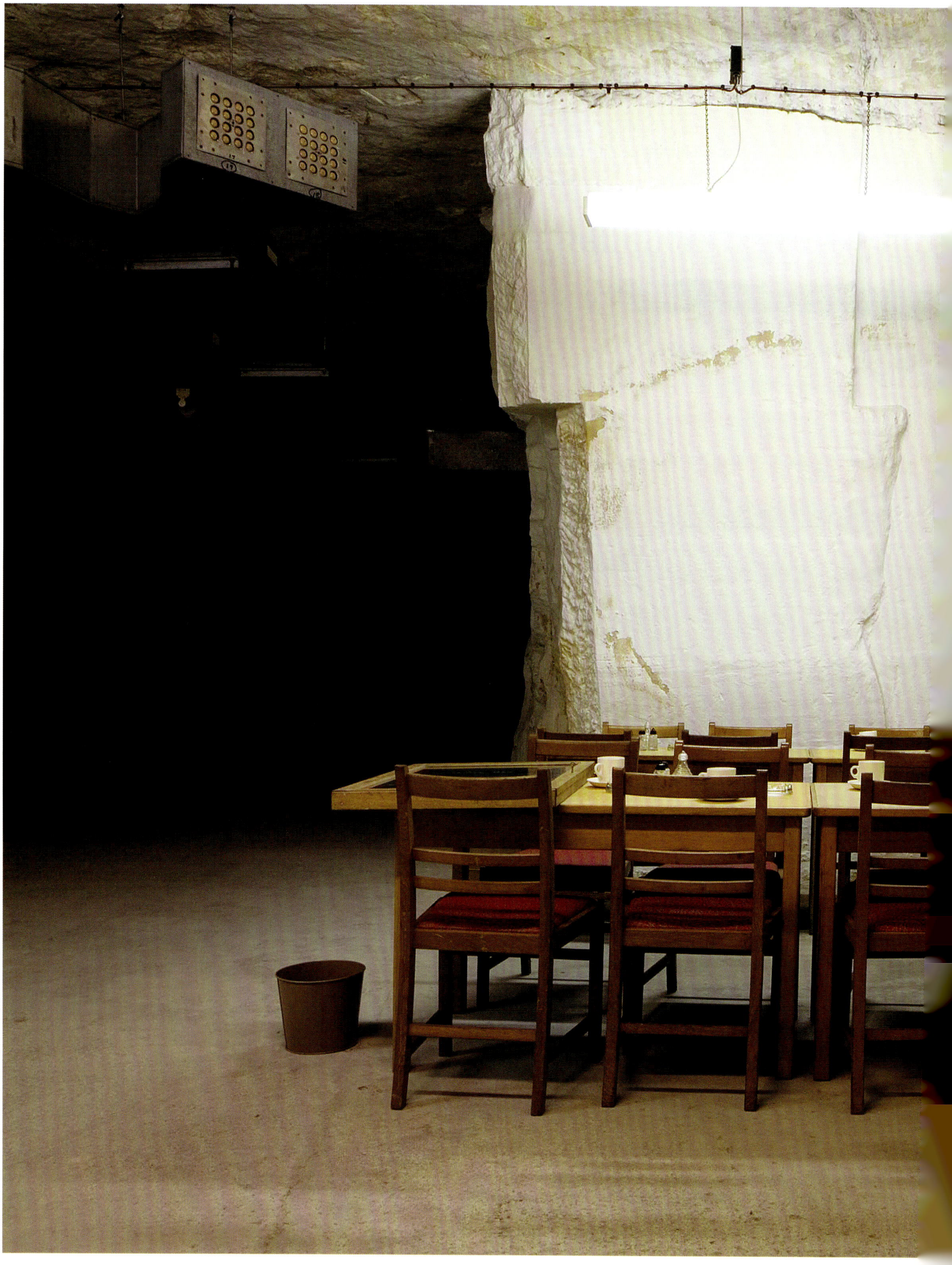

LEFT:
Canteen, Burlington Bunker, Corsham, Wiltshire, England
The 35-acre bunker could support its personnel with no outside contact for three months, with an underground lake providing water that could be treated to make it safe for drinking. For 30 years, it had the second largest, but unused, telephone exchange in Britain.

OVERLEAF:
The KGB Residency, Karlshorst, Berlin, Germany
The KGB residency in East Berlin was the largest KGB building outside the USSR. A former hospital building, it was part of the 160-acre Soviet compound at Karlshorst, which included the USSR's Berlin garrison. It was abandoned when the last Russian forces left Germany in 1994.

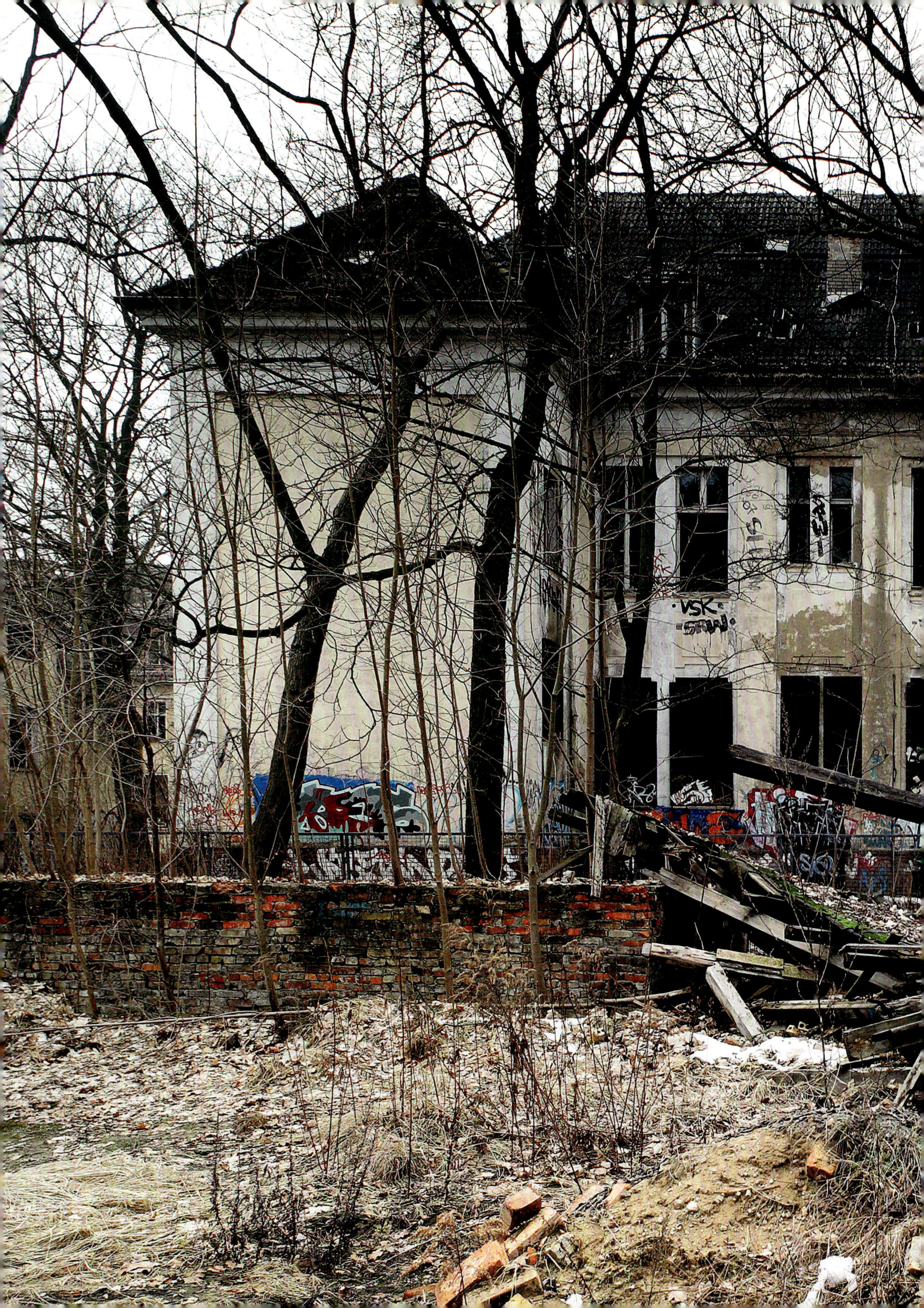
VSK

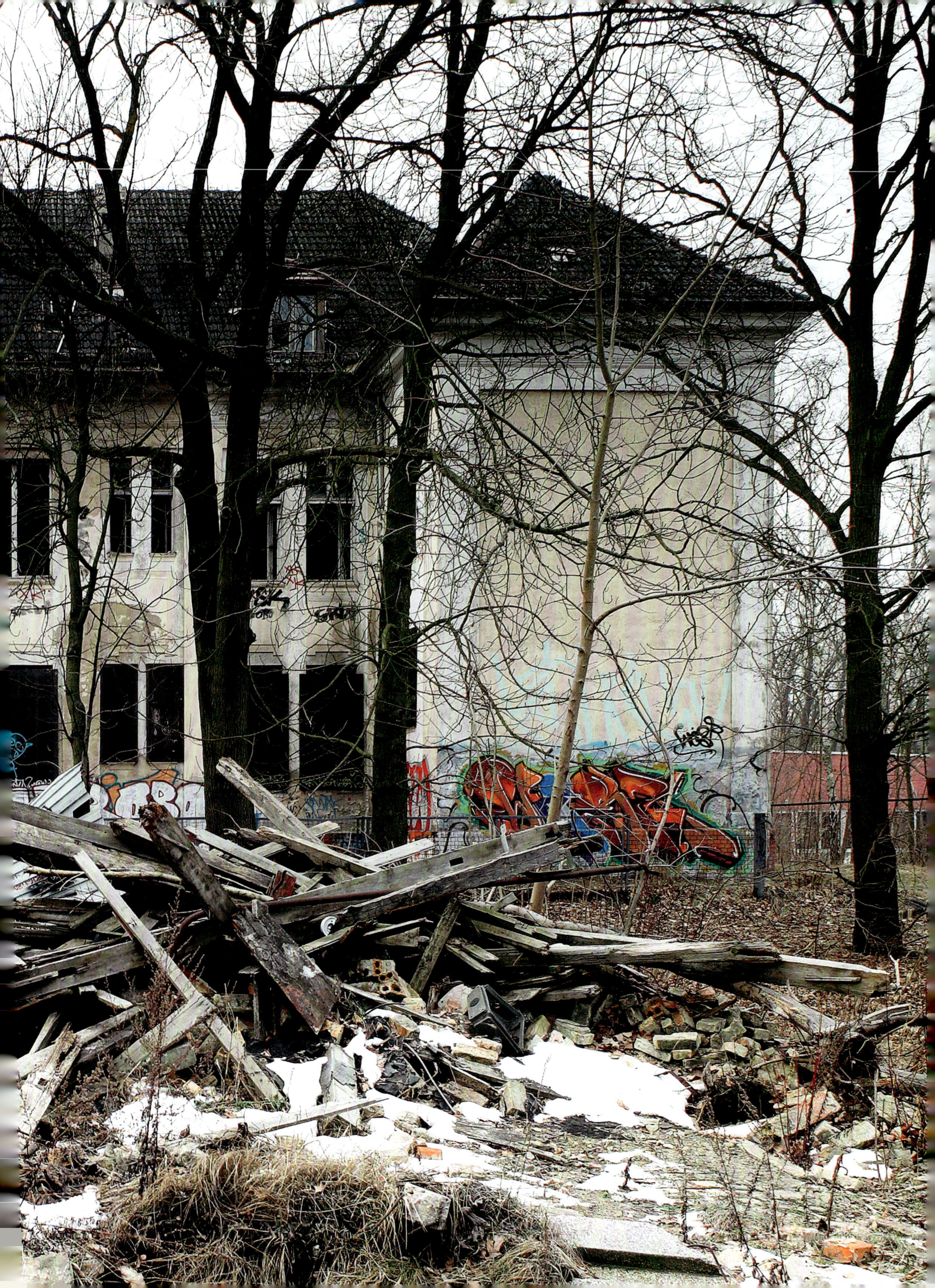

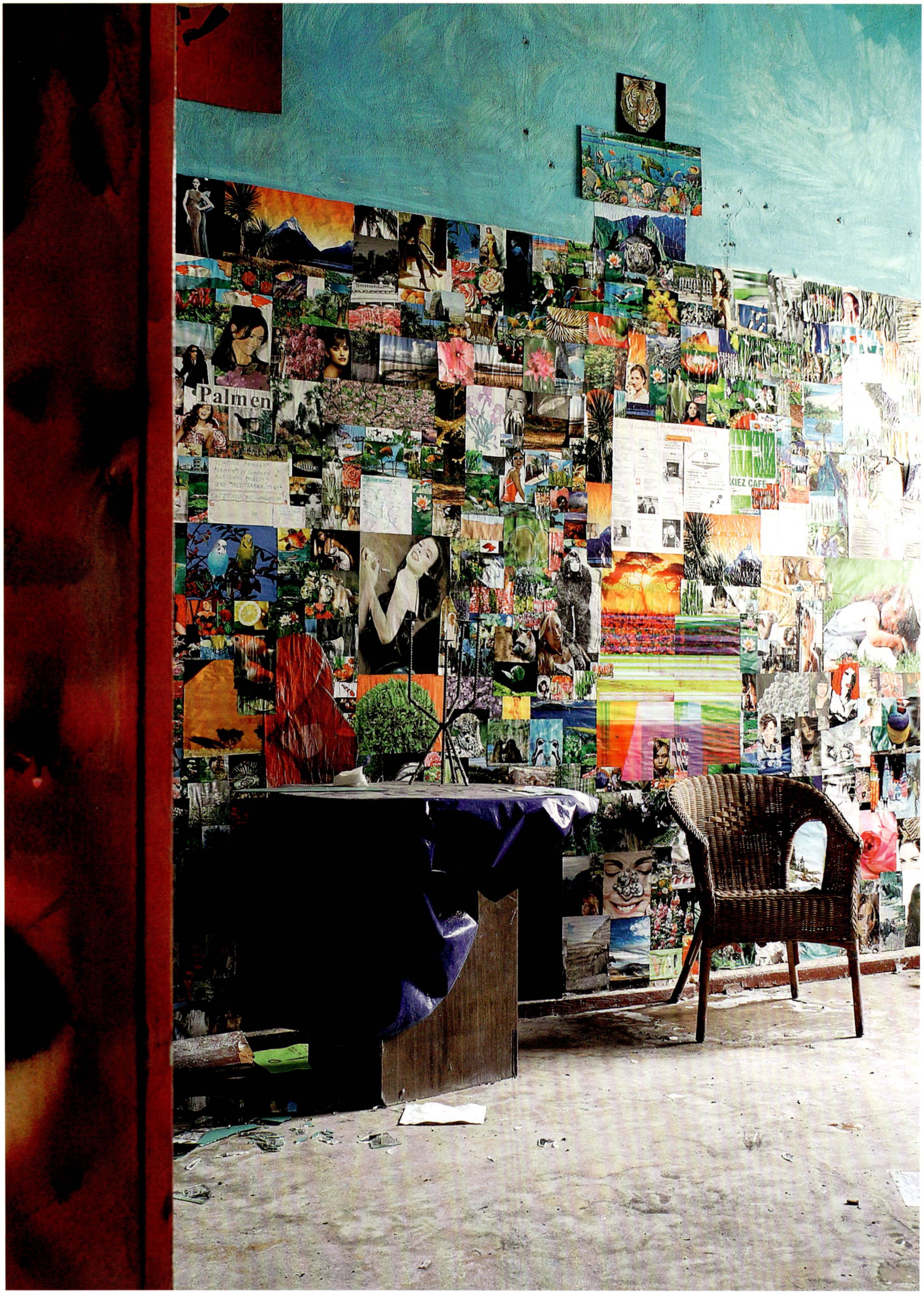
Palmen
KIEZ CAFE

ALL PHOTOGRAPHS:
The KGB Residency, Karlshorst, Berlin, Germany
For 20 years, the former KGB residency was boarded up and a destination only for urban explorers. Now, though, the whole Soviet compound is being redeveloped for housing.

Soviet tanks, Kabul Military Training Centre, Afghanistan
A graveyard of military hardware. Soviet tanks and armoured personnel carriers stand rusting many years after the Soviet retreat from Afghanistan in 1989.

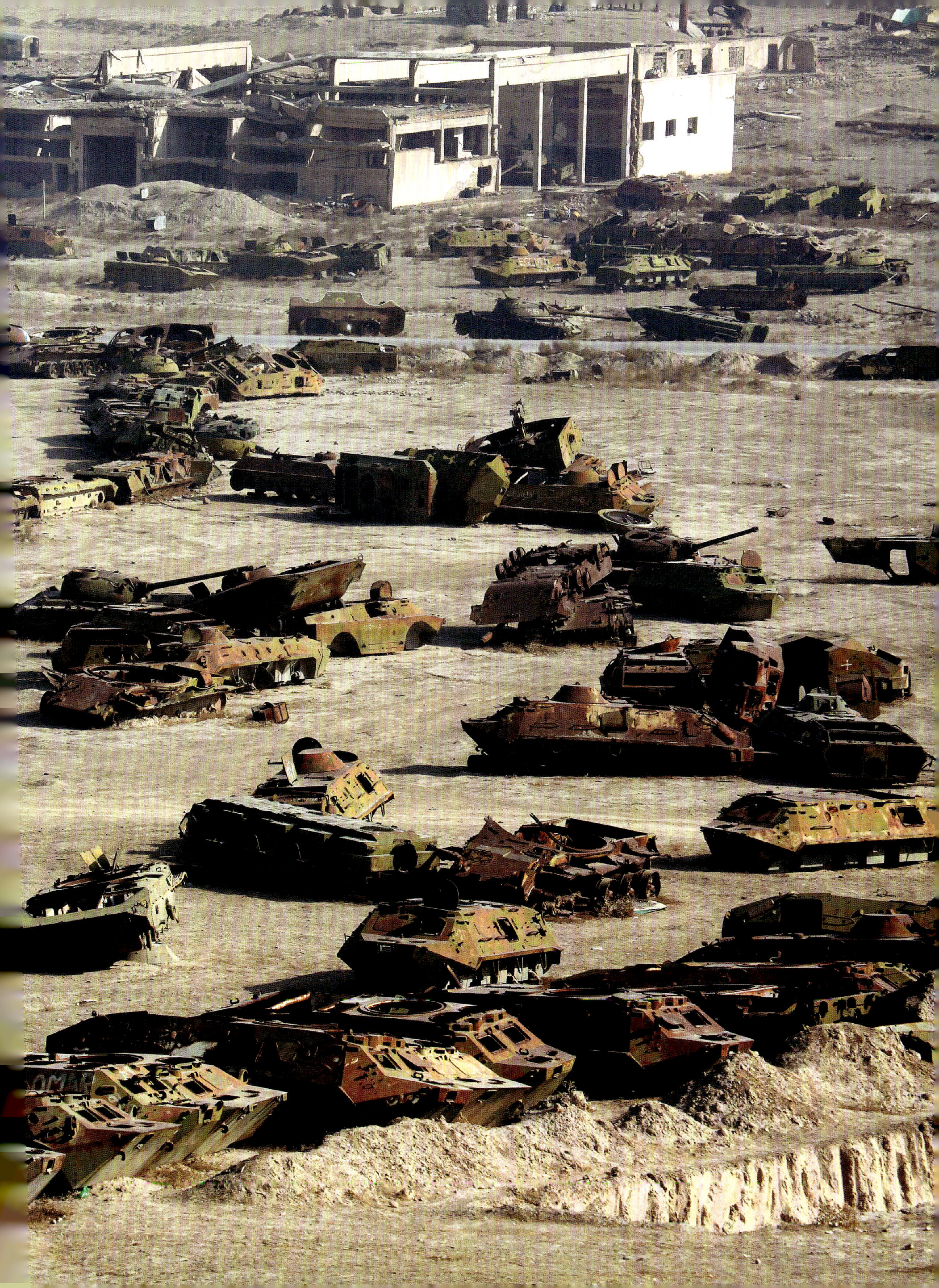

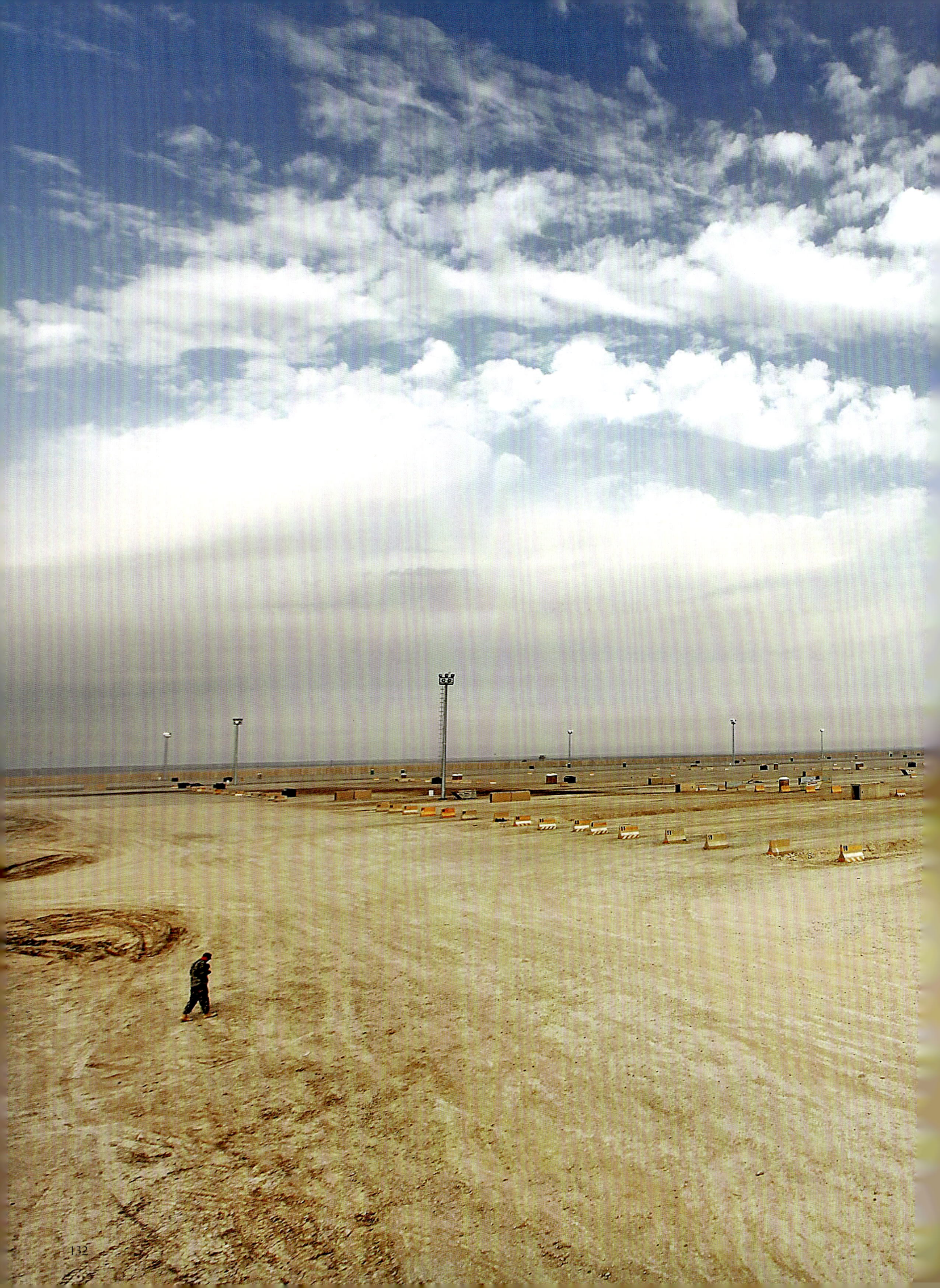

Camp Adder, Nasiriyah, Iraq
Bound for Kuwait, the last US troop brigade in Iraq leaves Camp Adder in December 2011. The ancient Babylonian city of Ur and its ziggurat temple is located within the perimeter of the base. After the US left, Camp Adder, also known as Talil Air Base, was returned to the Iraqi Air Force.

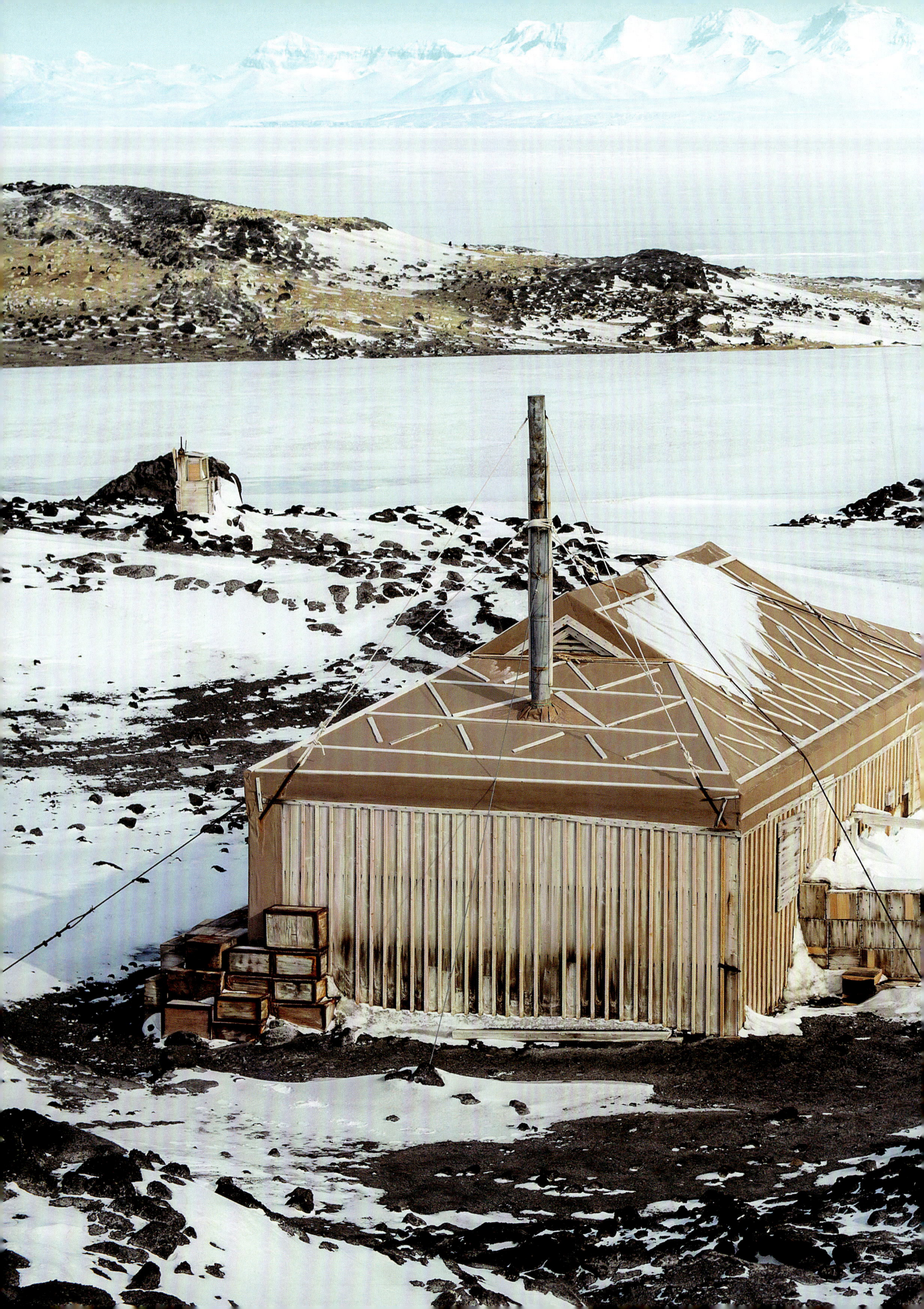

Ernest Shackleton's Hut, Cape Royds, Ross Island, Antarctica
During their 1907–09 Nimrod Expedition, Ernest Shackleton's team built this hut at Cape Royds. Shackleton didn't return to the hut after his failed attempt to lead the first team to reach the South Pole, but instructed that it be left in good working condition for any future parties.

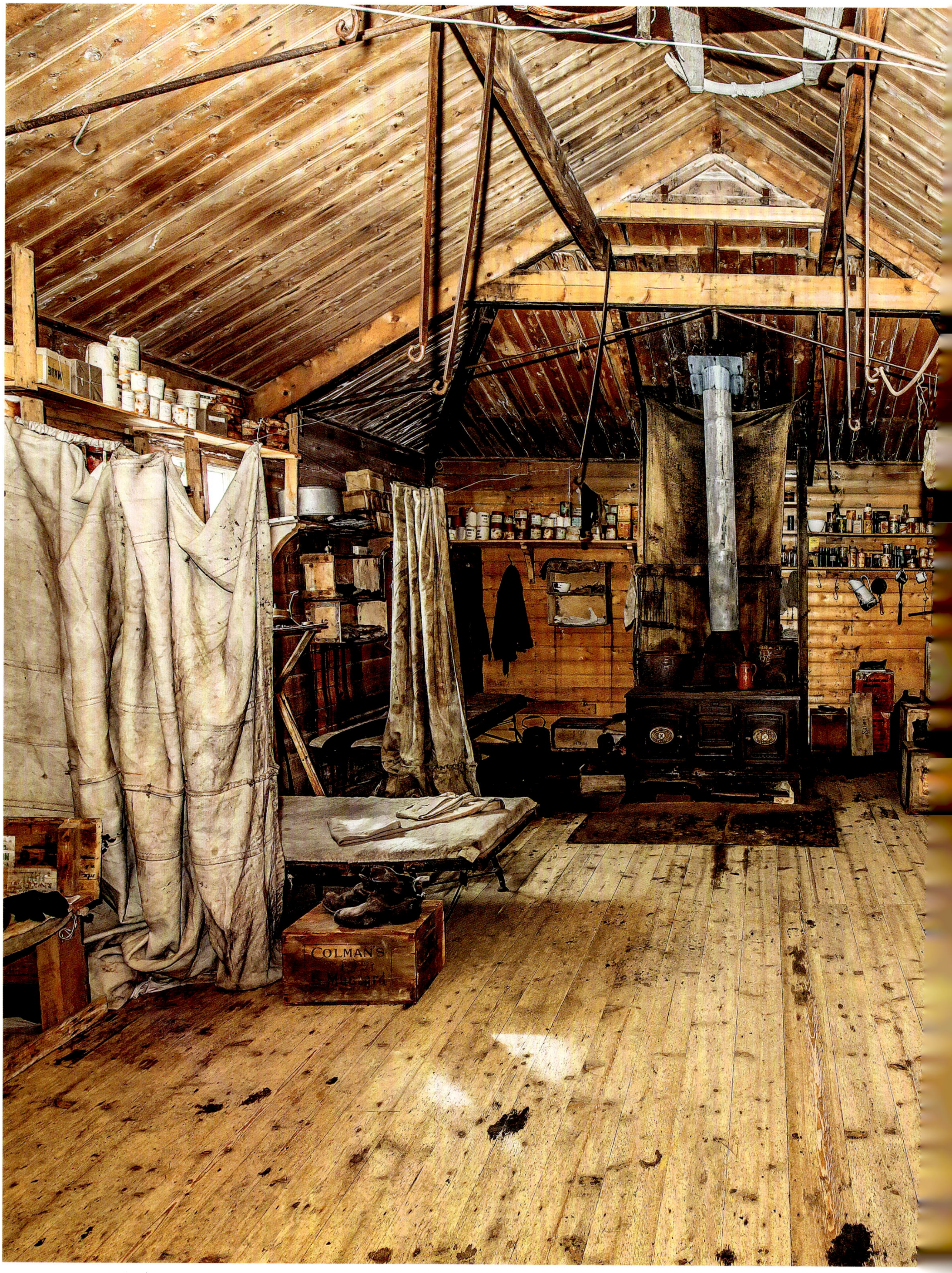
COLMAN'S

LEFT:

Ernest Shackleton's Hut, Cape Royds, Ross Island, Antarctica
When members of Shackleton's Nimrod Expedition left the Cape Royds hut, they pinned a letter in a conspicuous place, stating, for any future visitors, that there were sufficient provisions and equipment to last 15 men for a year. Raymond Priestley, who was with Shackleton, would return during Robert Scott of the Antarctic's 1910–13 expedition to find the hut exactly as he'd left it two years earlier.

Maunsell Forts, Red Sands, Thames Estuary, England
Though not all remain standing today, the World War II Maunsell Forts at Red Sands were arranged in groups of seven – six armed and in a semi-circle and a look-out tower set slightly apart. After being abandoned in 1958, some of the Maunsell Forts were later used as pirate radio stations.

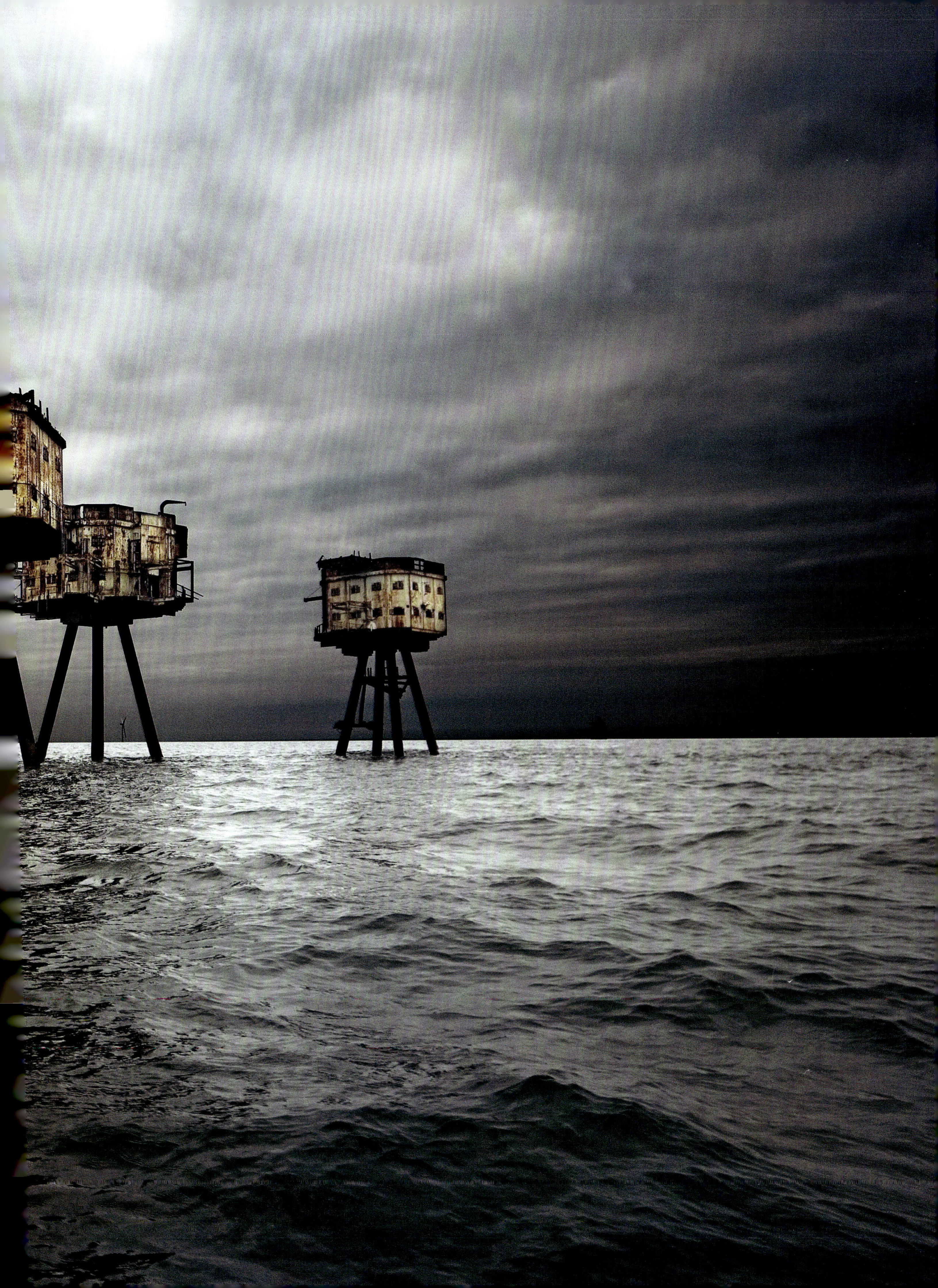

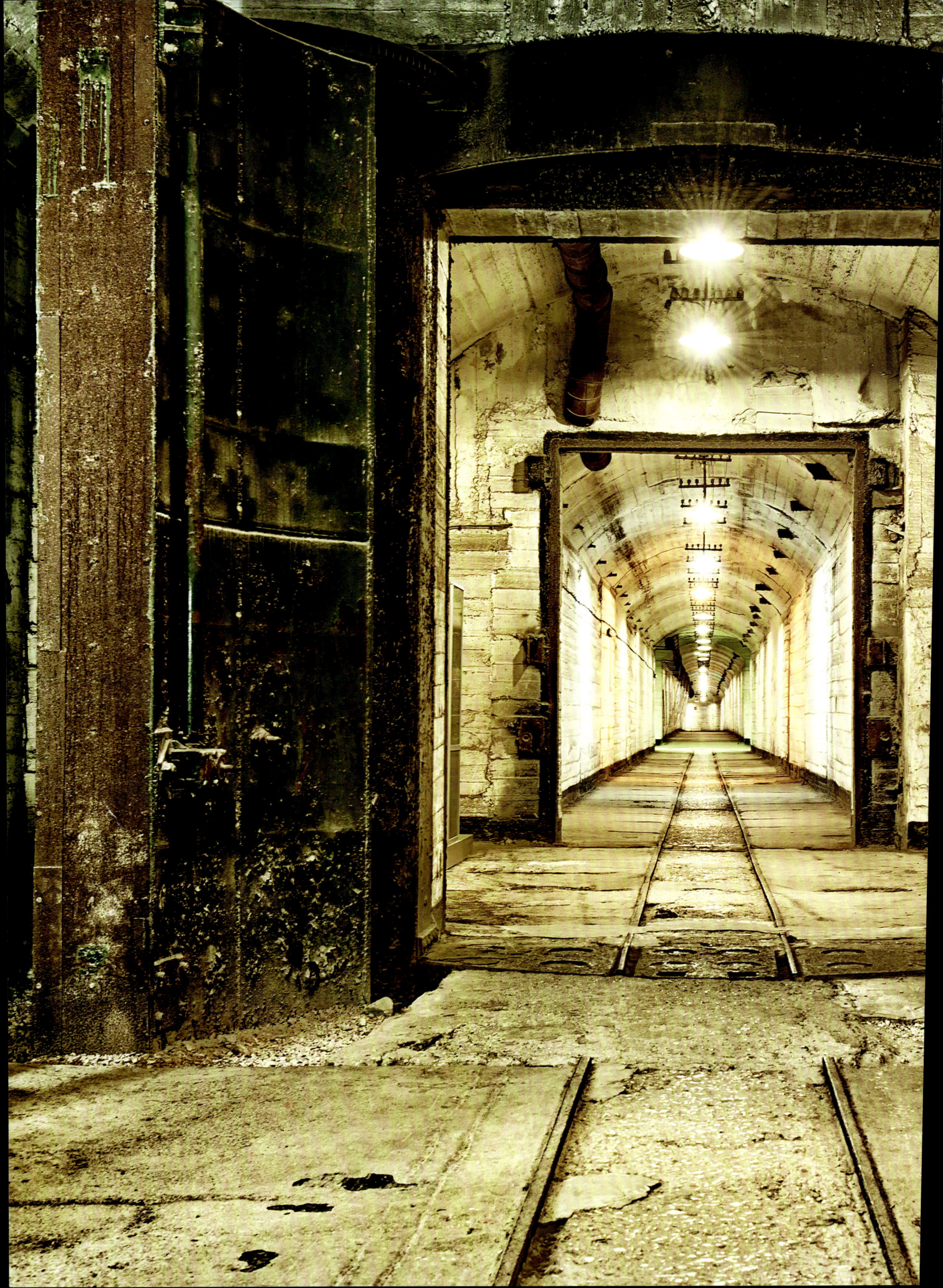

ALL PHOTOGRAPHS:
Balaklava Submarine Base, Crimea, Russia
Hidden inside a mountain in the port of Balaklava, this former top-secret nuclear submarine base was designed to survive a direct nuclear hit, and could support 3,000 people with supplies for a month.

Its full purpose as the home of the Soviet Union's Black Sea Fleet wasn't just a secret from the West, but even from high-ranking employees. A tour guide who'd worked at the base for five years with level-two security clearance – one below the highest – hadn't known that the submarines carried nuclear warheads.

'It was in our culture then not to ask about what didn't concern us,' she said. 'A common saying at the time was: "The less you know, the better you sleep."'

The base was decommissioned in the early 1990s following the break-up of the Soviet Union.

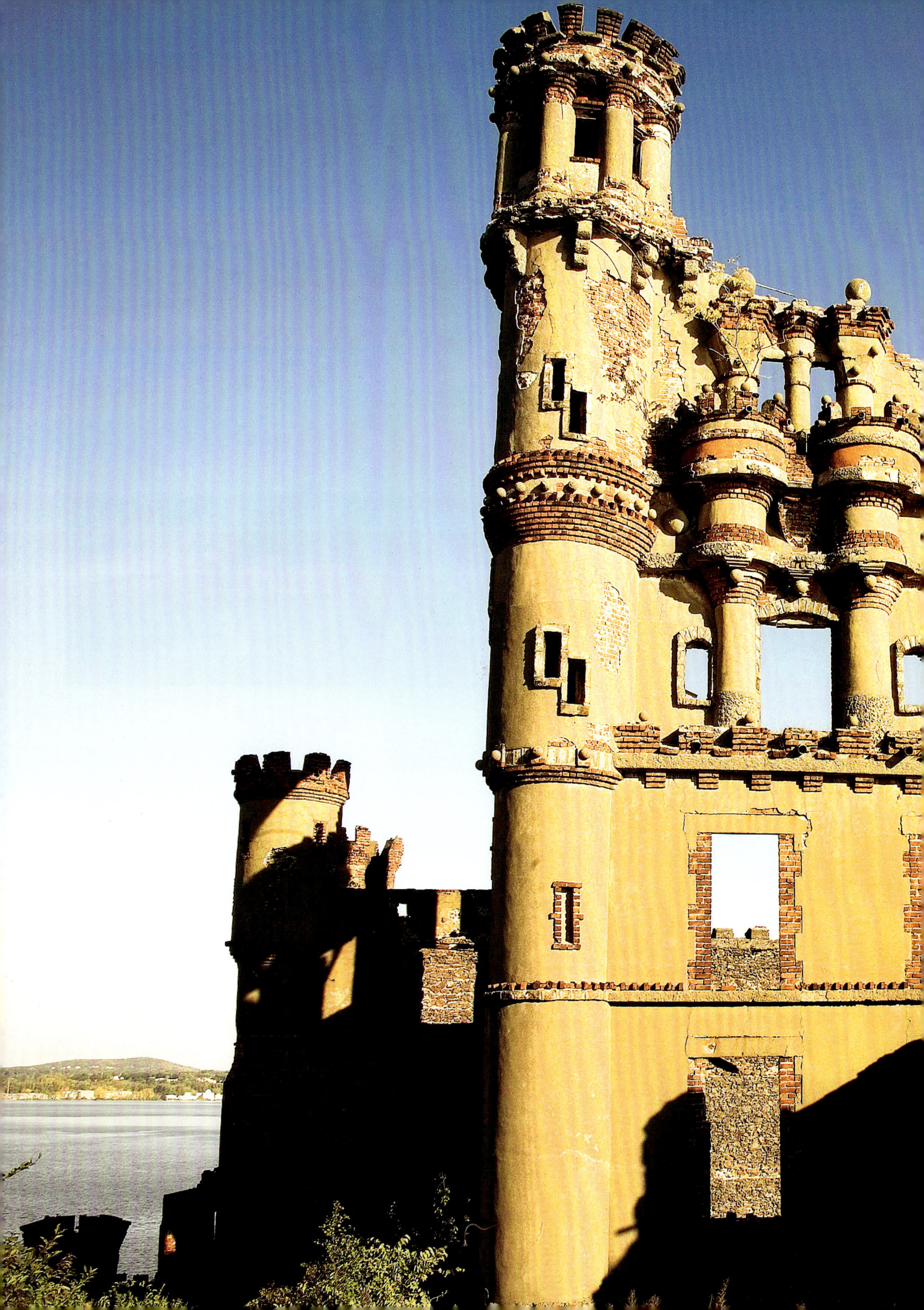

Bannerman Castle, Pollepel Island, Hudson River, New York State, USA

Francis Bannerman bought Pollepel Island in 1900 as a storage base for his business in military surplus goods – which included munitions. Building a castle there, he had the words 'Bannerman's Island Arsenal' emblazoned across one wall. Keeping munitions was, however, a risky business, and in 1920 an explosion destroyed part of the building. After legislation later tightened the sale of military weapons to civilians, Bannerman's business declined. By the early 1950s, the island was essentially vacant.

RIGHT:
British Antarctic Survey Base, Detaille Island, Antarctica
Occupied between 1956 and 1959, this base housed geologists and meteorologists – before having to be evacuated when sea ice and poor weather made rescue by ship impossible.

OVERLEAF:
British Antarctic Survey Base, Detaille Island, Antarctica
A glimpse into the past. Photographed more than 50 years after it was shut down, the base really has been frozen in time, the sub-zero climate preserving the hut as it was when last used.

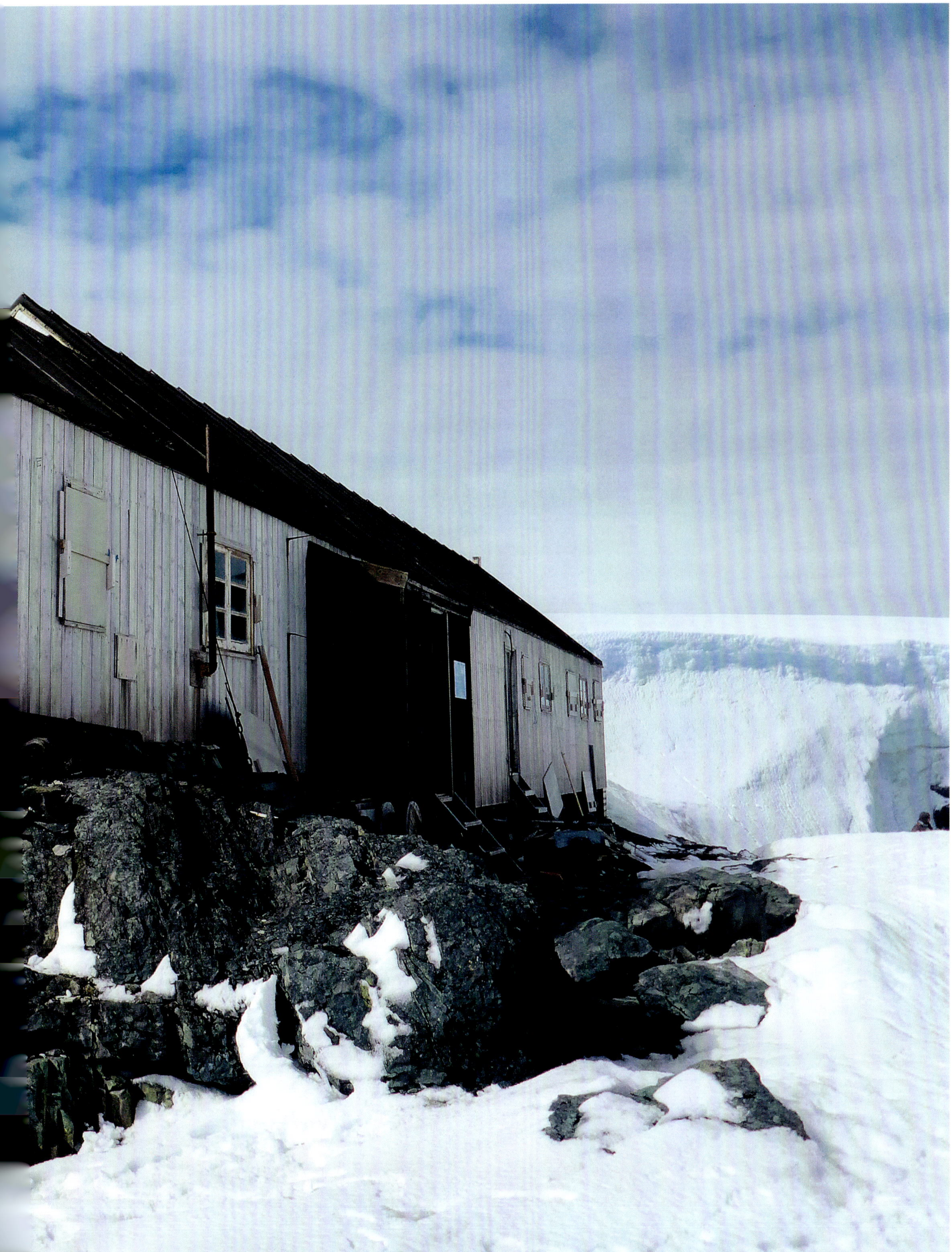

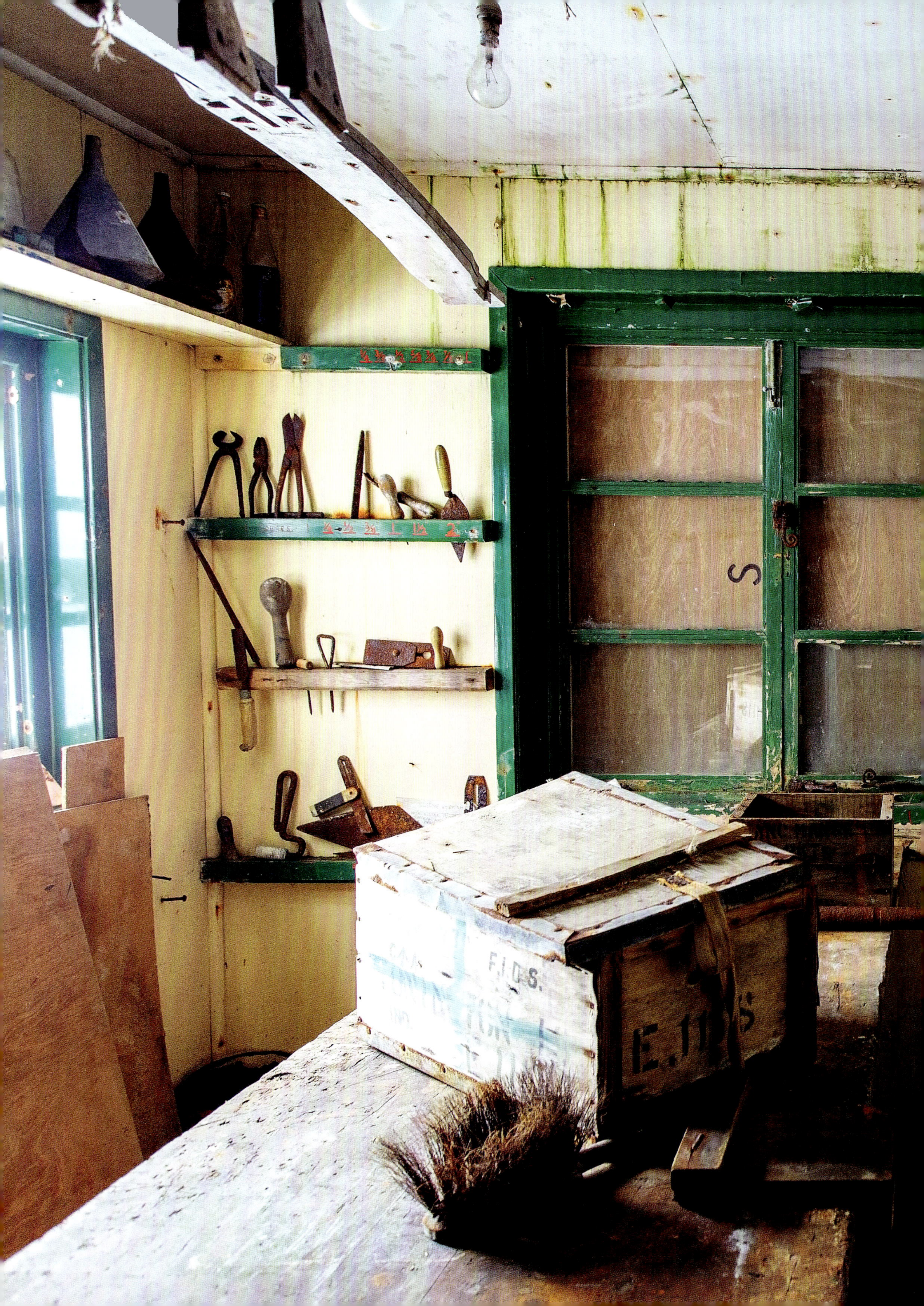
F.I.D.S.

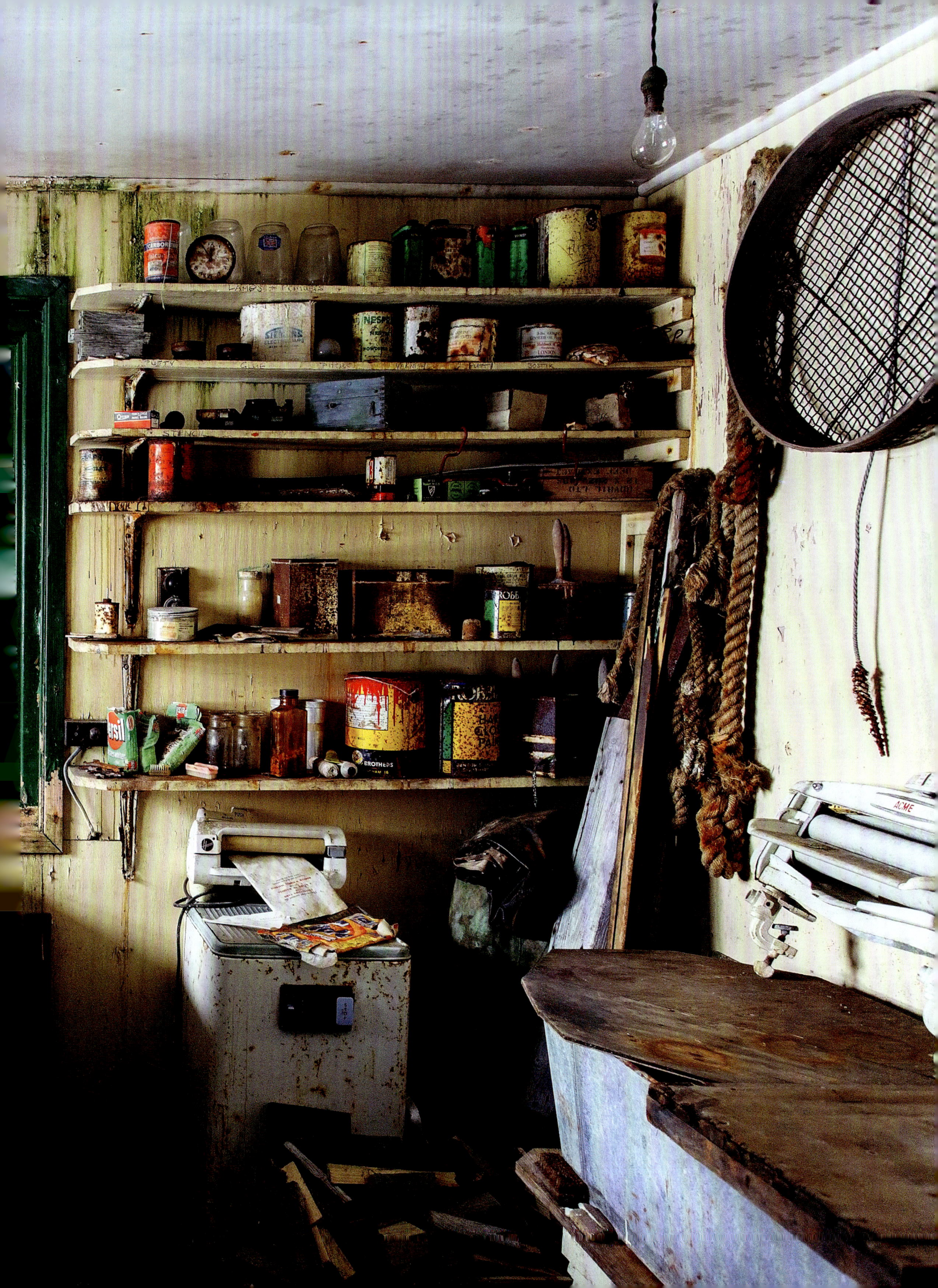
ACME
BROTHERS

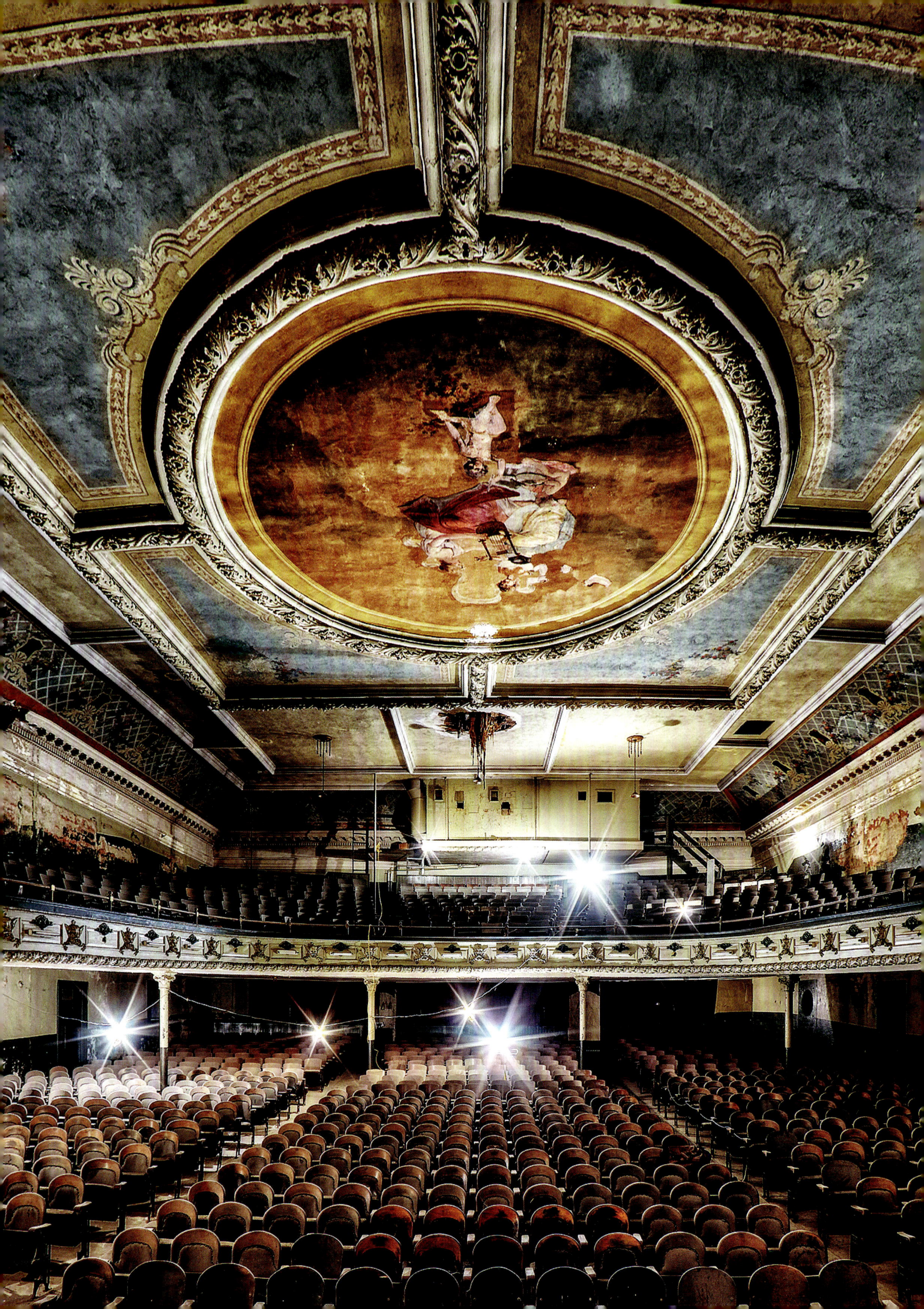

Recreational & Retail Buildings

Theatres, cinemas, amusement parks and zoos may be designed to present and celebrate the arts, to thrill a crowd or share the wonders of the natural world, but when abandoned they can quickly come to look more forlorn than anywhere else. Faded fairground rides now entwined in weeds appear eerie and opulent theatres and cinemas look violated when their stucco begins to collapse. While, devoid of shops and busy shoppers, once ordered and perhaps rather sterile malls begin to develop a new, and wild, life when nature repossesses them. The roller coasters, zoos, theatres, cinemas and shopping malls on these pages may no longer draw large crowds, but, as they have aged and turned into curiosities, they have begun to attract a new, smaller audience. Whether it be urban explorers, photographers, reporters or graffiti artists, either keen to preserve the past or simply inquisitive, this new crowd find a beauty in these bizarre structures. Like the forgotten silent movie star in the film *Sunset Boulevard* 'still waving to a parade which had long since passed her by', these aren't worlds in which the circus left town, but places where the town left the circus.

LEFT:
Orpheum Theatre, New Bedford, Massachusetts, USA
Built in the Beaux-Arts style, the Orpheum opened in 1912 as a 1,500-seat vaudeville theatre and was later used as a cinema. The building, which also housed a ballroom and a shooting range, closed in 1958. A campaign is underway to restore it.

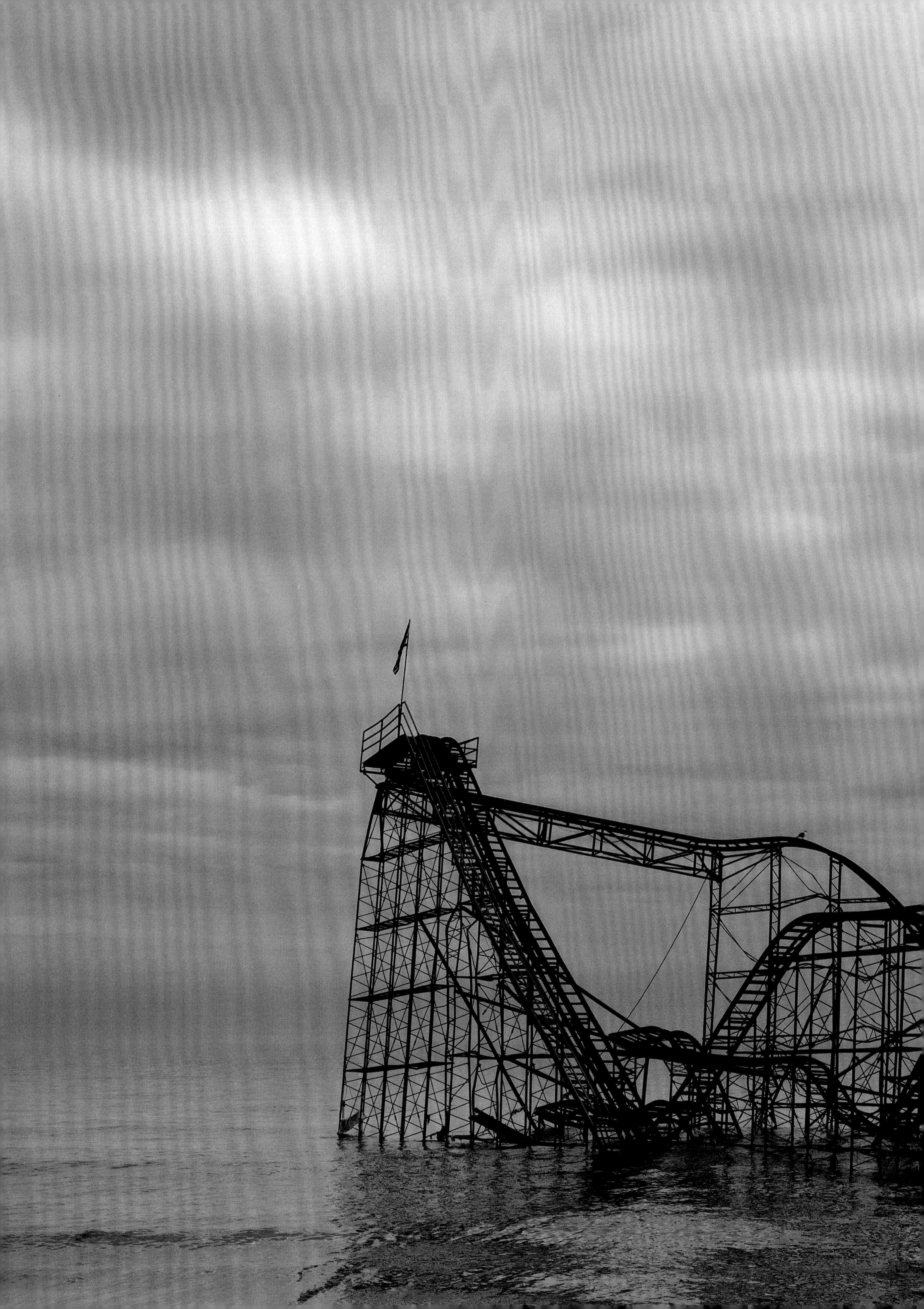

Roller coaster, Seaside Heights, New Jersey, USA
Before Hurricane Sandy hit in 2012, the Jet Star roller coaster was an end-of-the-pier attraction. Unfortunately, the storm pulled down much of the pier, leaving the ride in the Atlantic Ocean.

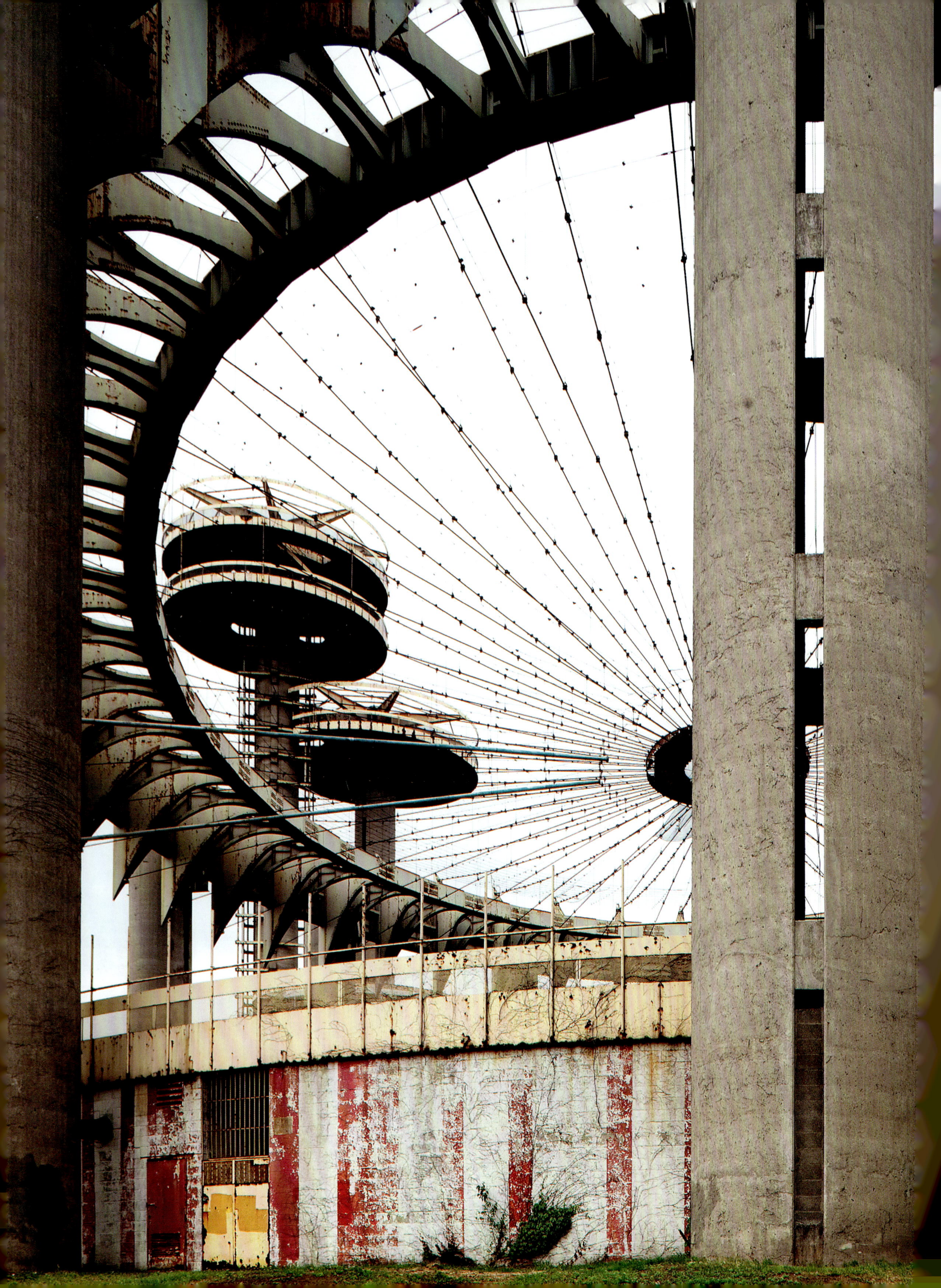

LEFT:

New York State Pavilion, 1964 World's Fair, New York, USA

These pillars once supported the world's largest cable suspension roof, while beneath them, on the oval floor of the 'Tent of Tomorrow' pavilion, was a giant map of New York State. After the fair closed, however, no new purpose could be found for the pavilion and the three observation towers behind it, other than as occasional film and TV locations. By the late 1970s the roofing tiles had become unstable and had to be removed, leaving the floor map open to the elements – ruining it. Plans are underway to restore the pavilion if funds can be raised. In the meantime, the steel framework of the 'Tent of Tomorrow' was recently repainted its original yellow colour.

OVERLEAF:

Six Flags Amusement Park, New Orleans, Louisiana, USA

Following Hurricane Katrina's storm surge in August 2005, Six Flags New Orleans was submerged for more than a month in up to 2m (7ft) of salty water. With the metal and wood structures on most of the rides ruined by long term salt immersion, it was announced the following year that the park would not be reopened.

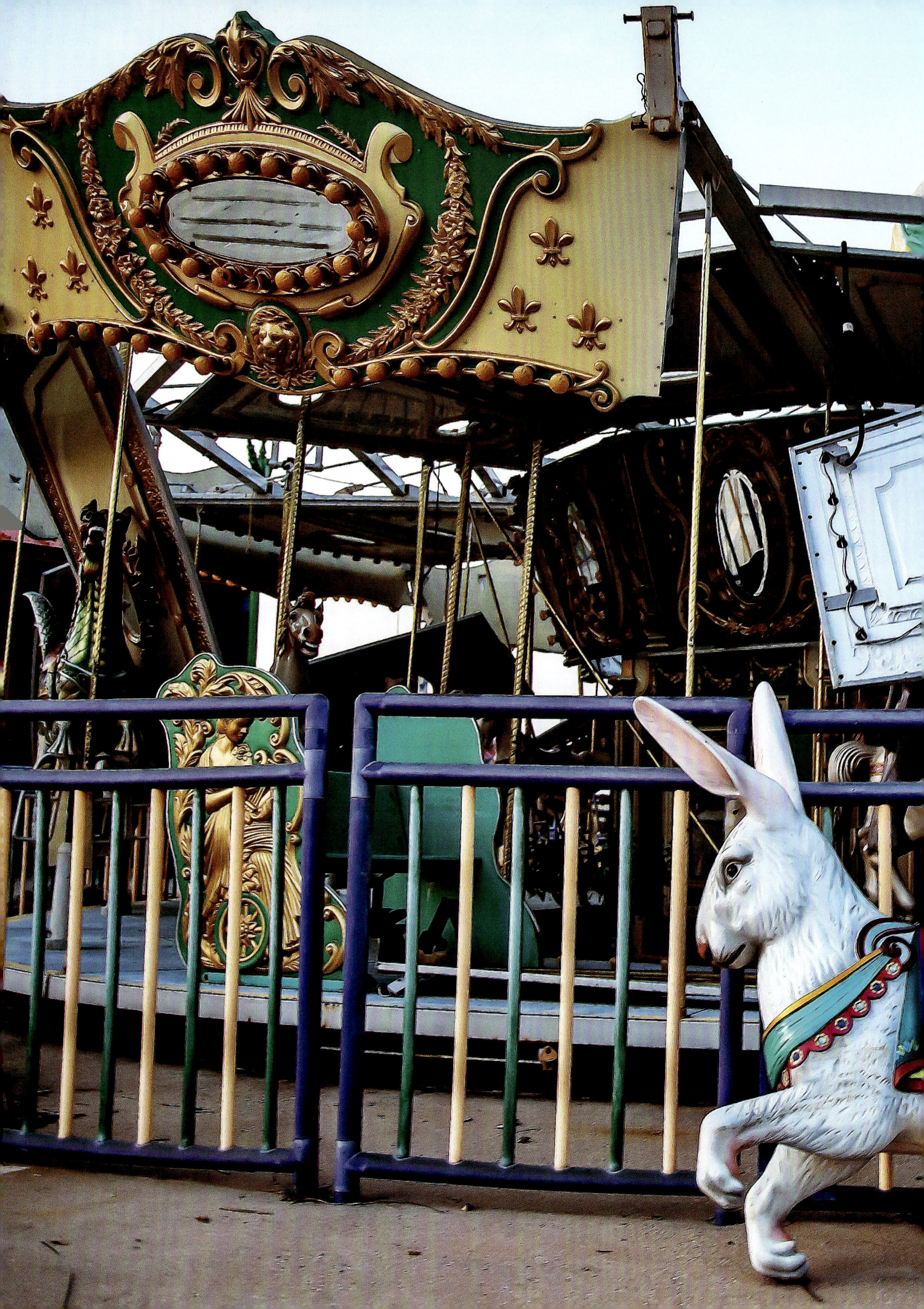

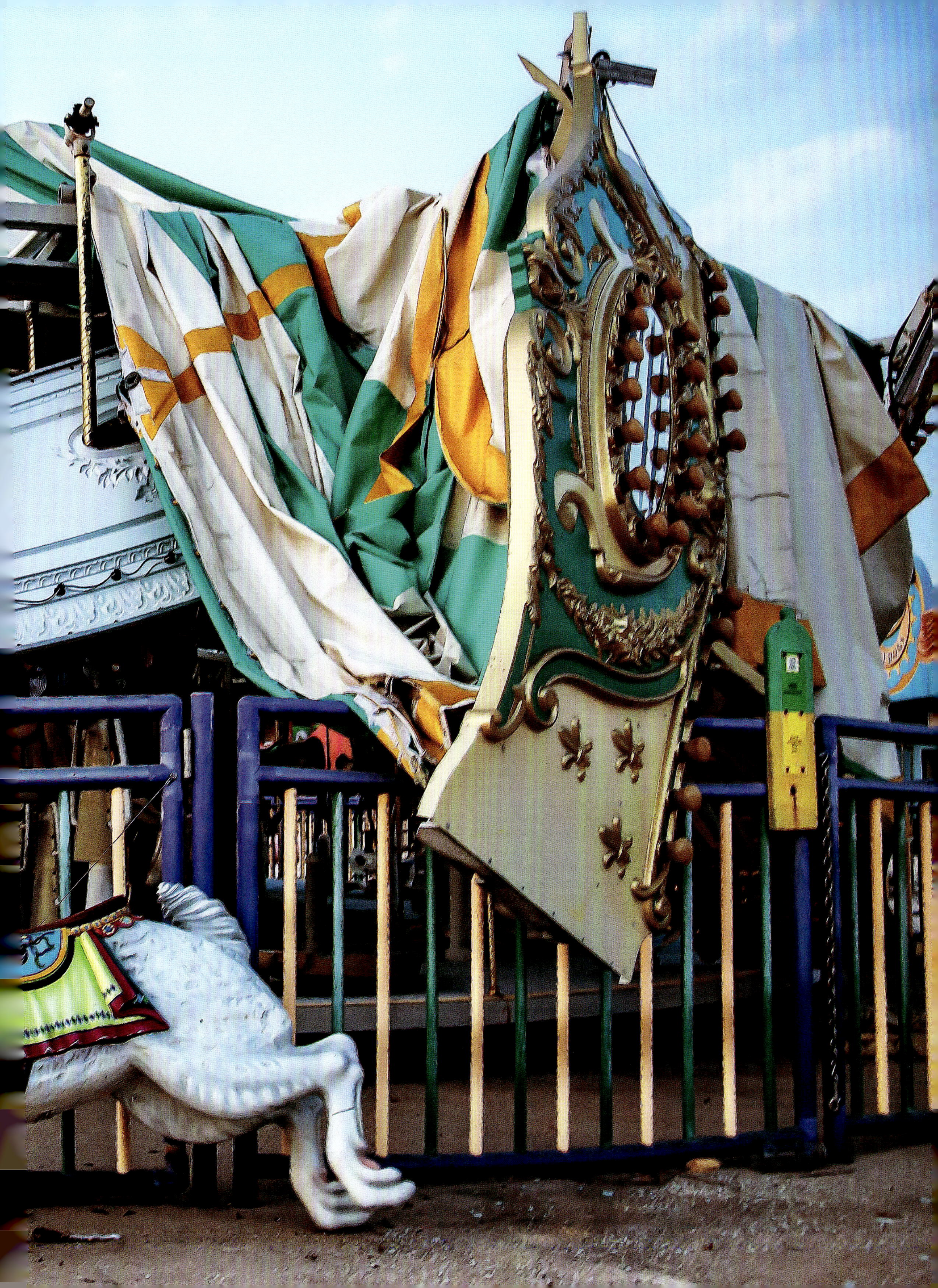

ALL PHOTOGRAPHS:
Six Flags Amusement Park, New Orleans, Louisiana, USA
The photograph on the far right shows the level of flooding two weeks after Hurricane Katrina passed. In the years afterwards, some of the rides that were on higher, drier ground were removed and reassembled at other fairgrounds. The City of New Orleans now owns the site and is seeking ways to redevelop it.

OVERLEAF:
Spreepark, Berlin, Germany
Opened in 1969, East Berlin's amusement park was expanded in a 1990s reunified Berlin with new rides, but, running at a loss, it closed in 2002. Since then, its rusting, animal-themed attractions, nestling within the park's encroaching woodland, have become an attraction for urban explorers.

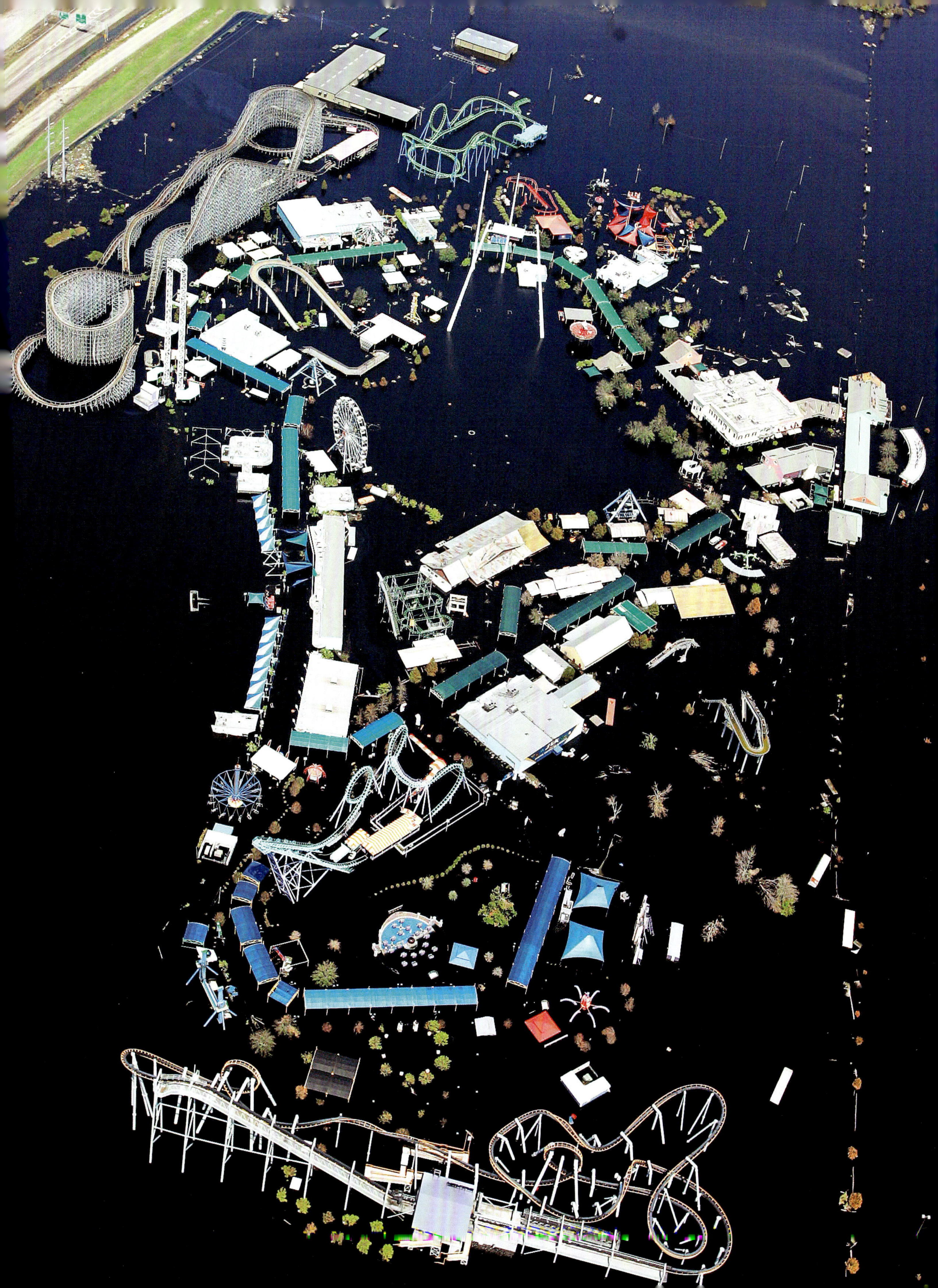

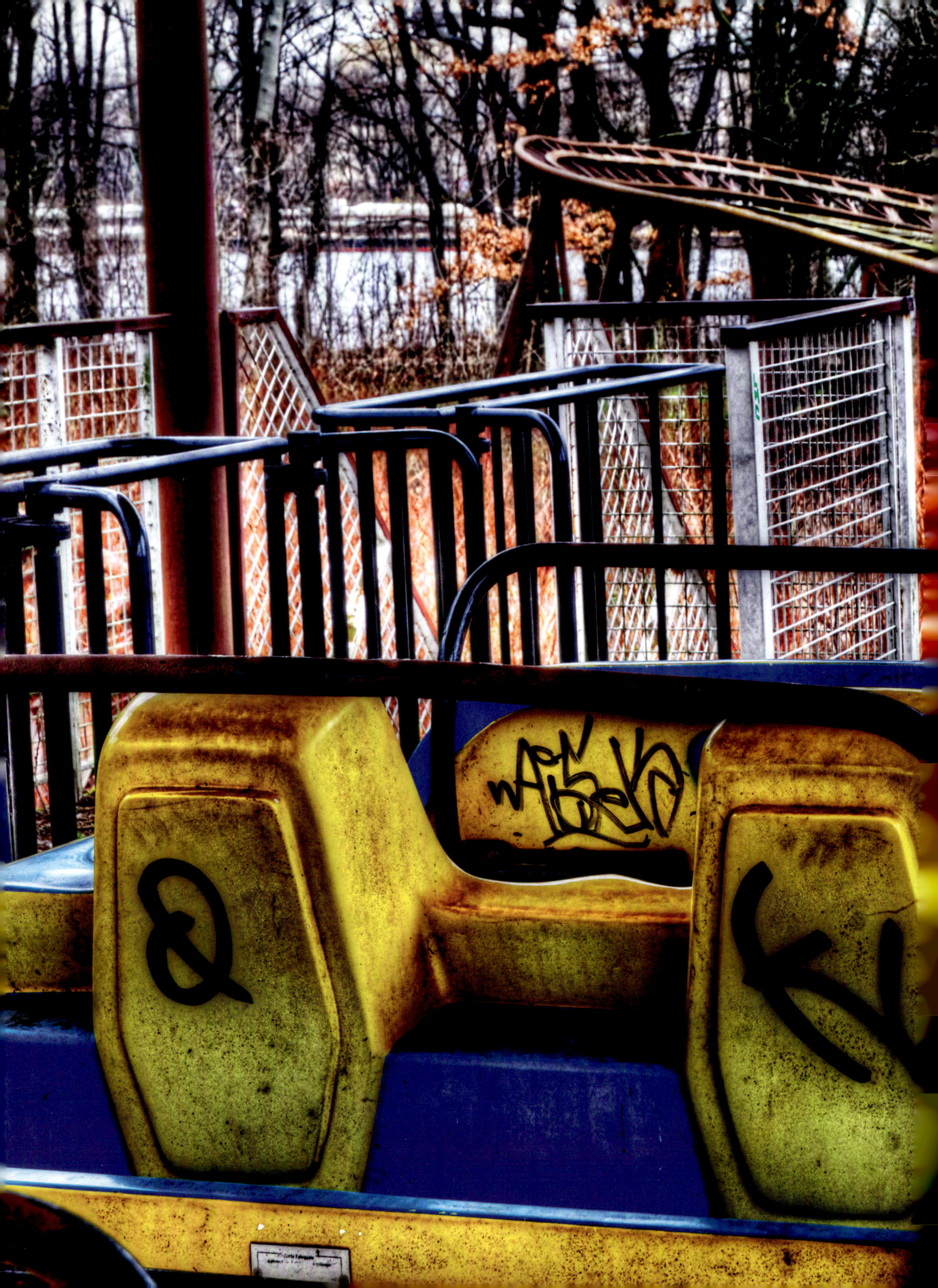

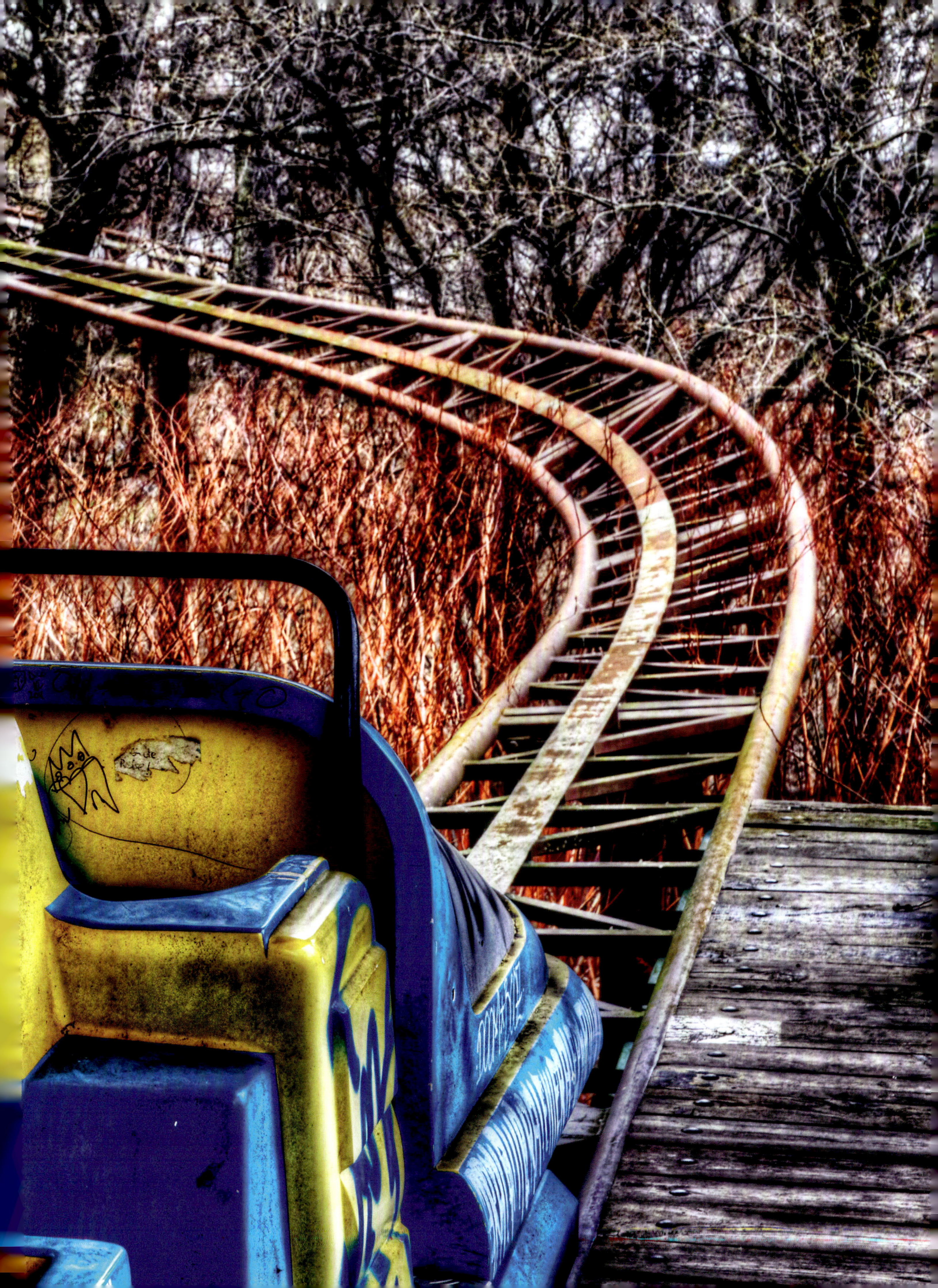

Igosu 108, Biwako Tower Amusement Park, Shiga, Japan
At 108m (354ft) tall, the Igosu 108 big wheel was the largest in the world when it opened at Biwako Tower in 1992. Today it is virtually all that remains of the amusement park, which closed in 2001.

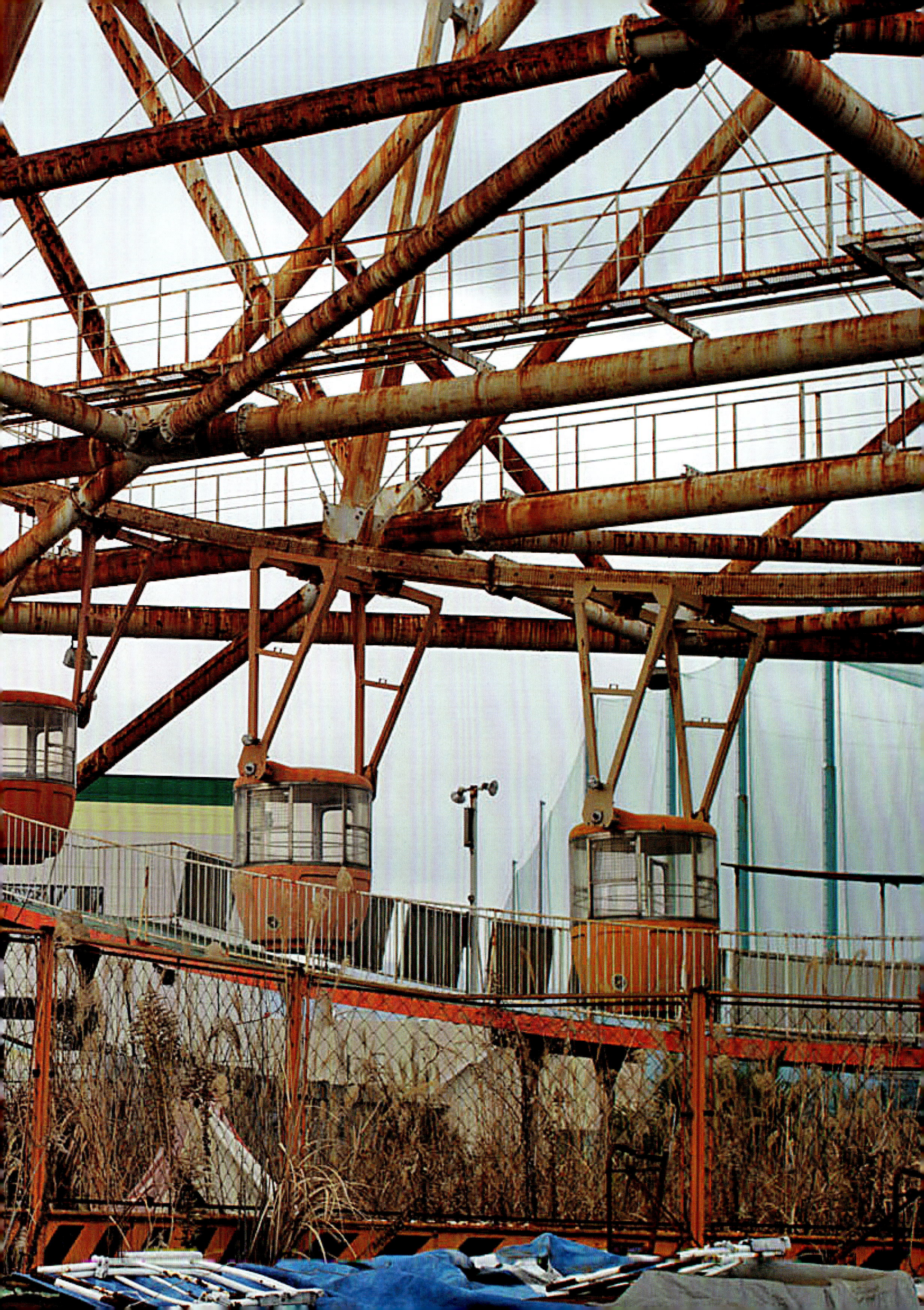

Nara Dreamland, Nara, Japan
Modelled on Disneyland, Nara Dreamland was built in the 1960s but closed in 2006 due to low visitor numbers. Today the monorail tracks carry creeping vines rather than passengers, weeds entwine the turnstiles and the cheery Americana street looks like a ghost town.

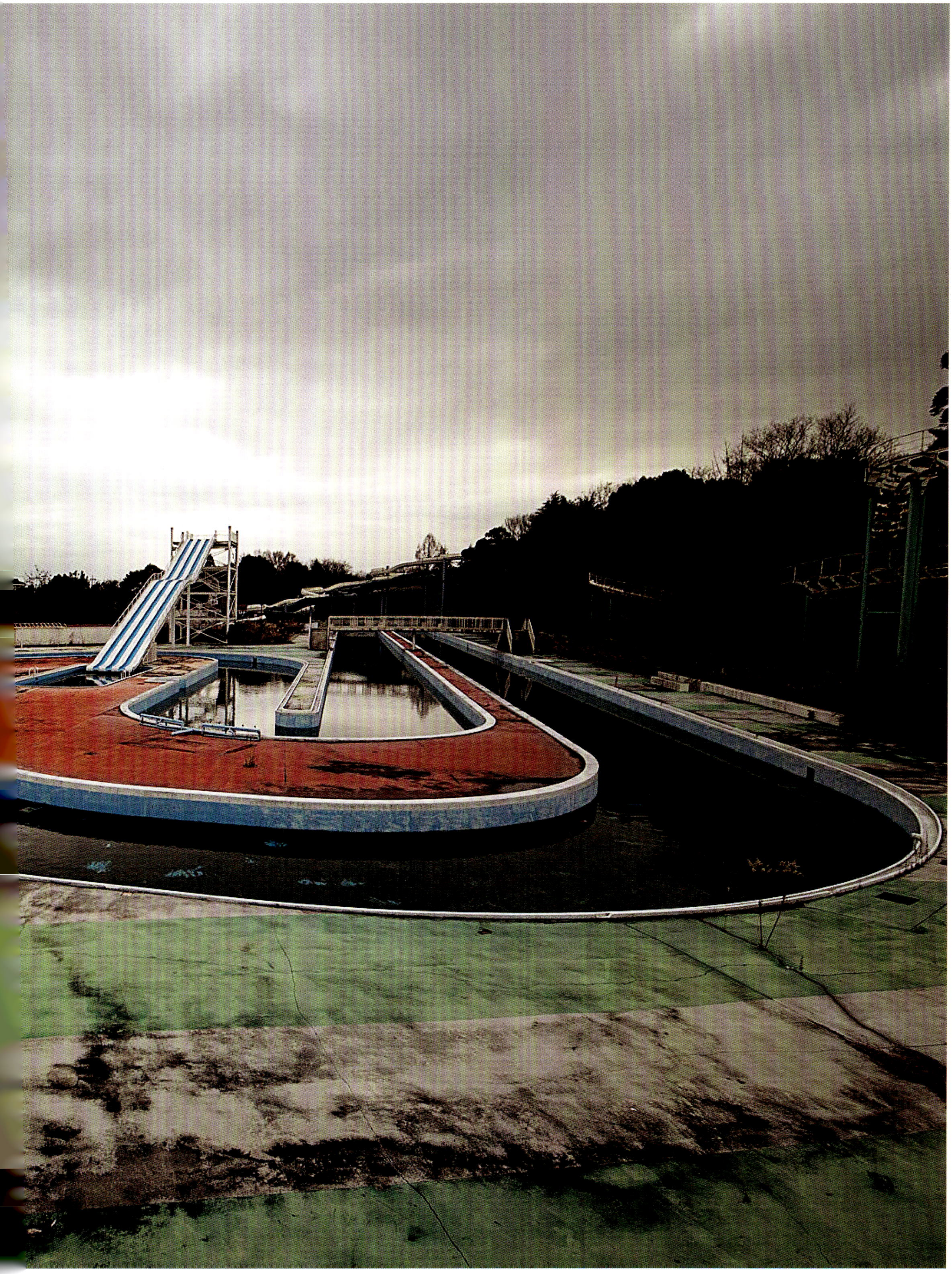

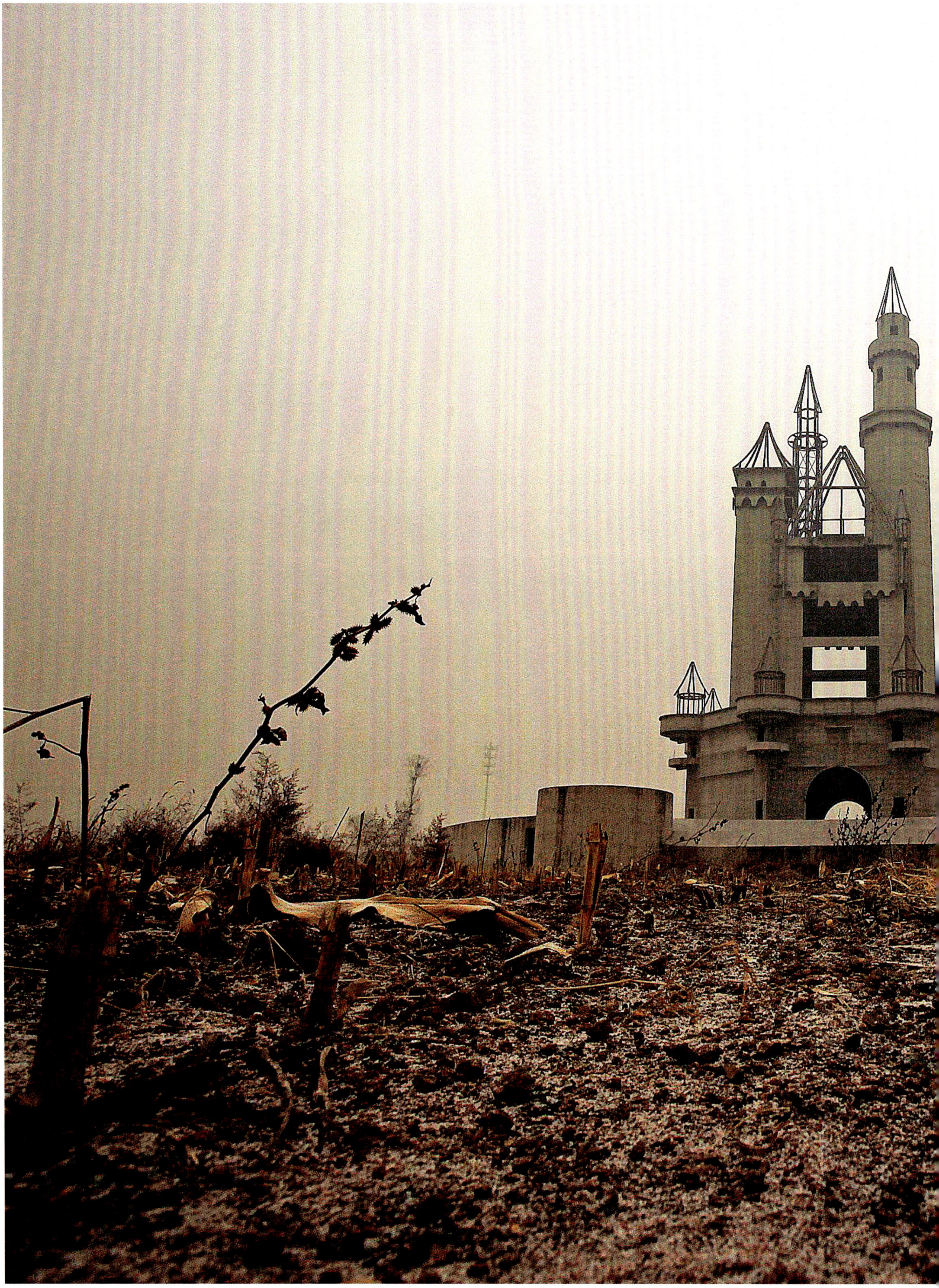

RIGHT:
Wonderland Amusement Park, near Beijing, China
Not all fairy-tales end happily. Construction at the Wonderland Amusement Park, which was planned to be the largest in Asia, was stopped in 1998 amid financial difficulties. The surrounding land was reclaimed by local farmers and in 2013 the site was demolished.

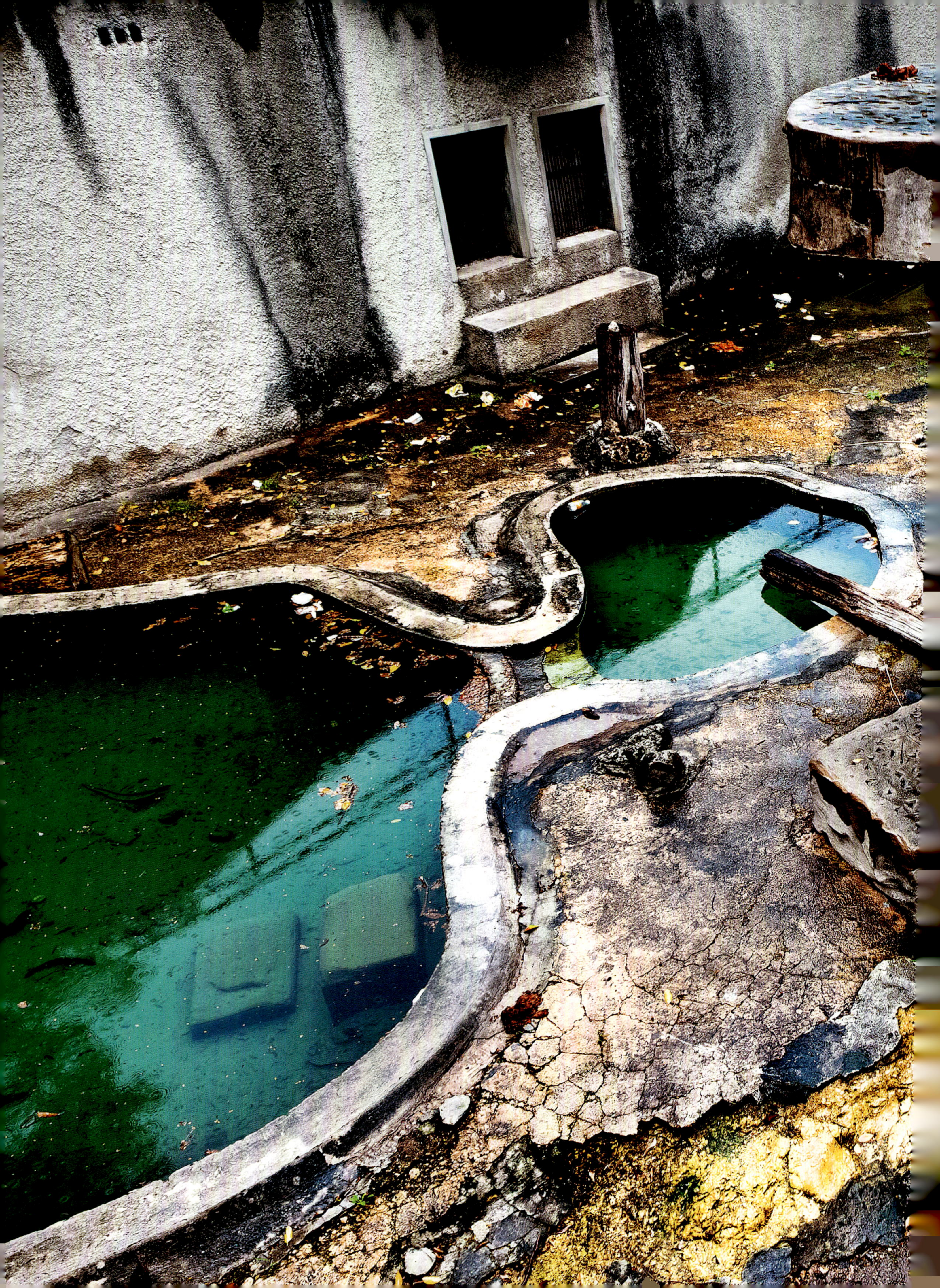

LEFT:
Havana Zoo, Cuba
The empty bear pit photographed in 2011. The zoo remains open, but has struggled in recent years, with many of the enclosures unoccupied or poorly kept.

RIGHT:
Havana Zoo, Cuba
An empty fountain with a broken statue, photographed in 2011. Founded in 1939, Havana Zoo, also known as Zoo 26, has struggled since the economic decline of the 1990s and competition following the opening of a large national zoological park outside the capital.

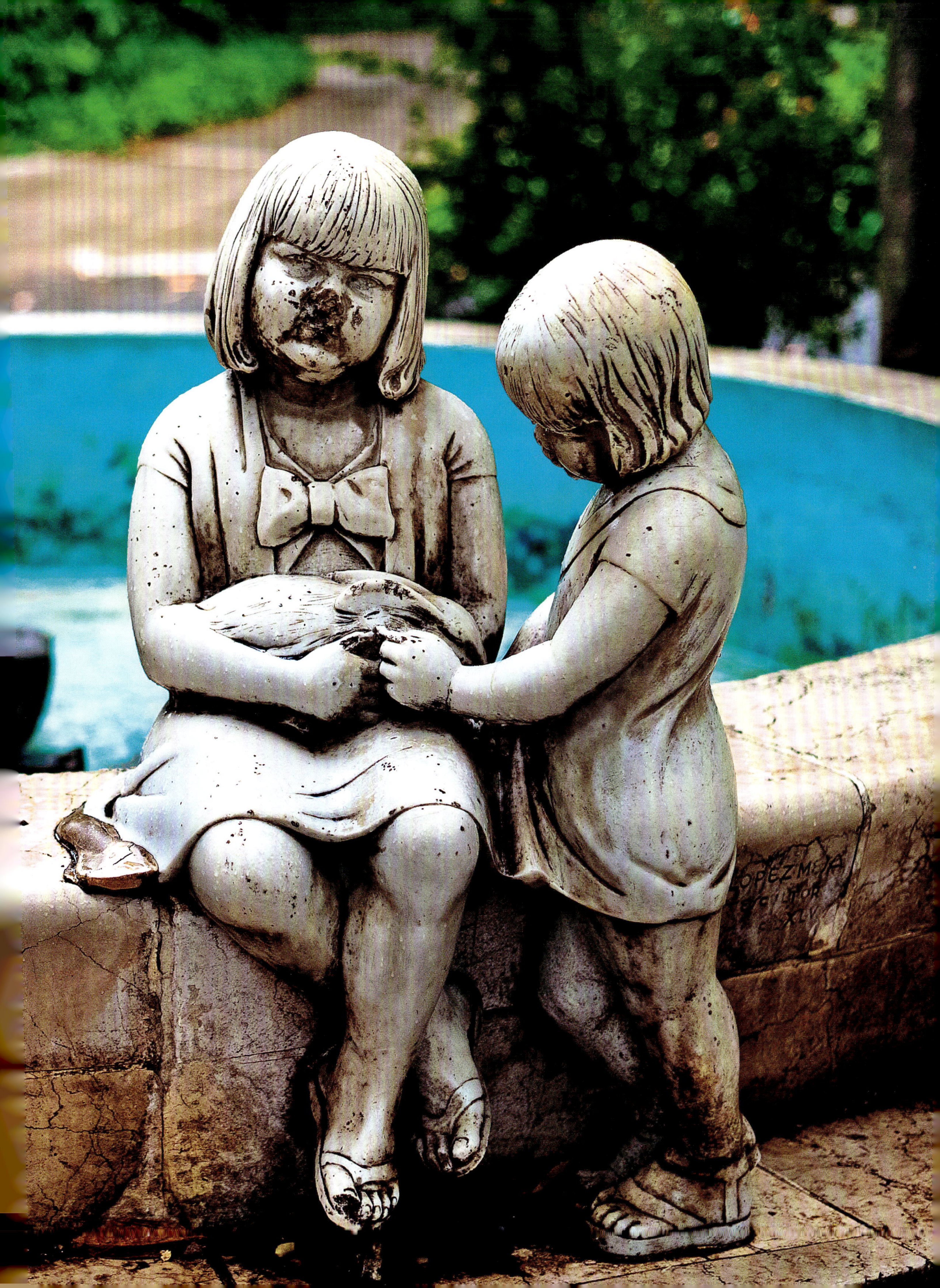

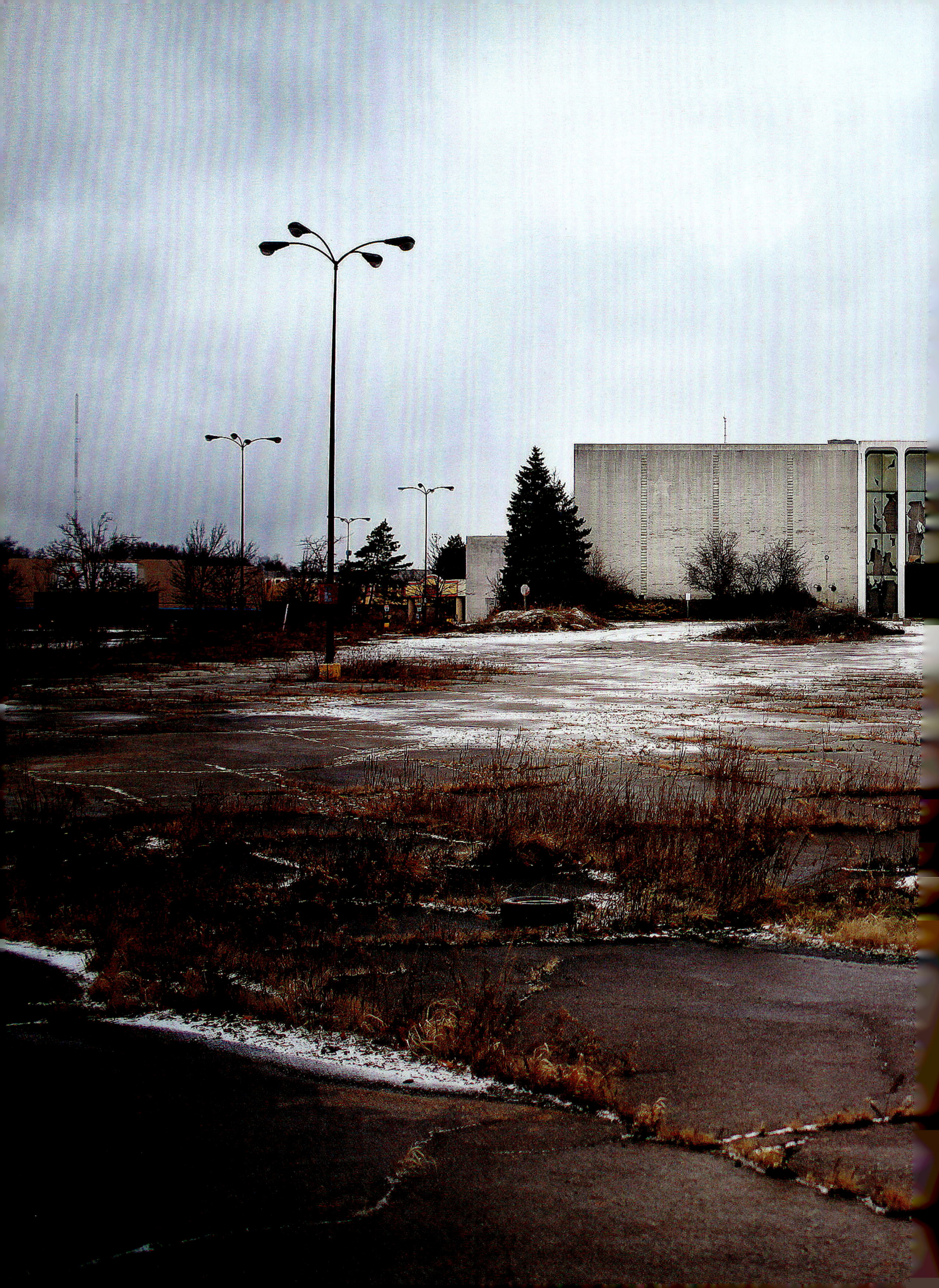

Rolling Acres Mall, Akron, Ohio, USA
Akron's mall was opened in 1975, but fell into decline in the 1990s, with its last shop closing on New Year's Eve, 2013. The indoor plants now grow wildly and snow piles up on the escalators where the roof has fallen in.

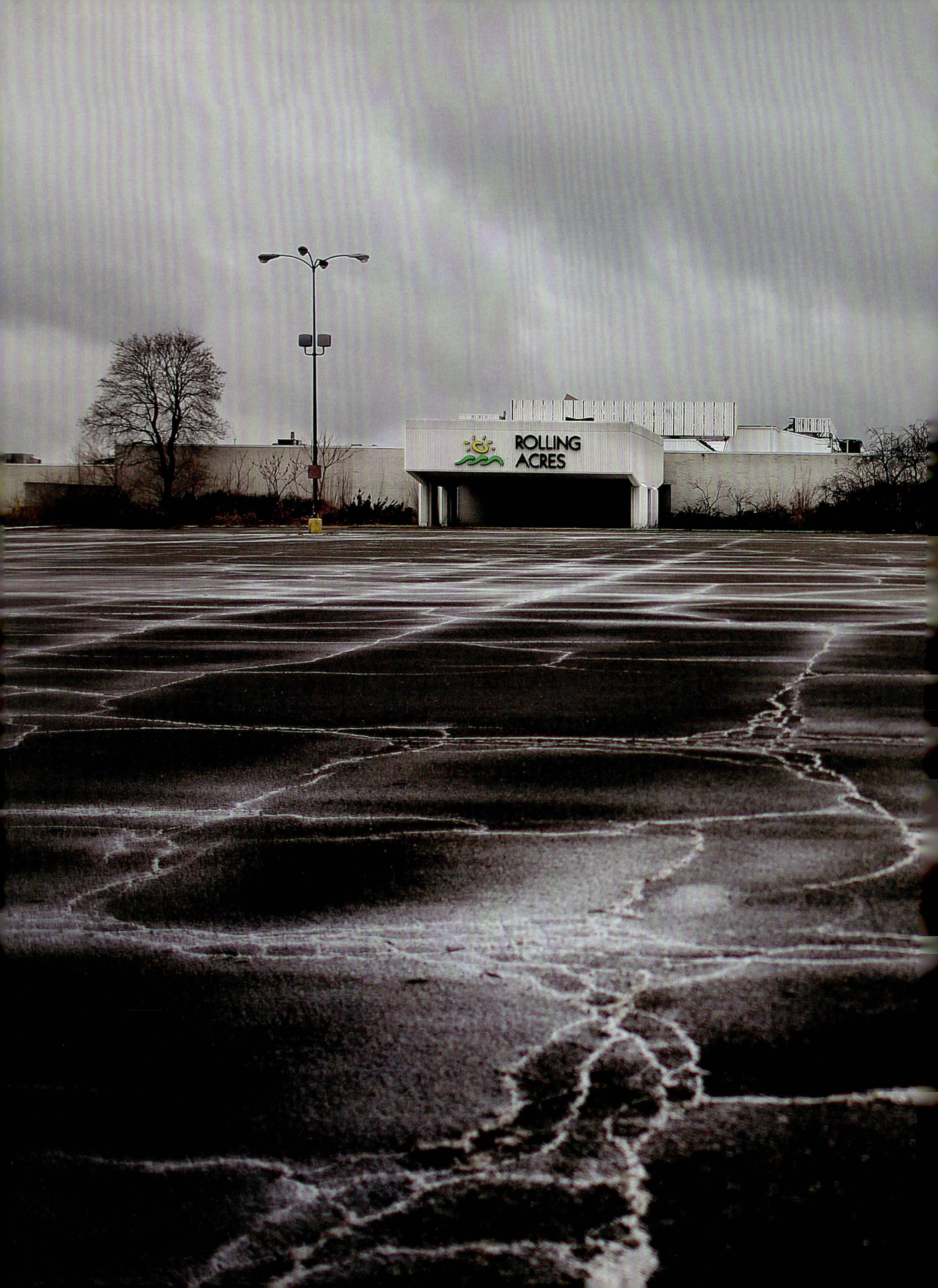
ROLLING
ACRES

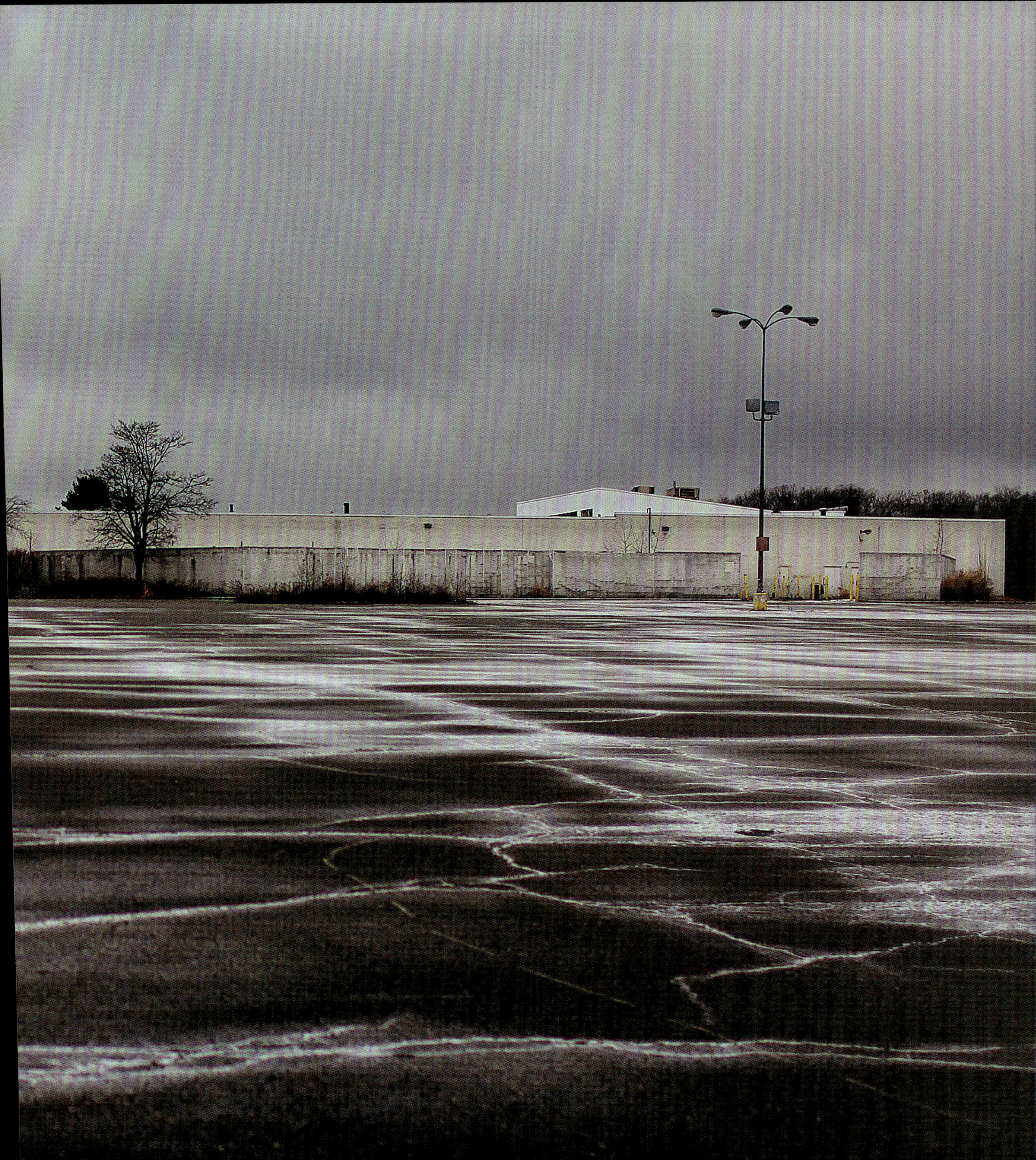

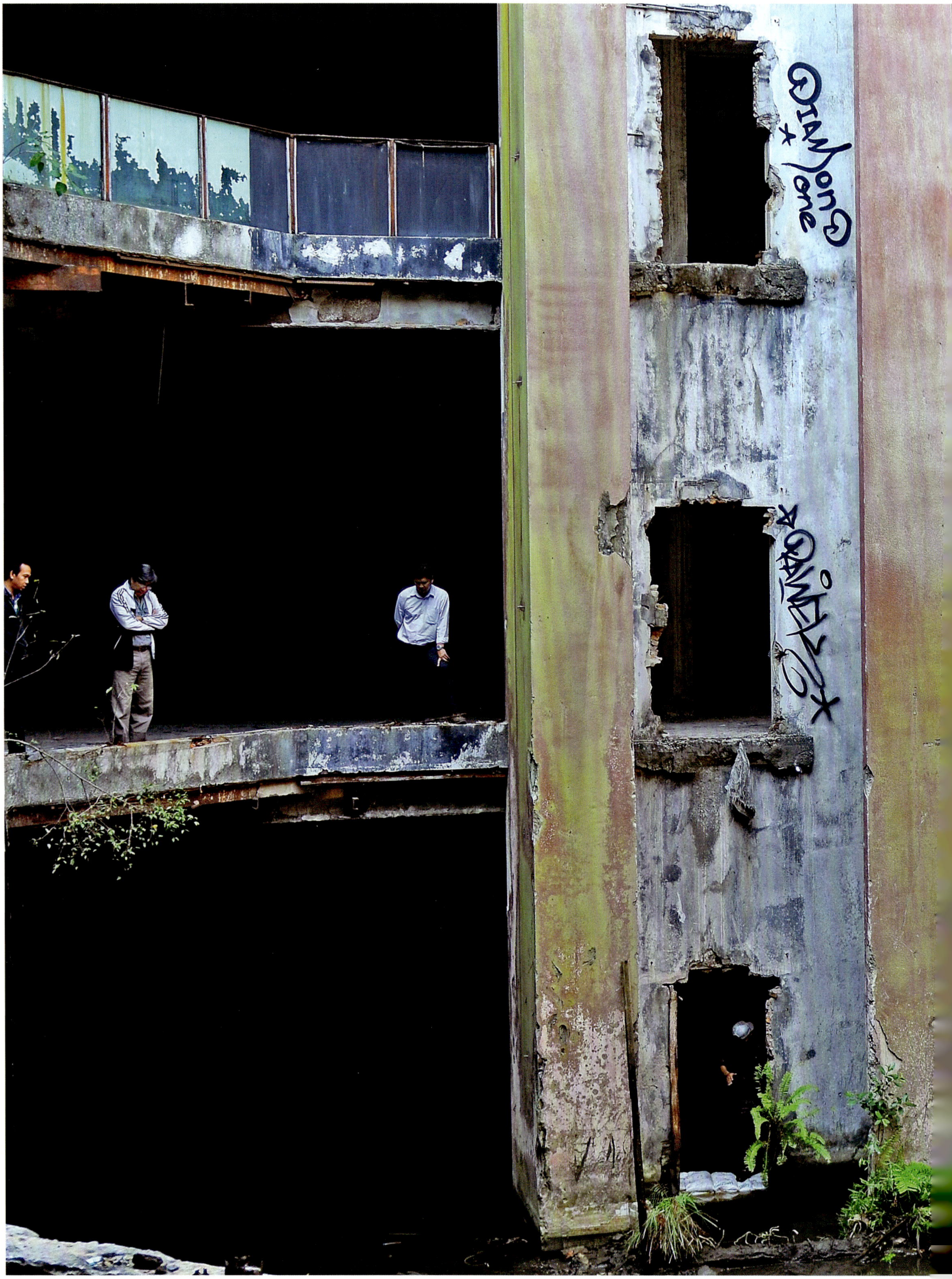

LEFT:

New World Mall, Bangkok, Thailand

How to create a self-sustaining urban aquarium. When the roof fell in on the abandoned New World Mall, the building began filling with rain water. This attracted thousands of mosquitoes, so, to combat them, the locals introduced a small population of exotic koi and catfish species. The fish thrived – it's estimated that there were 3,000 of them – but in January 2015 they were removed and released in preparation for the mall to be demolished.

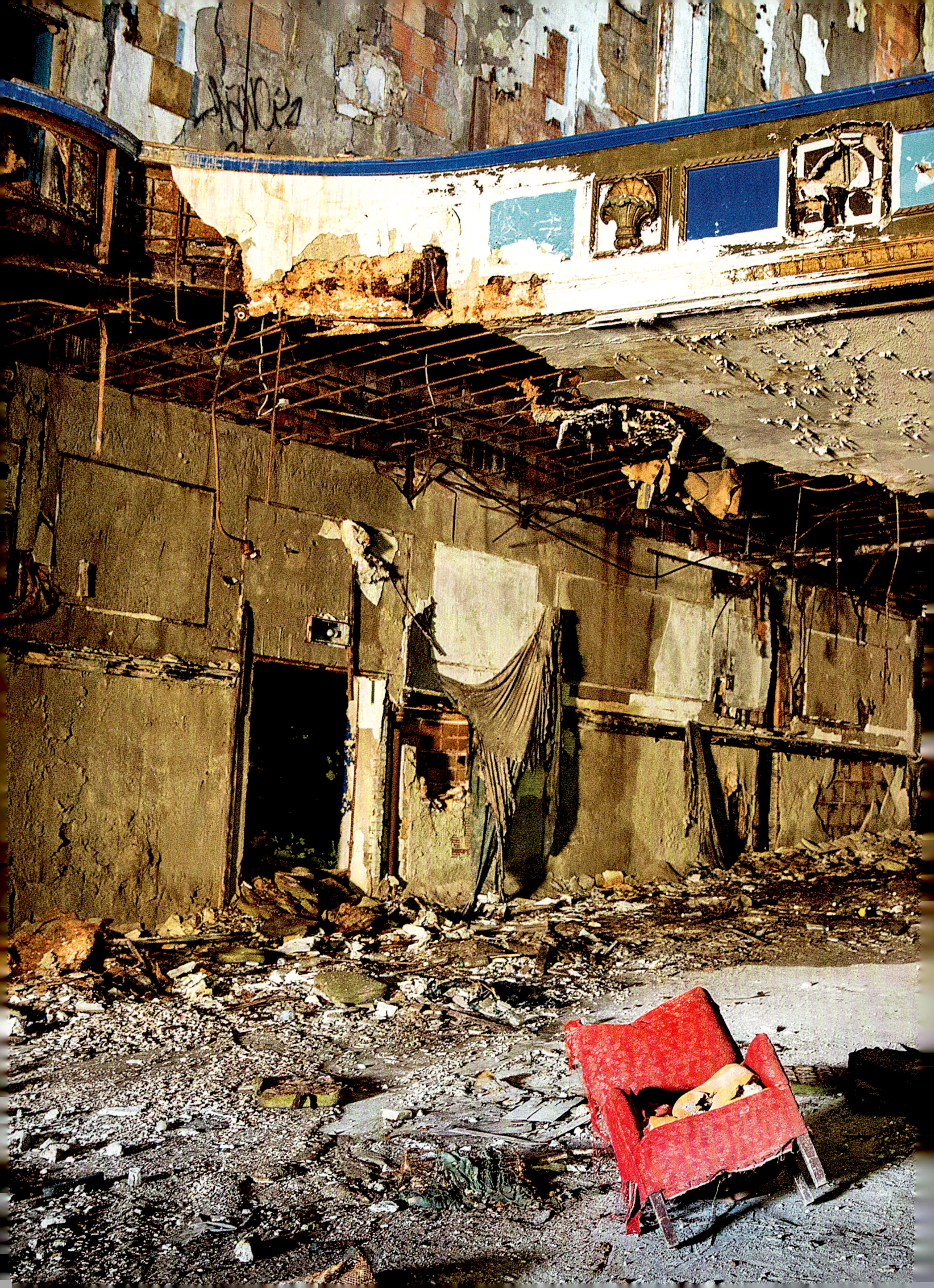

LEFT:

Eastown Theatre, Detroit, Michigan, USA

First a cinema, then a music venue and, in its later years, a church, the Eastown Theatre ultimately became one of Detroit's 78,000 abandoned buildings. Opened as a 2,500-seat cinema in 1931, its baroque interior had chandeliers, sculptures, tapestries and a ballroom. With the cinema closing in 1967, the theatre reopened two years later, minus the seats, as a rock venue. Gradually falling into disrepair, it was abandoned in 2004, suffered extensive fire damage in 2010 and was demolished in 2015.

OVERLEAF:

Orpheum Theatre, New Bedford, Massachusetts, USA

Owned by the French Sharpshooter's Club of New Bedford, this theatre was leased to the Orpheum Circuit of vaudeville theatres and cinemas. In 1928, Orpheum became part of Radio-Keith-Orpheum, better known as RKO, the Hollywood movie studio and distribution company. The Sharpshooter's sold the building in 1962.

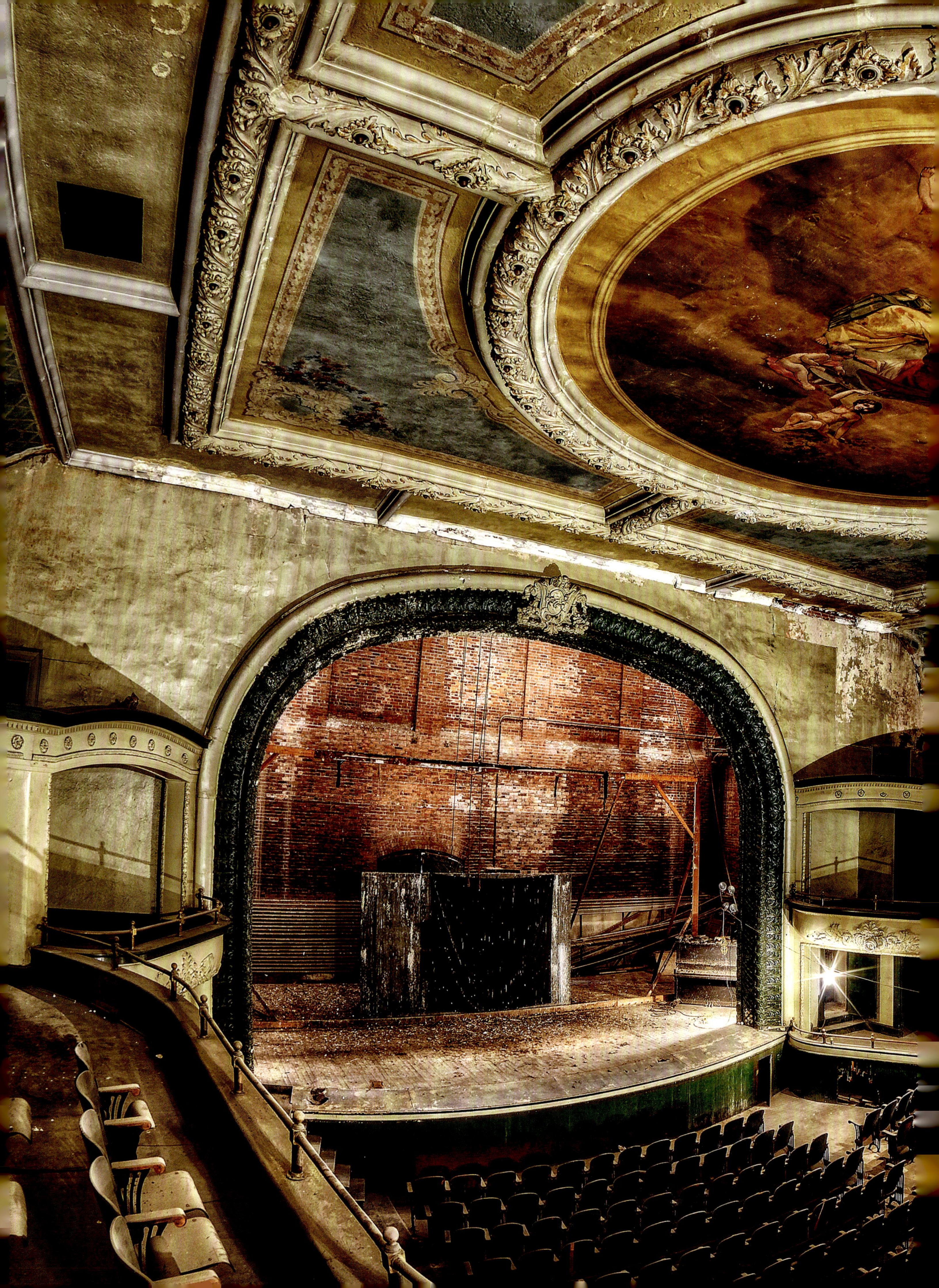

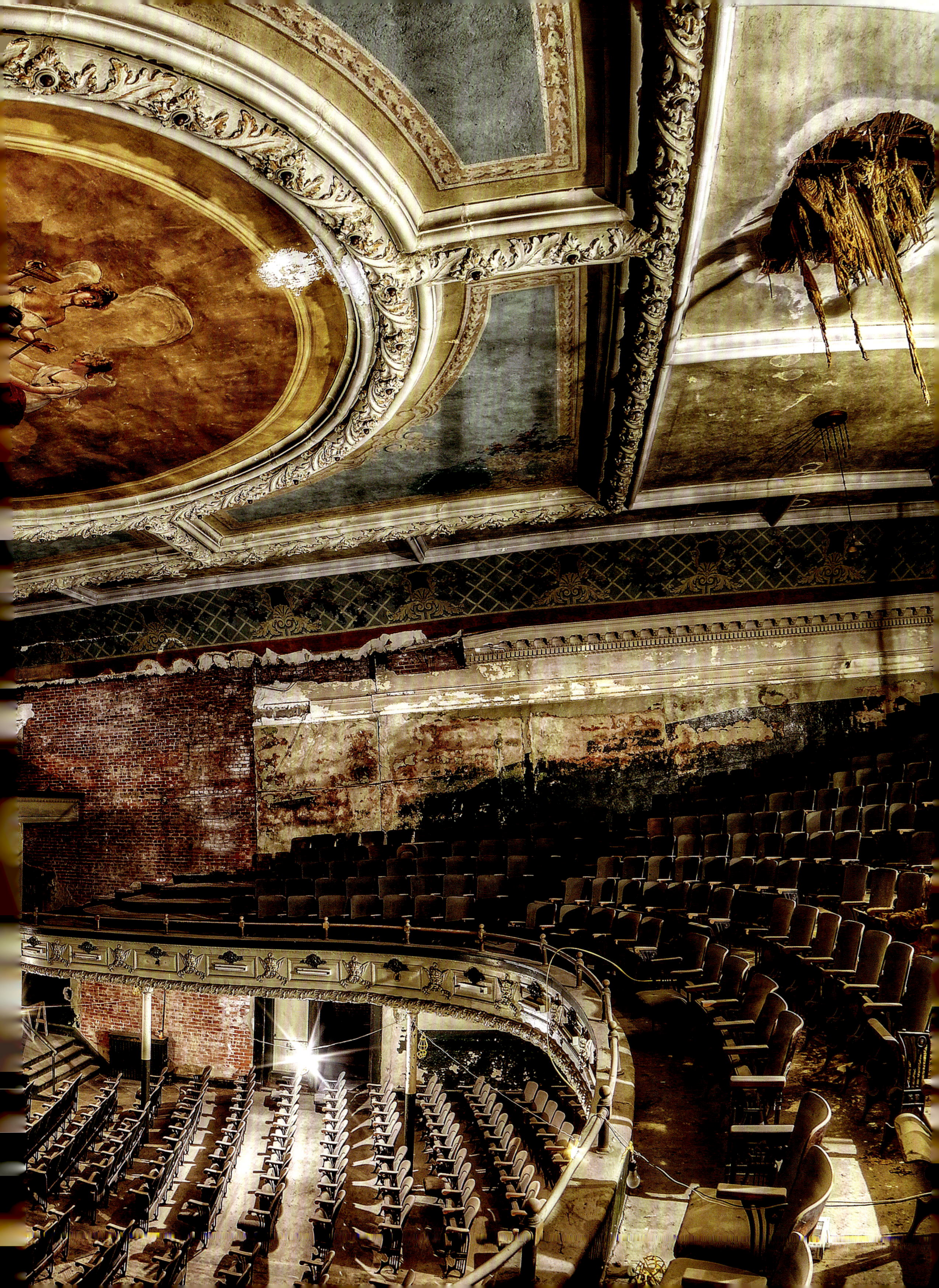

Mos Espa film set, near Tozeur, Tunisia
A long time ago in a galaxy far, far away… Well, in the 1990s, in the Tunisian desert, this set was built for *Star Wars: The Phantom Menace*. A second other-worldly *Star Wars* set has already been buried by the shifting sands of the Sahara, which might cause future archaeologists a little puzzlement if it's ever rediscovered.

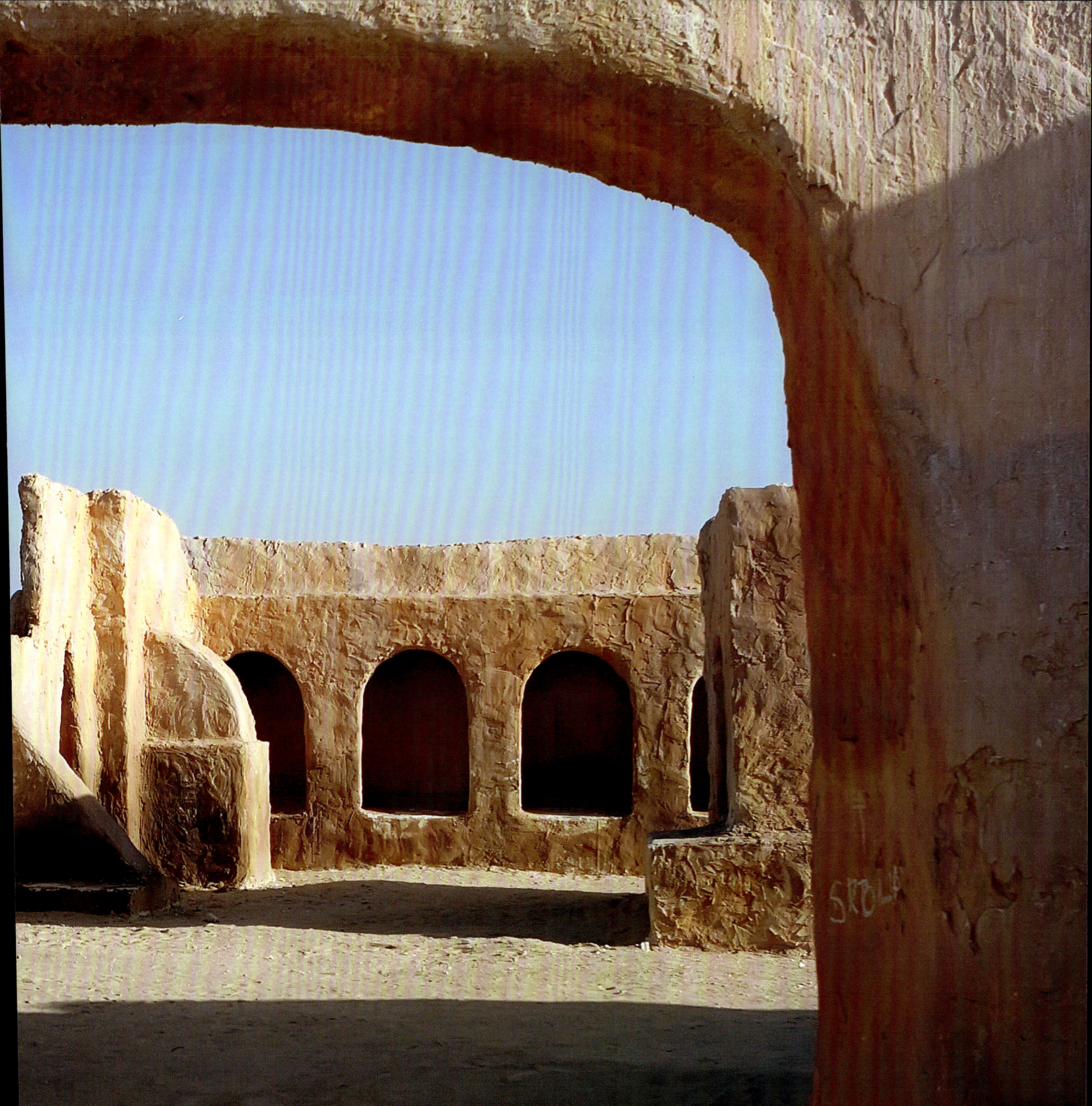

**Mos Espa film set,
near Tozeur, Tunisia**
Until the Arab Spring and later terrorist attacks in Tunisia, the *Star Wars: The Phantom Menace* set was a popular destination for tourists keen to visit film locations. More domes and fantastical fibreglass structures from *Star Wars* lie half-buried in the desert beyond.

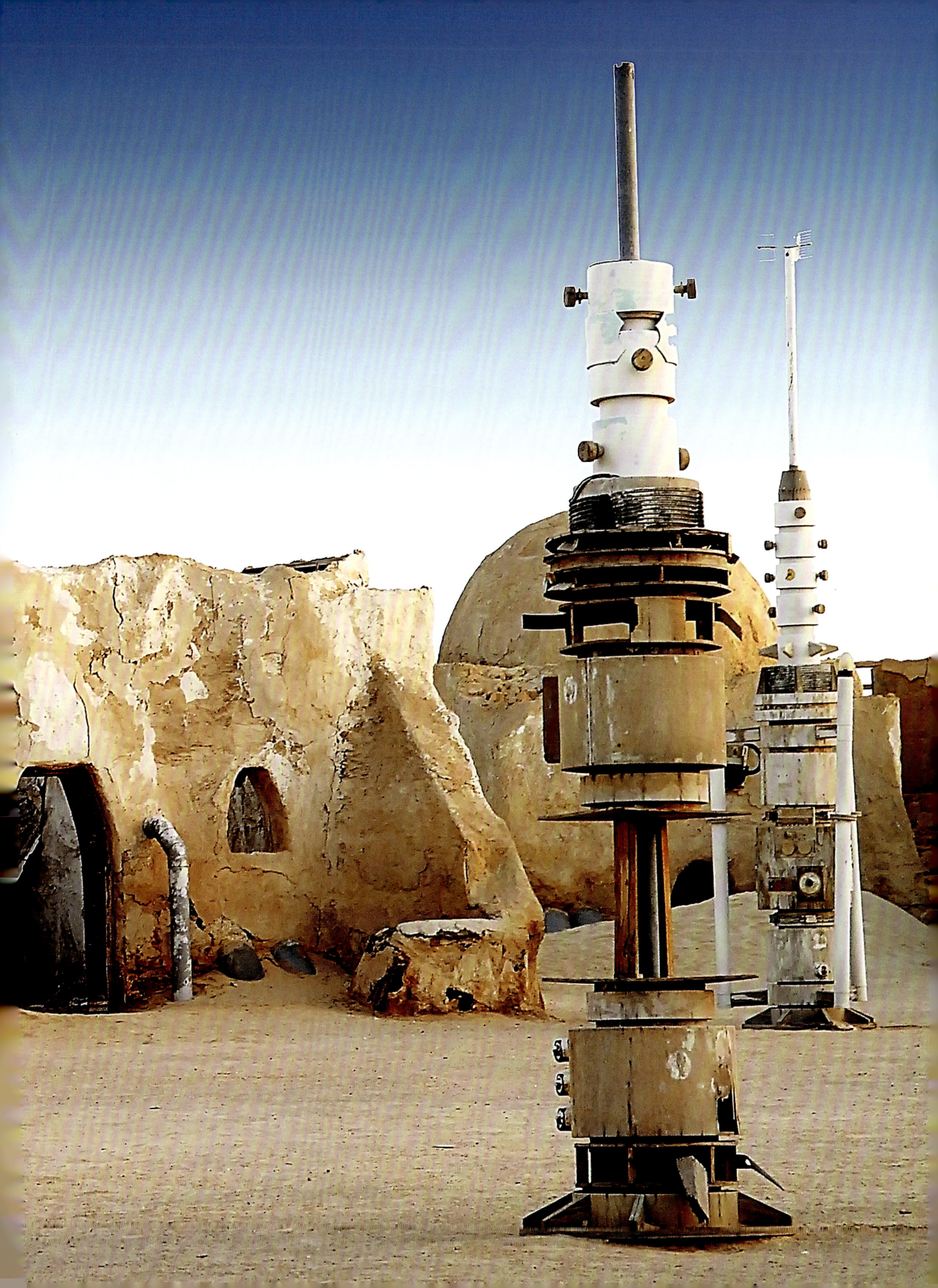

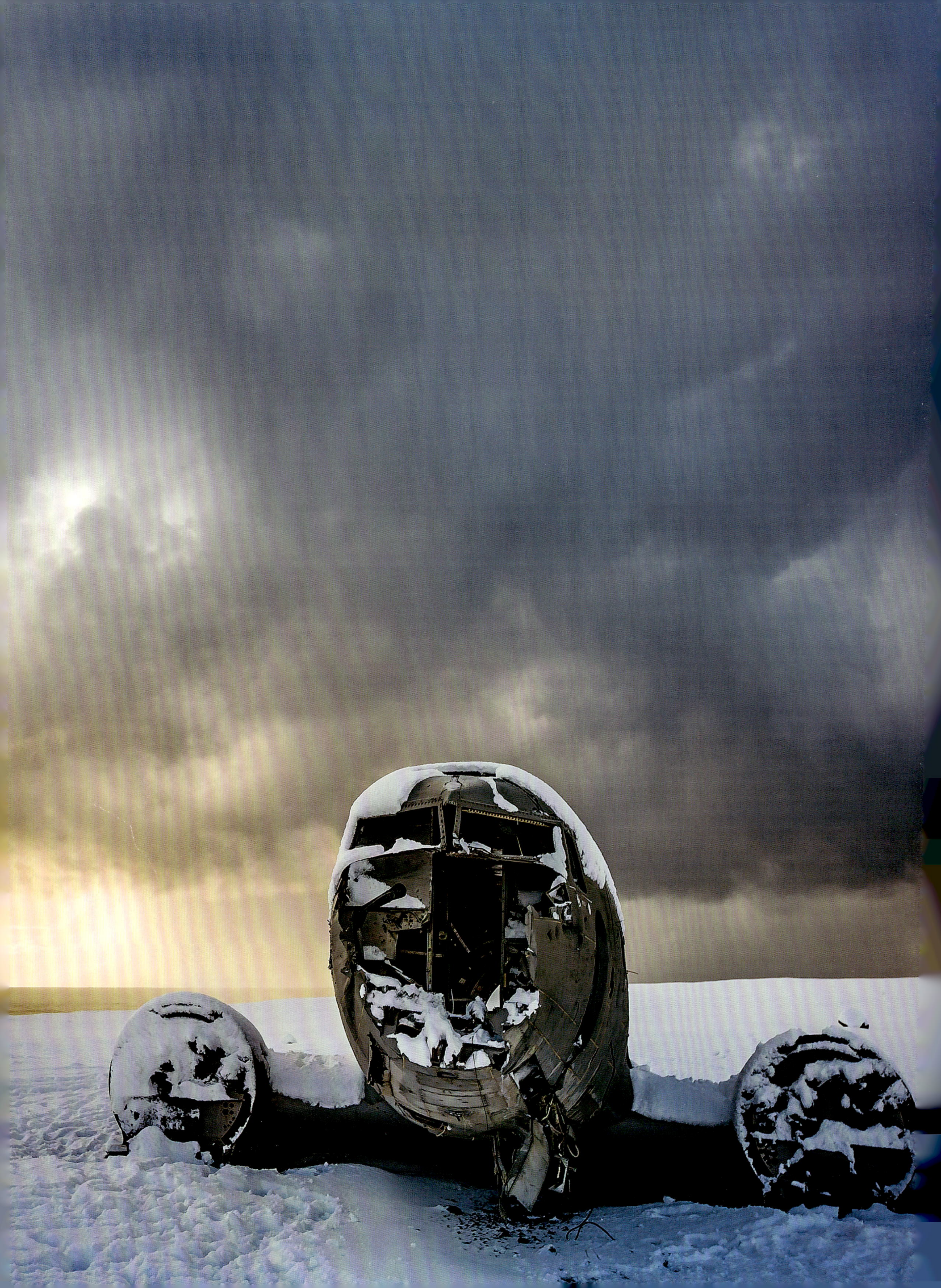

Transport

Perhaps more interesting than a railway that goes somewhere is a railway that used to go somewhere. Where did it go? Why did it stop? And, can we still trace its route?

With forgotten trains, trams, crashed aircraft, hidden subterranean stations, wrecked ships, disused railways, broken bridges, vintage petrol stations, lighthouses about to tumble into the sea and even an abandoned newly built airport, the photographs here range across industrial and passenger transport, from mining railways in the Andes to the New York Subway, London and Paris. With bizarre relics of locomotives half-buried in the desert, beautiful ghost stations glimpsed through a train window and tracks that lead off into mysterious tunnels come tales of people who disappeared, of economic collapse and of grand, possibly corrupt, follies. They still paint the runway at Spain's Ciudad Real Airport, even though the airport closed in 2012. But they're not refreshing the lines to help aircraft to land. Quite the opposite: they're painting yellow crosses on the tarmac to make it clear to any pilots that this isn't the airport they're looking for. These are the strange stories of the transport that stopped.

LEFT:
Douglas Super DC-3 cargo plane, Sólheimasandur, Iceland
On 24 November 1973, a US Navy cargo plane was forced to crash land on Sólheimasandur's volcanic black sand beach – and there it has remained. All the crew members survived.

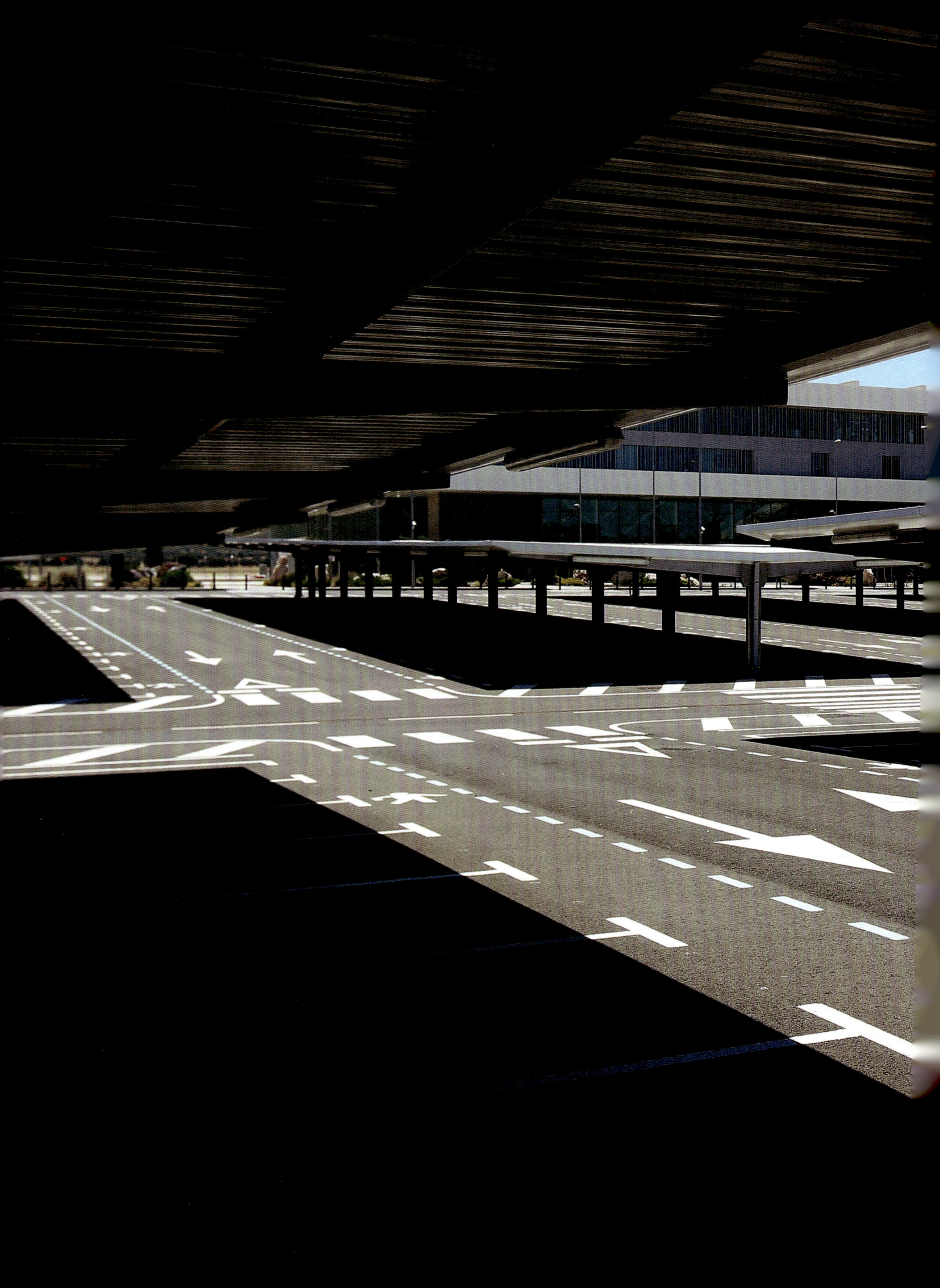

Ciudad Real Central Airport, Spain
It may look like a new car park that is yet to open, but actually it's one that has already closed. Ciudad Real Central Airport, 120 miles (200km) south of Madrid, closed in 2012 after just three years, its management having gone into receivership.

TAXI

Exit
Salida
Arrivals
Llegadas
Check-in
Facturación
Ciudad Real

ALL PHOTOGRAPHS:
Ciudad Real Central Airport, Spain
The first privately funded airport in Spain, Ciudad Real was planned and financed during the construction boom in the 1990s and early 2000s, but opened during the recession after 2008. International flights began in June 2010 – that is, with a sole Ryanair service to London, but by October even that was cancelled. Other airliners continued flying domestic flights until 2012.

The airport was intended to be an overflow for Madrid's main airport, but Ciudad Real is a two-hour drive from the capital. Added to that, positioned between Madrid and Córdoba, it was also supposed to be Spain's first airport linked to the country's AVE high-speed rail network – but no railway station was ever built there.

Some have suggested that the airport's building had only ever been to serve the construction industry. The bankruptcy report states: 'The loans taken out were enough to cover the construction phase, but no thought was given to the investment needed to make the airport function as a business.'

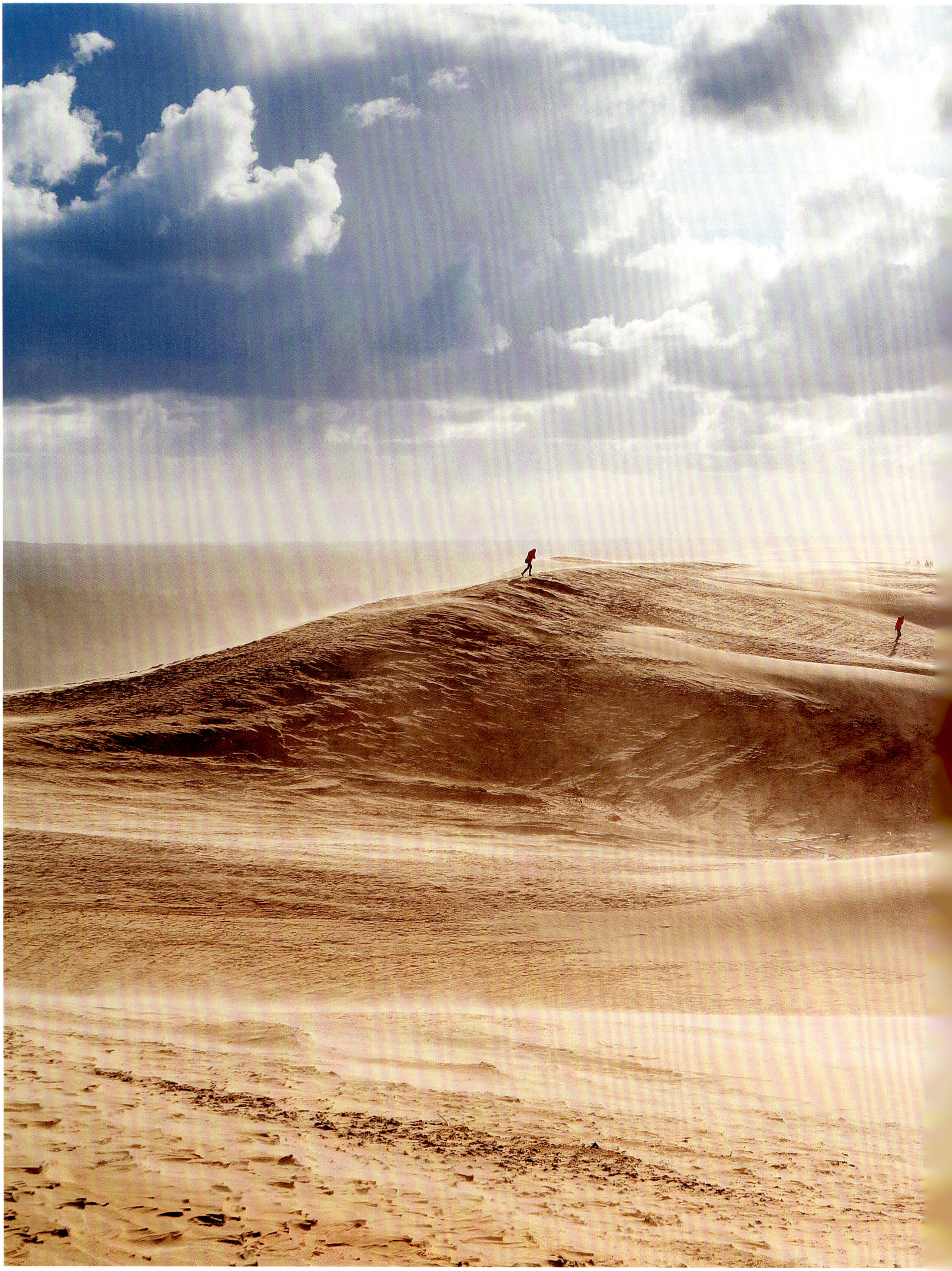

LEFT:
Rubjerg Knude Lighthouse, northern Jutland, Denmark
Situated on top of a cliff, the Rubjerg Knude Lighthouse was built in 1900 and ceased operating in 1968. With coastal erosion and continually shifting sands a major problem in the area, it is anticipated that by 2023 the cliff will have been eroded so far that the lighthouse will fall into the sea.

Great Isaac Cay Lighthouse, Bahamas
Built in the 1850s, the Great Isaac Cay Lighthouse stands on this eerie, giant coral head. On 4 August 1969, it was discovered that the two keepers posted there had disappeared. No trace of them has ever been found, but it's thought that they died in Hurricane Anna, which had passed a few days earlier. The keepers weren't replaced and the lighthouse was switched to an automated system.

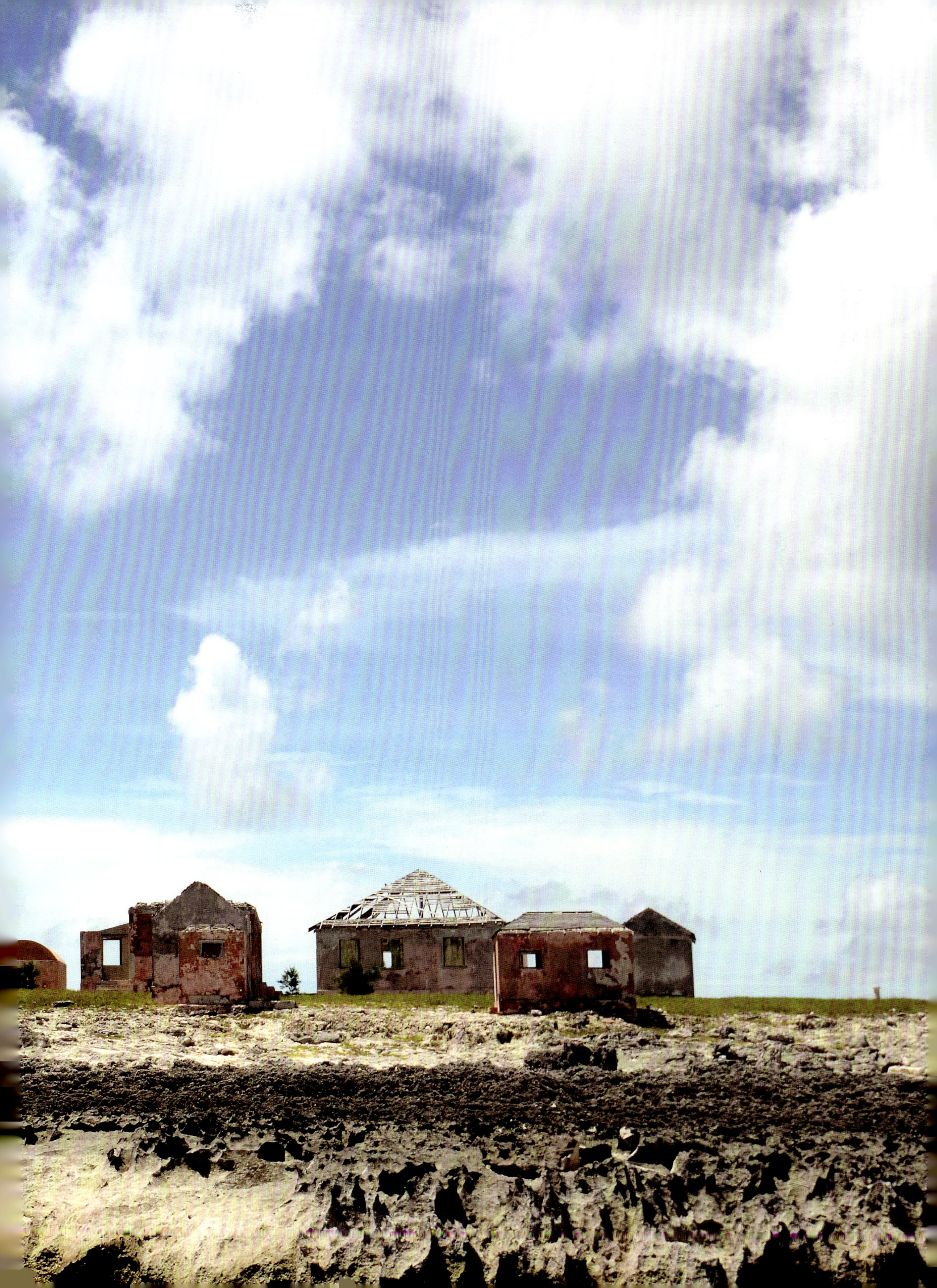

Wreck of the SS *American*, Fuerteventura, Canary Islands
While under tow to Thailand for refitting in 1994, the SS *American* was caught in a thunderstorm and ran aground when the tow snapped. Within two days, the 50-year-old ocean liner had broken in two. Since then the continual pounding of the waves has gradually broken up the rest of the ship. By 2013 the last pieces of the wreck could only be seen at low tide.

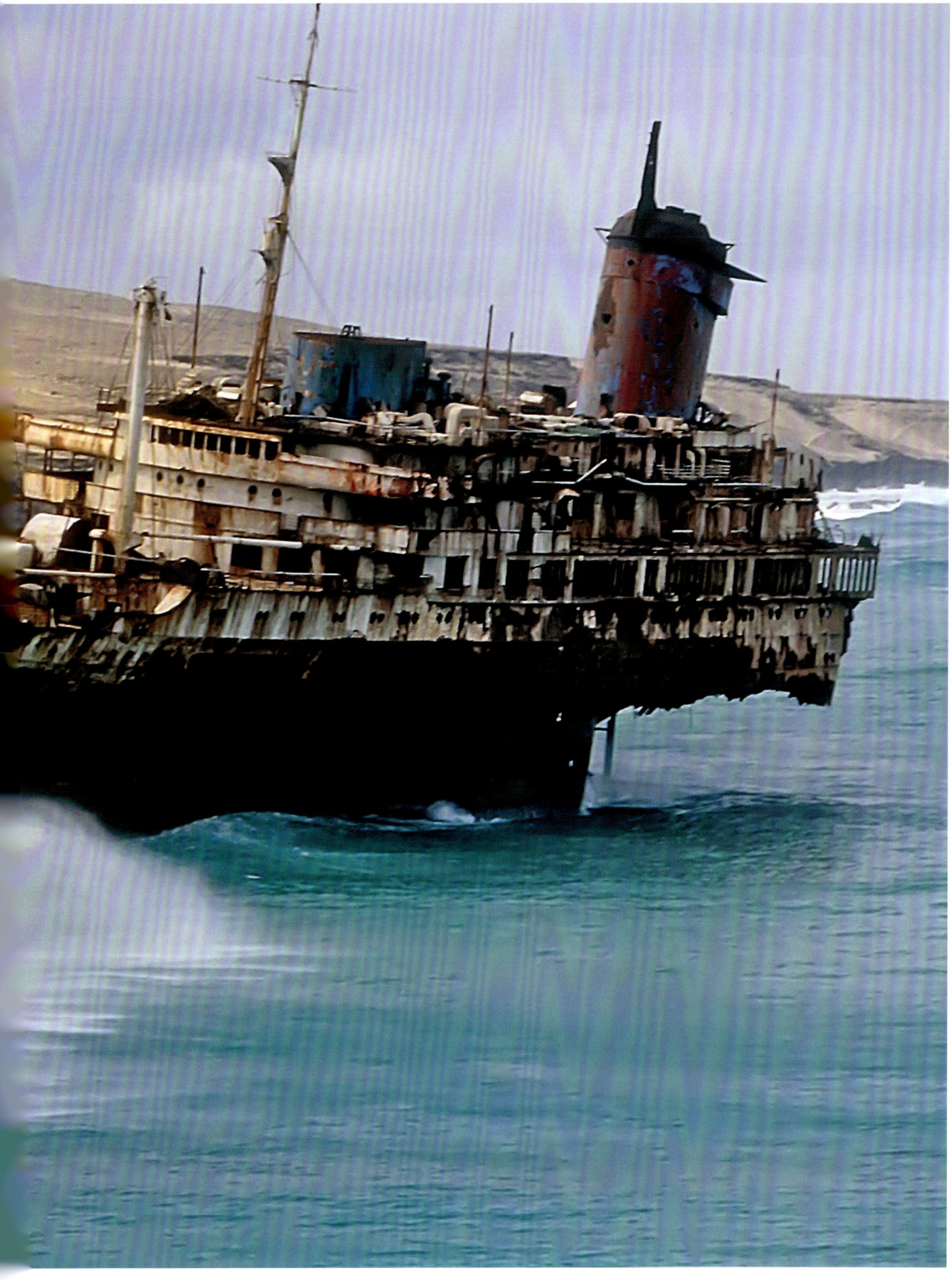

TOP LEFT:
Route 178, Trona, San Bernardino County, California, USA
Out of gas. Located in the Mojave Desert, Trona is a company town for Searles Valley Minerals, which extracts a variety of minerals from the nearby Searles Dry Lake.

BOTTOM LEFT:
Winnemucca, Humboldt County, Nevada, USA
It may look far from any road, but this petrol station is just off the Interstate 80 running through Nevada from Utah to California.

TOP RIGHT:
Sinclair Gas Station, Elberta, Utah County, Utah, USA
This station doesn't feature the Sinclair's trademark brontosaurus, but the green paint is the same tone as that used for their dinosaur.

BOTTOM RIGHT:
Pinedale, Sublette County, Wyoming, USA
Pinedale is popular for hunting, fishing, hiking and skiing.

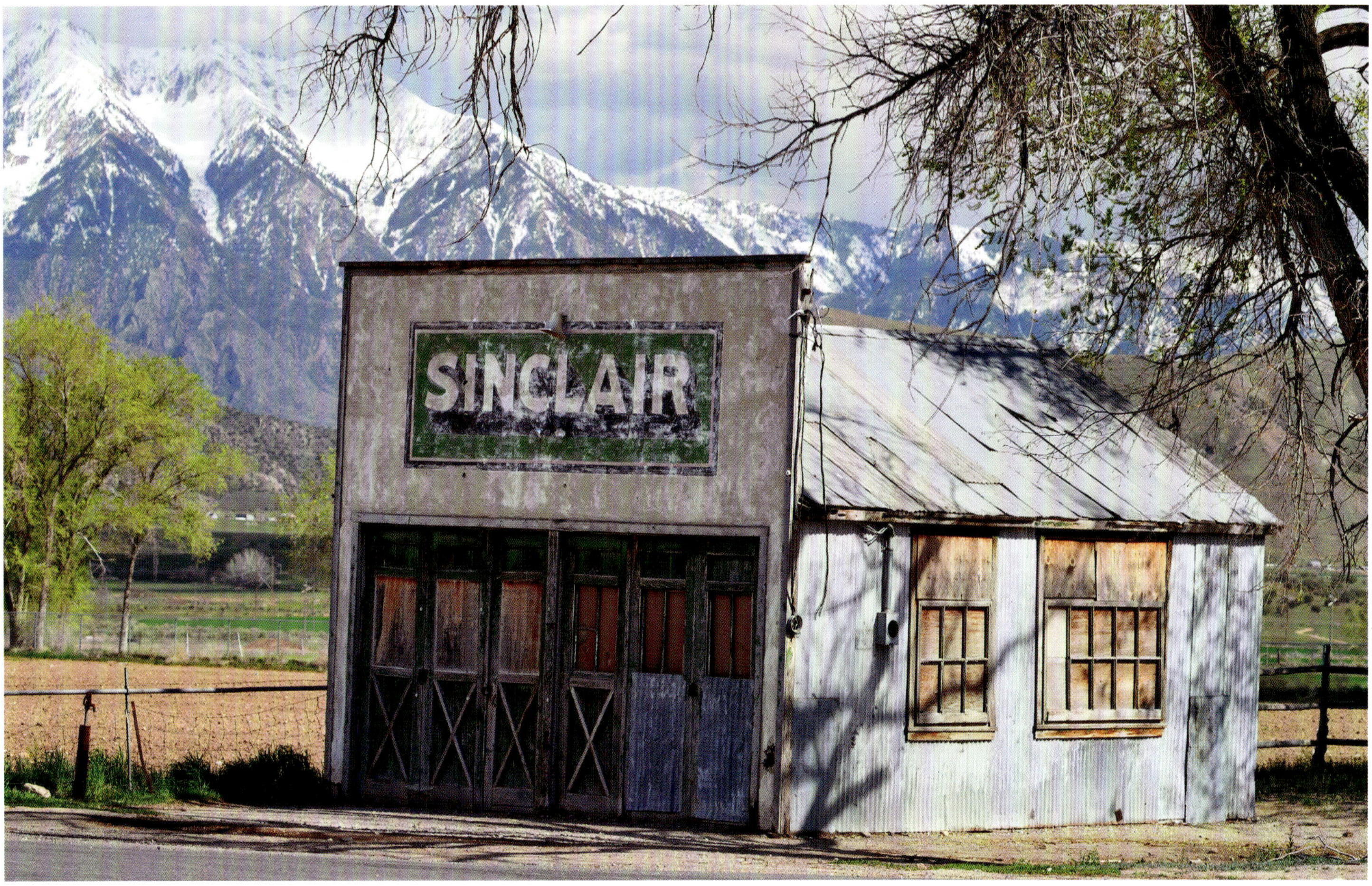
SINCLAIR

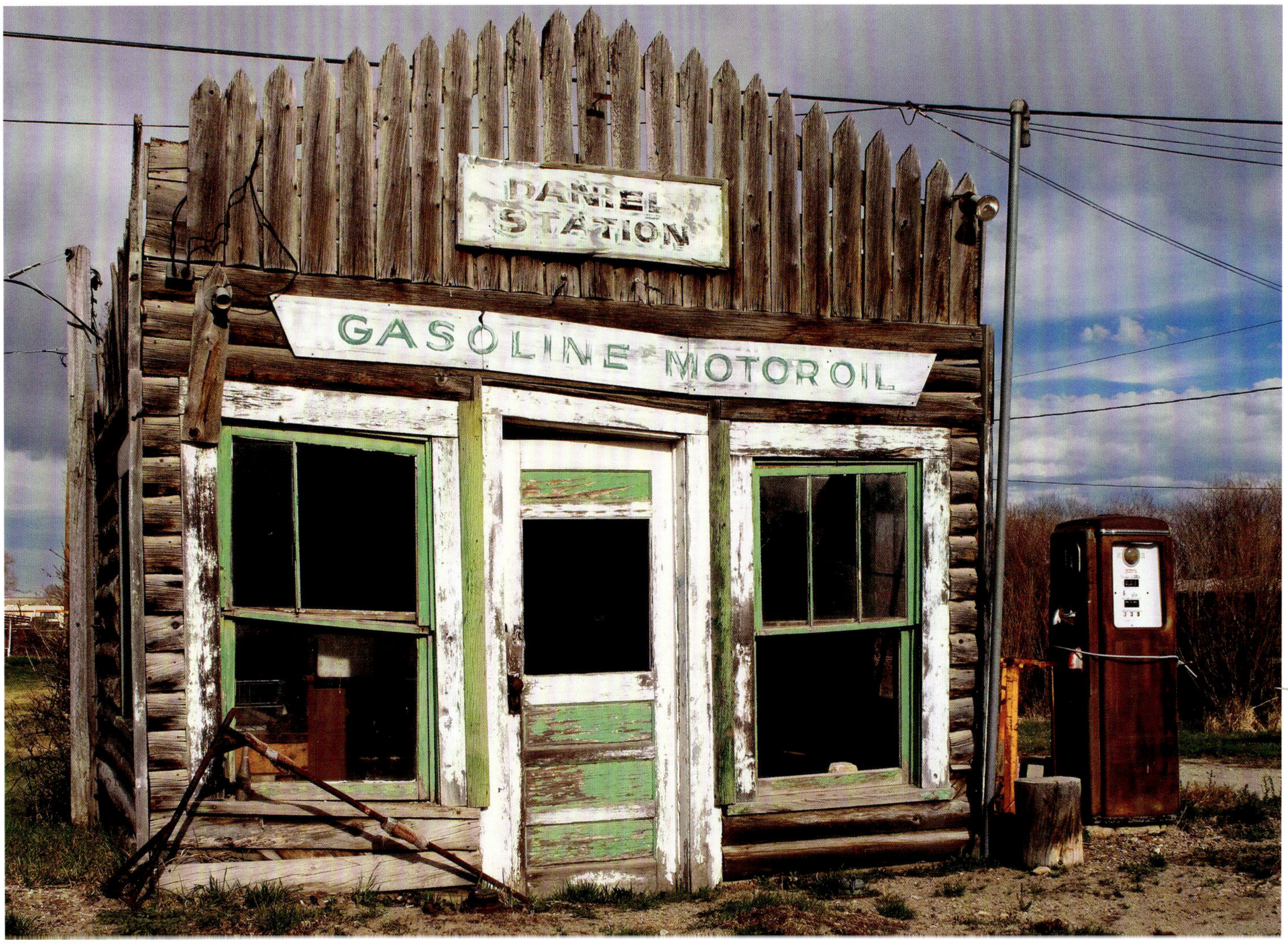
DANIEL STATION
GASOLINE MOTOR OIL

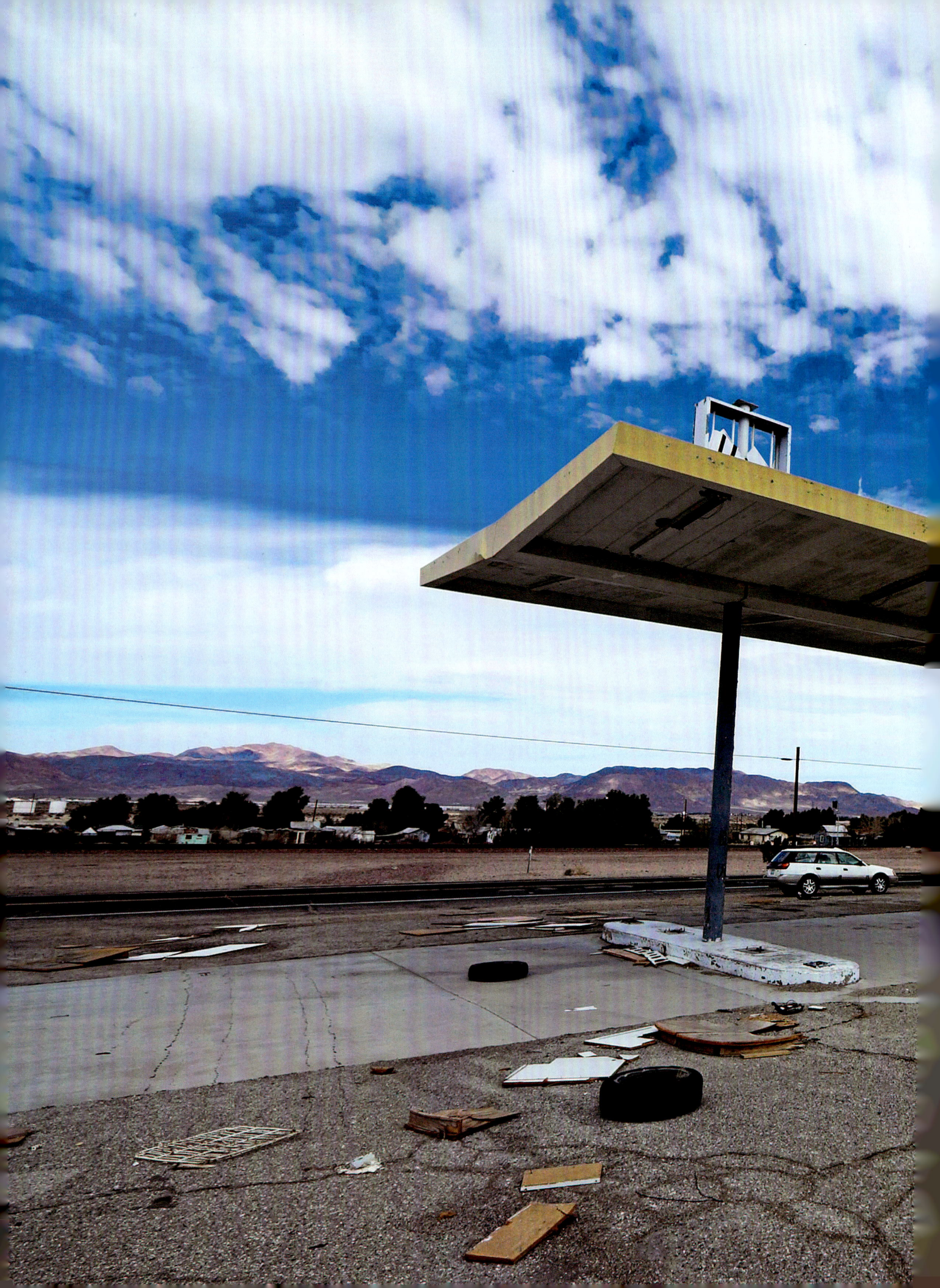

National Trails Highway, 'Historic Route 66', Daggett, San Bernardino County, California, USA
Linking Chicago with Los Angeles, Route 66 was the road taken by many to reach California, including those heading west during the 1930s Dust Bowl. After it had been replaced by the Interstate highways in 1985, Route 66 was removed from the United States Highway System, but surviving stretches are still marked 'Historic Route 66'.

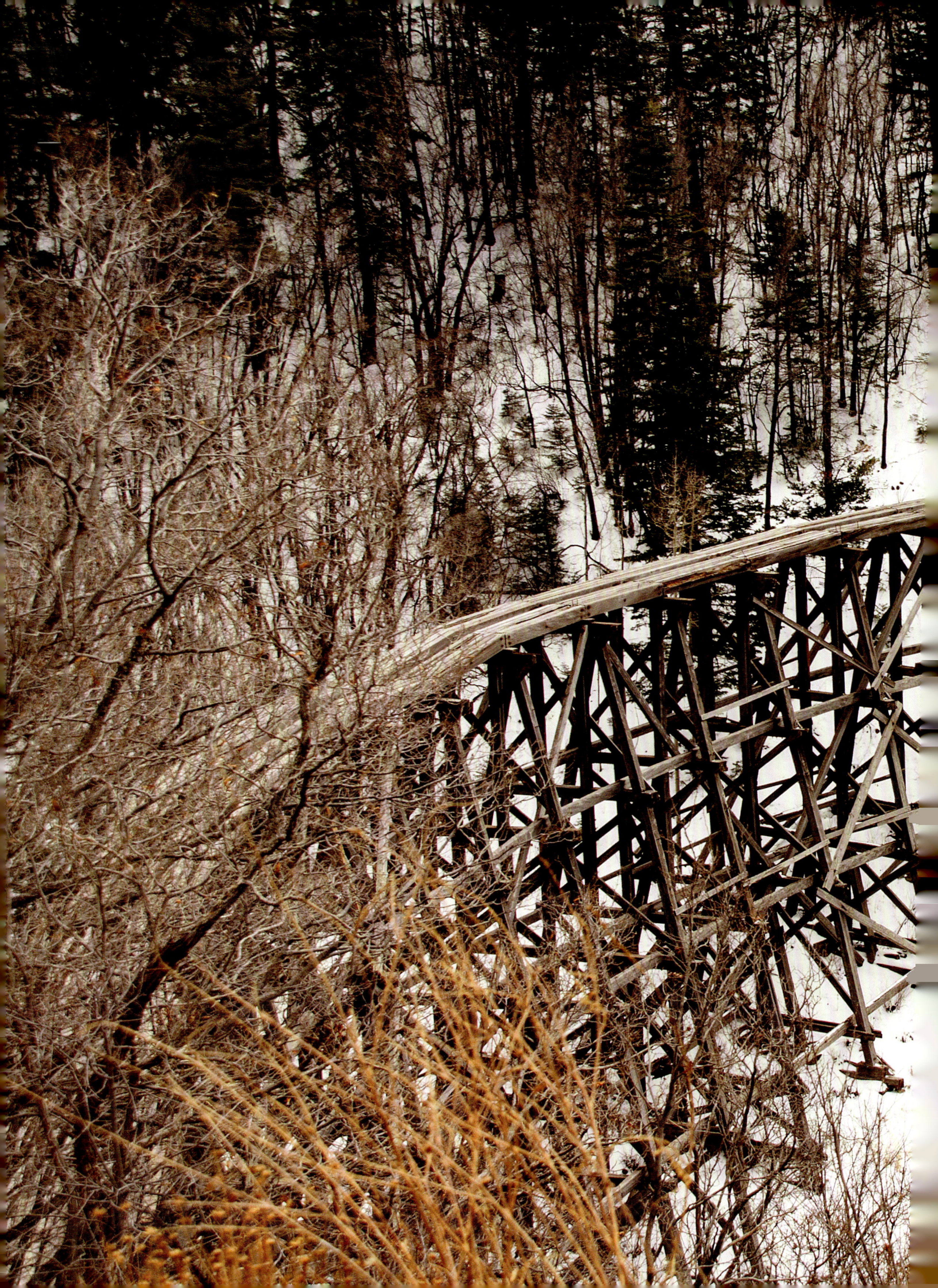

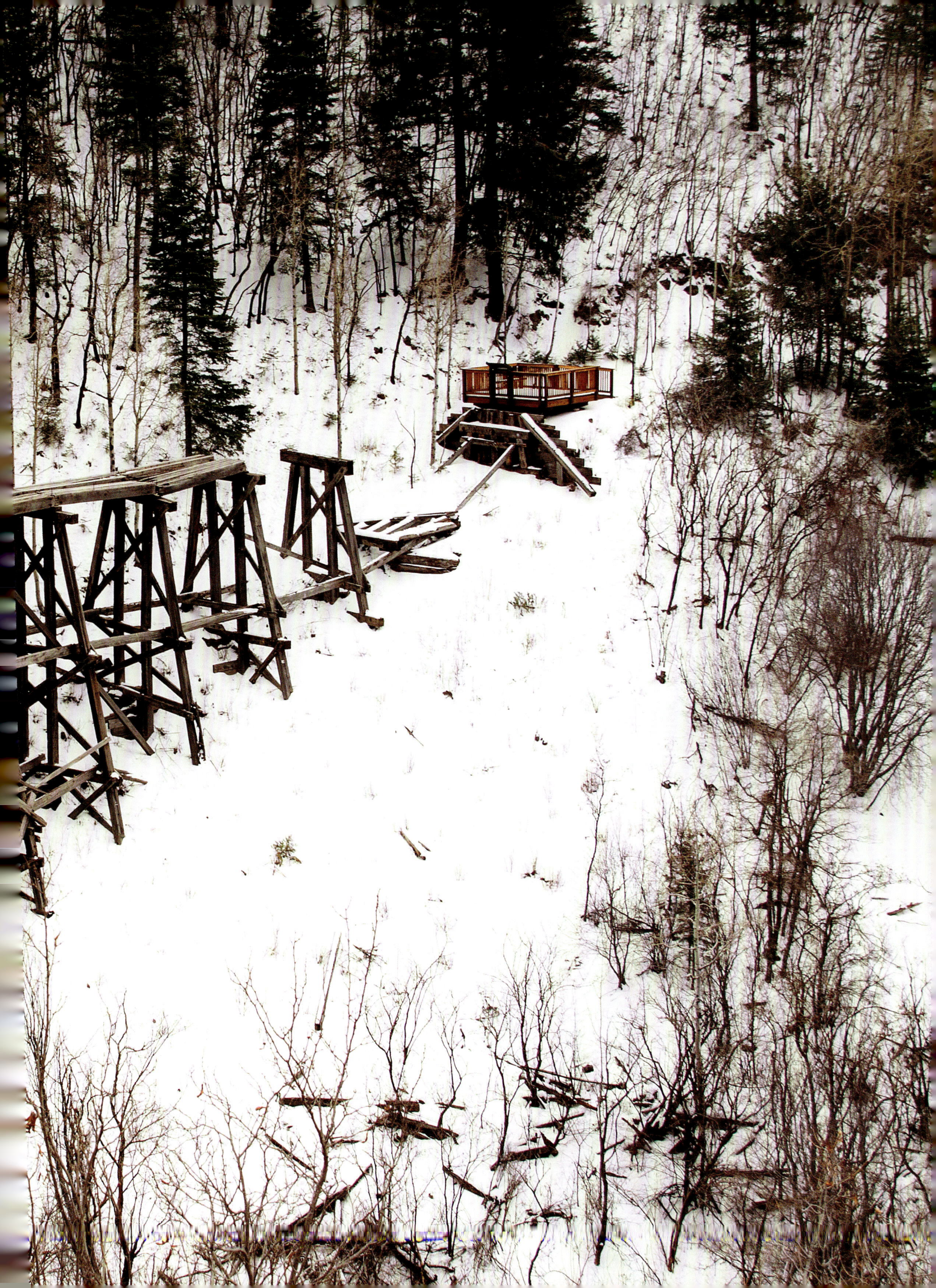

PREVIOUS PAGE:
'The Cloud-Climbing Railroad', nr Cloudcroft, New Mexico, USA
Opened in the 1890s the branch line carried tourists up to enjoy the views from the Sacramento Mountains. It was closed in 1948 after a decline in traffic.

TOP LEFT:
Independence Mine, Talkeetna Mountains, Alaska, USA
Gold was mined at the Independence Mine from 1886 until 1951. In 1964, the settlement was listed on the National Register of Historic Places and is now a state historic park.

BOTTOM LEFT AND TOP RIGHT:
Bahia Honda Bridge, Florida Keys, USA
After closure, the former railway and road bridge was left standing and two spans were removed to allow tall boats to pass through.

BOTTOM RIGHT:
East Coulee Bridge, Alberta, Canada
Built in 1936, the East Coulee Bridge served the Atlas Coal Mine until the mine closed in the 1970s.

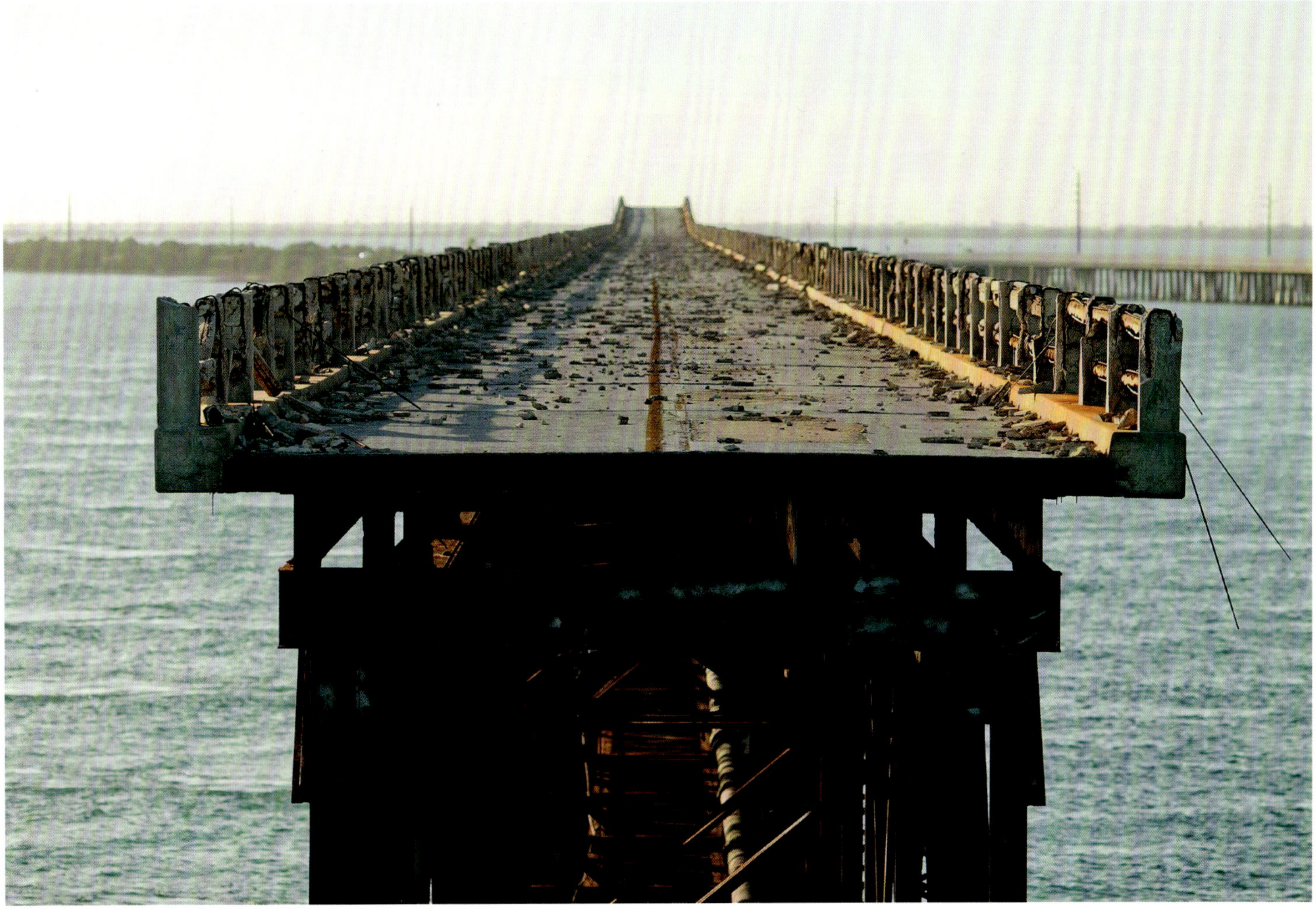

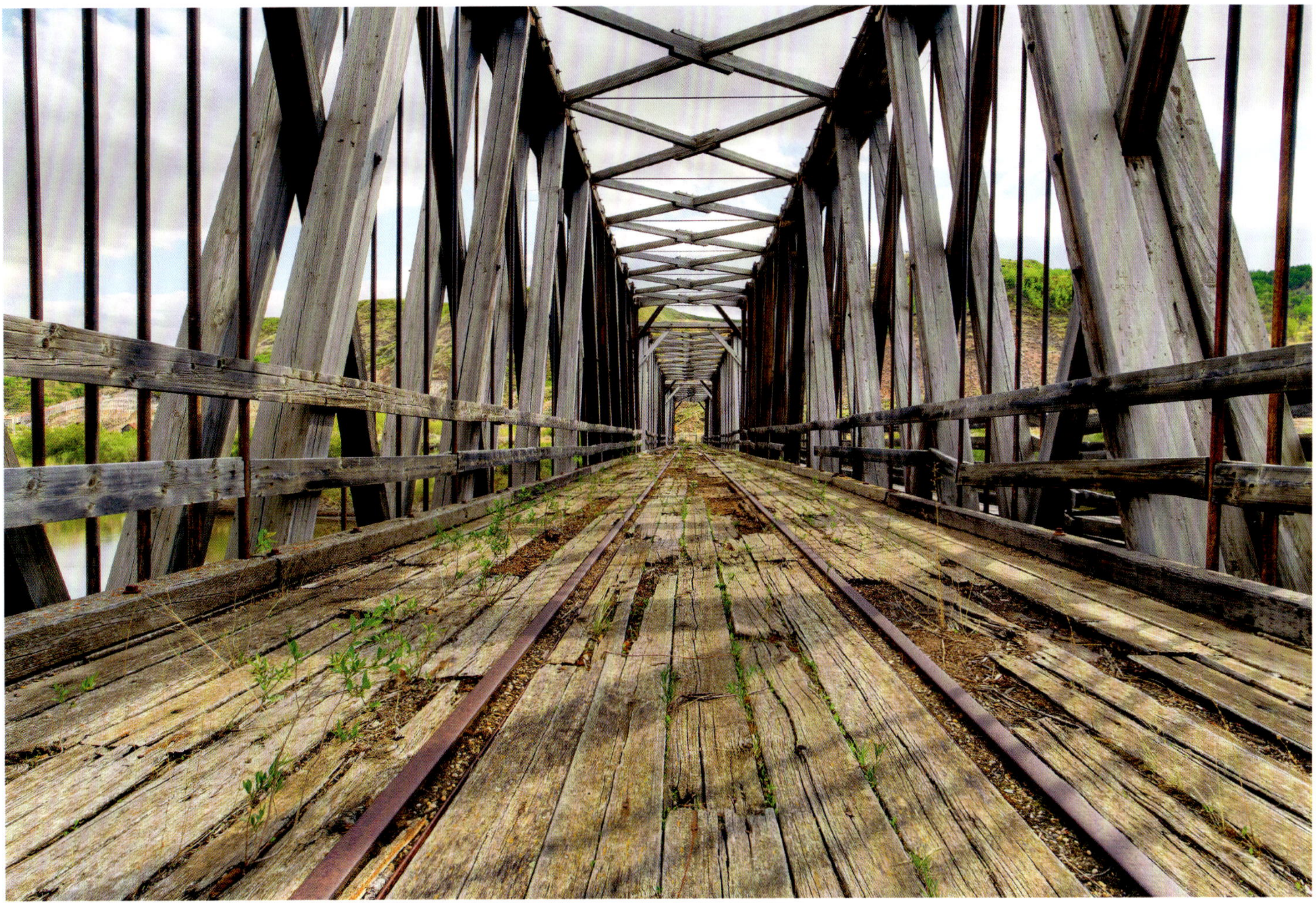

Disused platform, Chambers Street Subway Station, New York City, USA
Built in 1913 when Lower Manhattan was New York's principal business district, Chambers Street Station was designed to be a hub. By the mid-1920s, however, the subway network was drawing the city's population north, leaving Chambers Street behind. In 1931, half of the station was closed.

ERS ST.

City Hall Station, New York City, USA
Designed as a showpiece for New York's new subway system, City Hall Station opened in 1904. An elegant structure of Romanesque Revival style with skylights, coloured glass and brass chandeliers, its tightly curved platform meant that, in later years, longer subway carriages were unable to stop there – the carriage doors being a dangerous distance from the platform. Always a quiet station, passenger service was discontinued in 1945.

207

REJECTED
PANELS
HERE

11A

Aldwych Underground Station, London, England
A relic of a merger between two London Underground schemes, trains ran the single stop between Holborn and Aldwych from 1907 until 1994. During World War II, the platforms and tunnels were used as an air-raid shelter and to store antiquities from the British Museum.

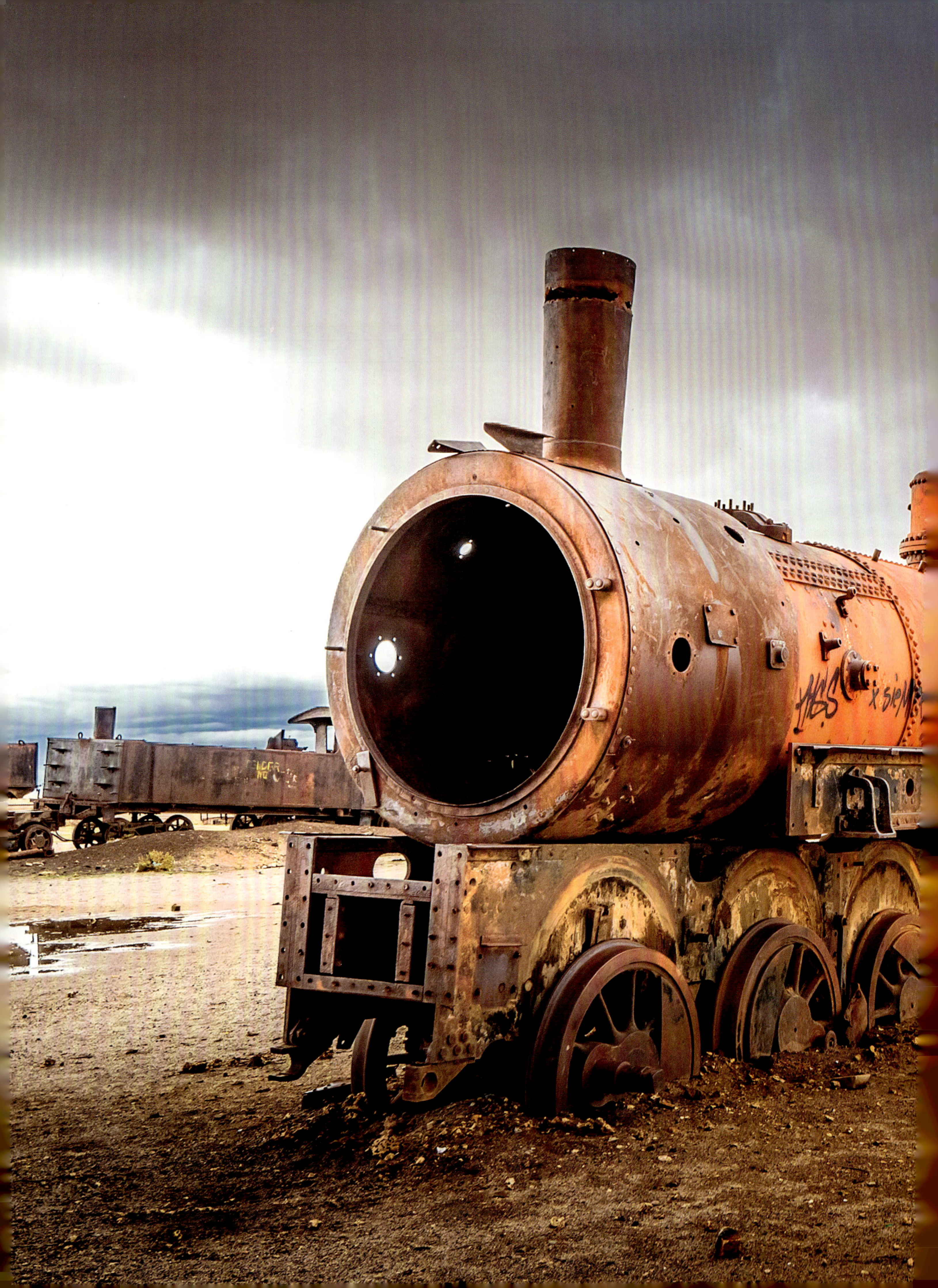

Uyuni Train Cemetery, Uyuni, Bolivia
In the late 19th century, the Andean town of Uyuni served as a distribution hub linking trains carrying minerals to Pacific Coast ports. After the mineral mining industry collapsed in the 1940s, the railways that served the mines fell into ruin, leaving the trains to the harsh winds blowing off the Uyuni flats, the world's largest salt plain. Today, though, the rusting, graffiti-covered hulks have become one of Uyuni's attractions.

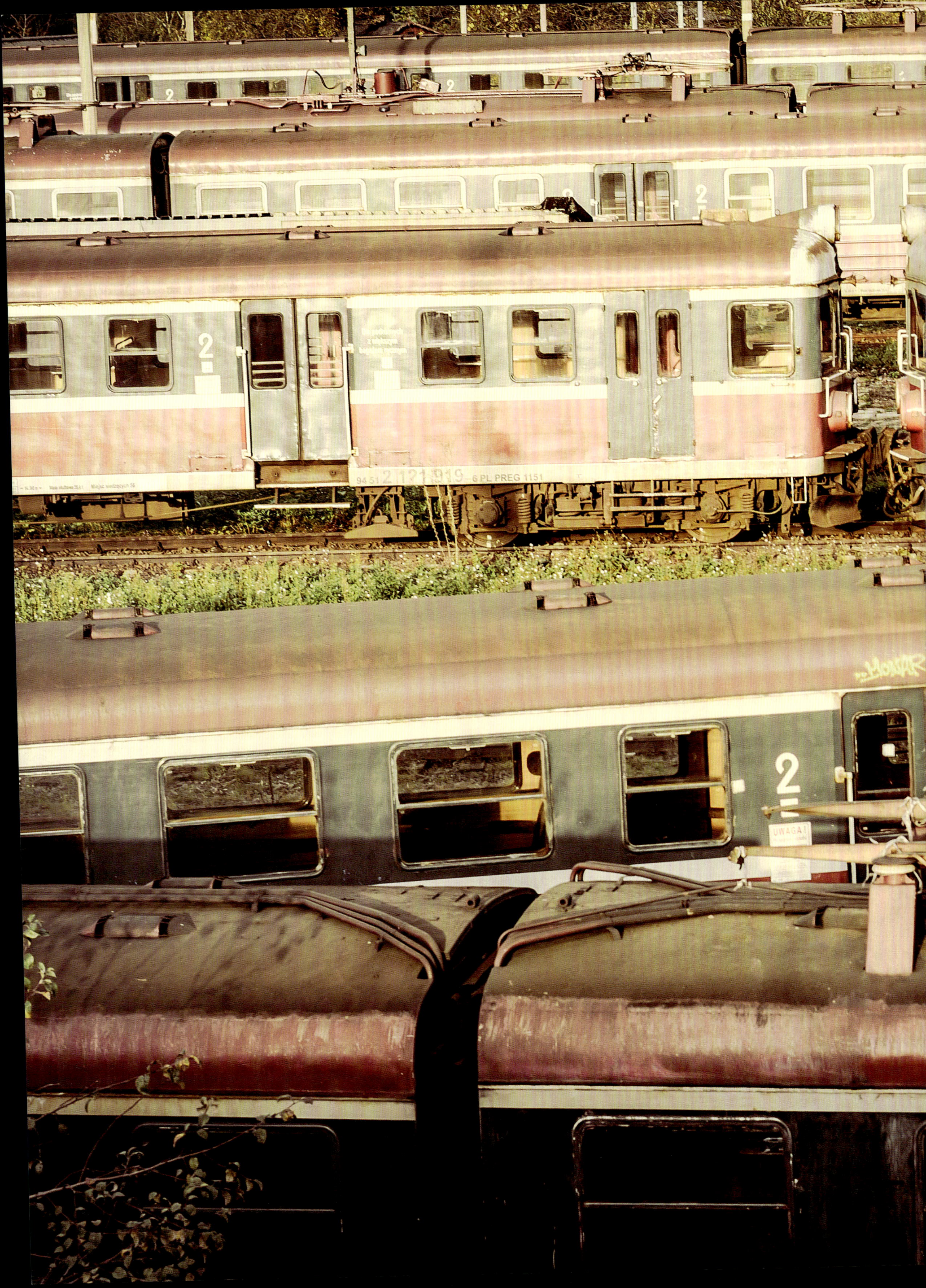
2
94 51 2 121 919-6 PL PREG 1151
2
UWAGA!

94 51 2 121 910 -5 PL - PREG 1151

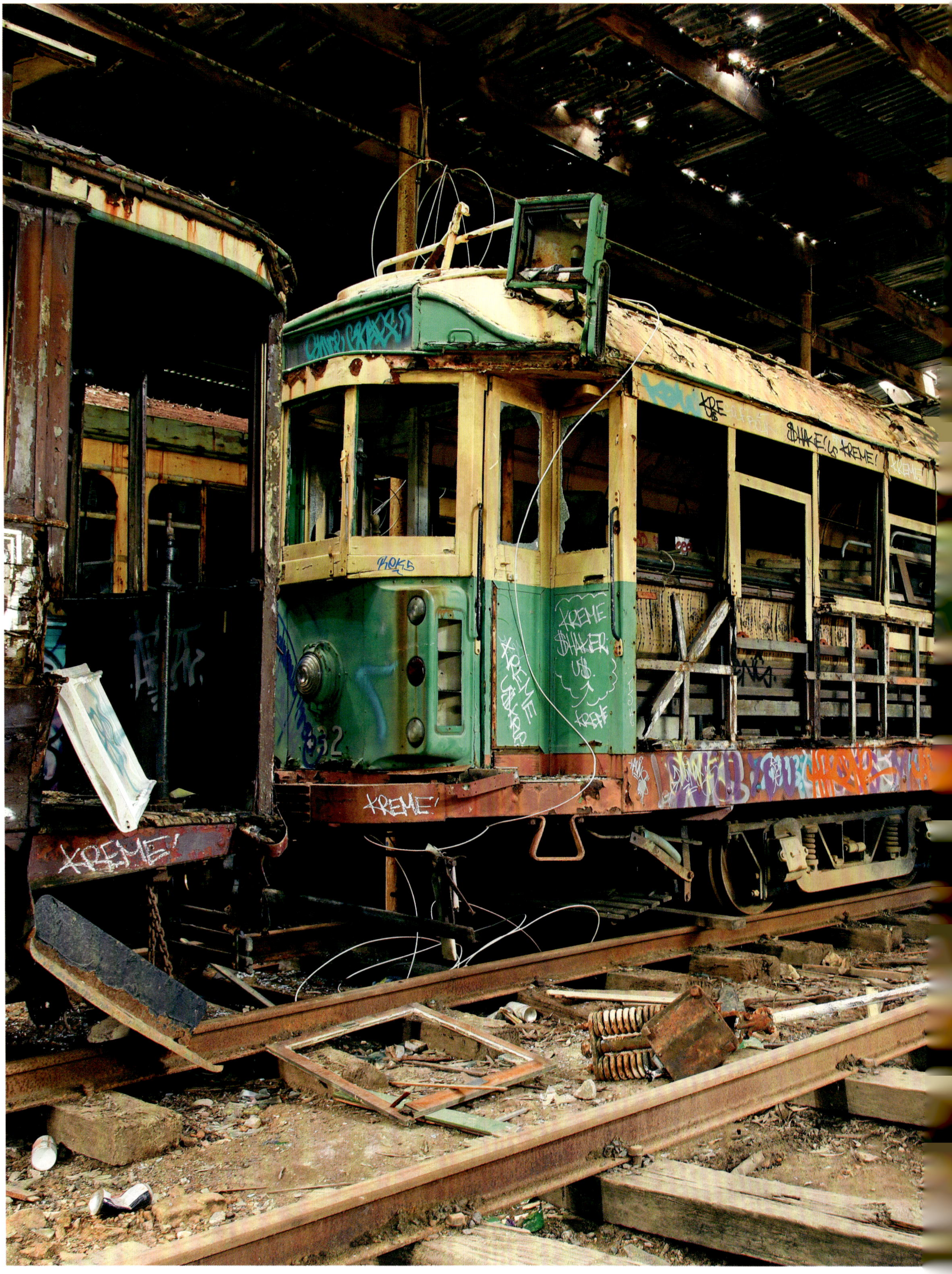
KREME!
KREME!

PREVIOUS PAGE:
Disused trains, Czestochowa, Poland
Electric trains of a type no longer in service stand abandoned in a railway depot.

LEFT:
Loftus Tram Shed, Sydney, Australia
The oldest trams in the Loftus Tram Museum's storage shed dated back to 1896. Last used in 1961, when Sydney shut down its tram system, they became, over the years, a target for vandals and graffiti artists. In 2015 a fire in the shed destroyed all the trams.

Canfranc Station, Spain
As the gateway between France and Spain, Canfranc Station, high in the Pyrenees, was designed in a grand Art Nouveau style, only to become an elegant anachronism. Built in 1928, international traffic at the station ceased in 1970 when a railway bridge on the French side collapsed and wasn't rebuilt. A couple of local trains still run each day on the Spanish side.

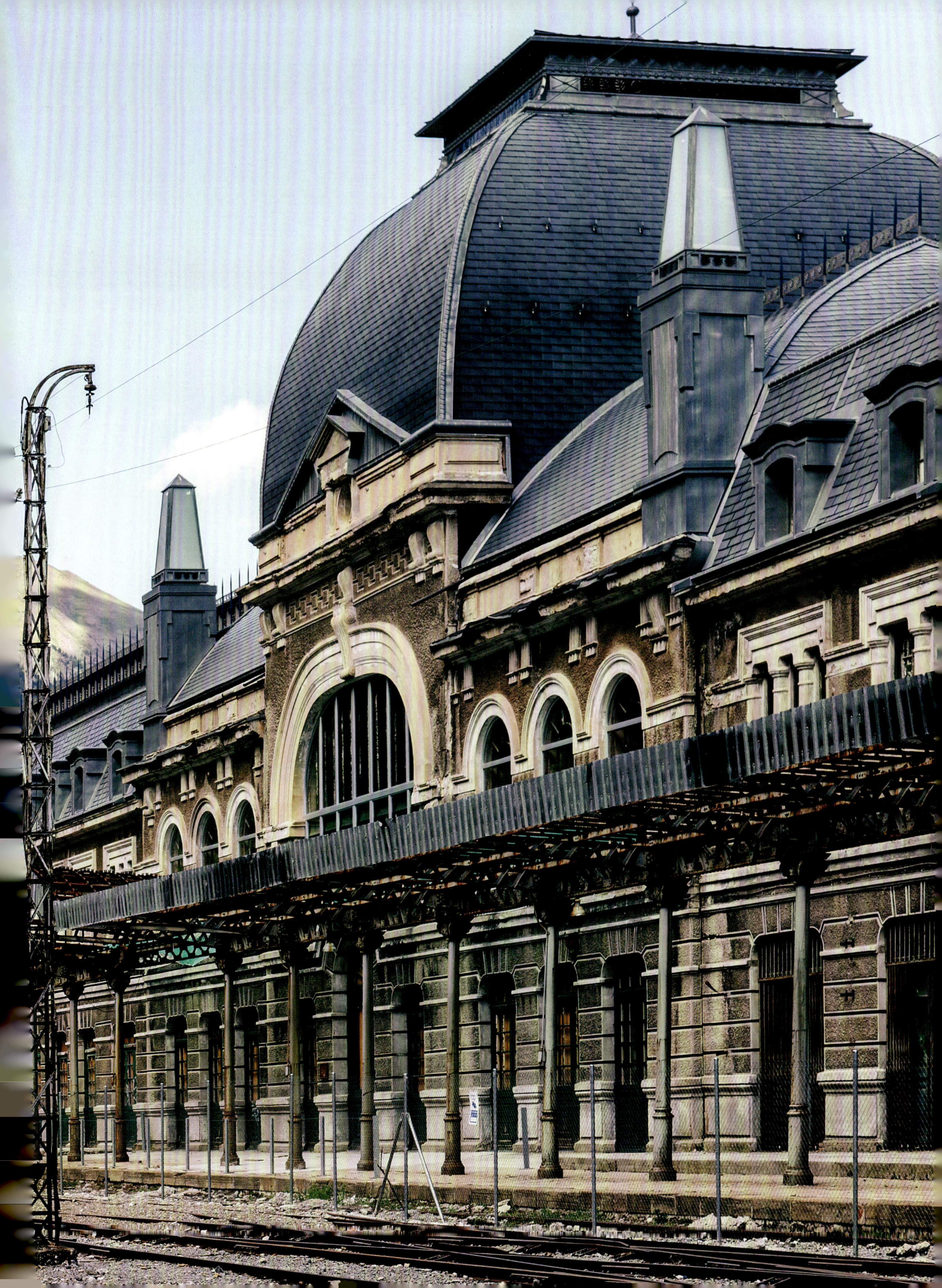

ALL PHOTOGRAPHS:
Canfranc Station, Spain
A large station was needed at Canfranc, not only because it was a border crossing with customs controls, but because, when it was built, French and Spanish trains ran on different gauges – passengers and freight crossing the border having to transfer from one train to another.

The interior of the station – beautiful wood-vaulted halls, customs offices and waiting rooms – are falling apart, the tracks are overgrown and the trains are wrecks.

One of the disused railway tunnels is now the site of a scientific research laboratory working on, among other projects, the search for dark matter.

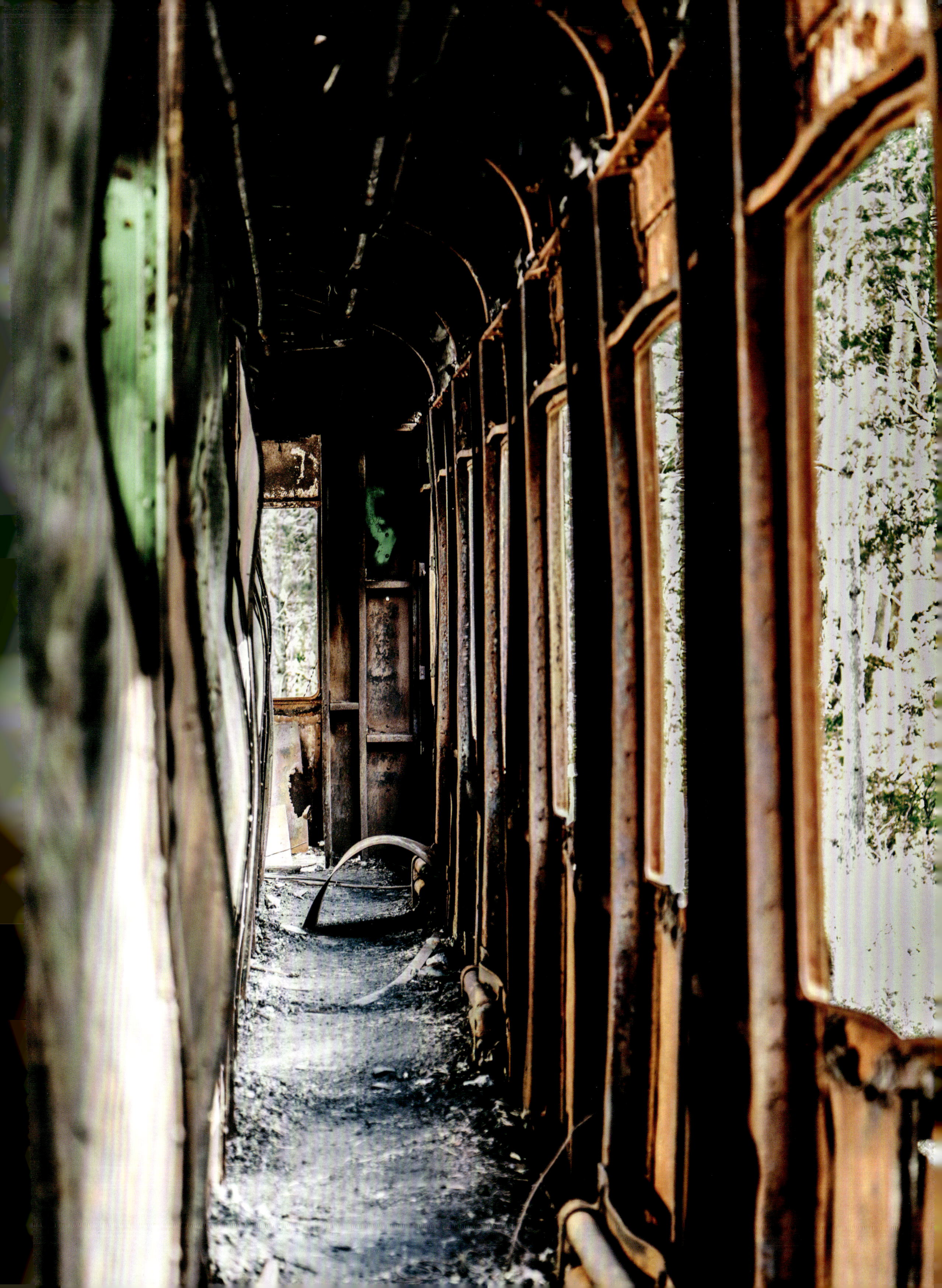

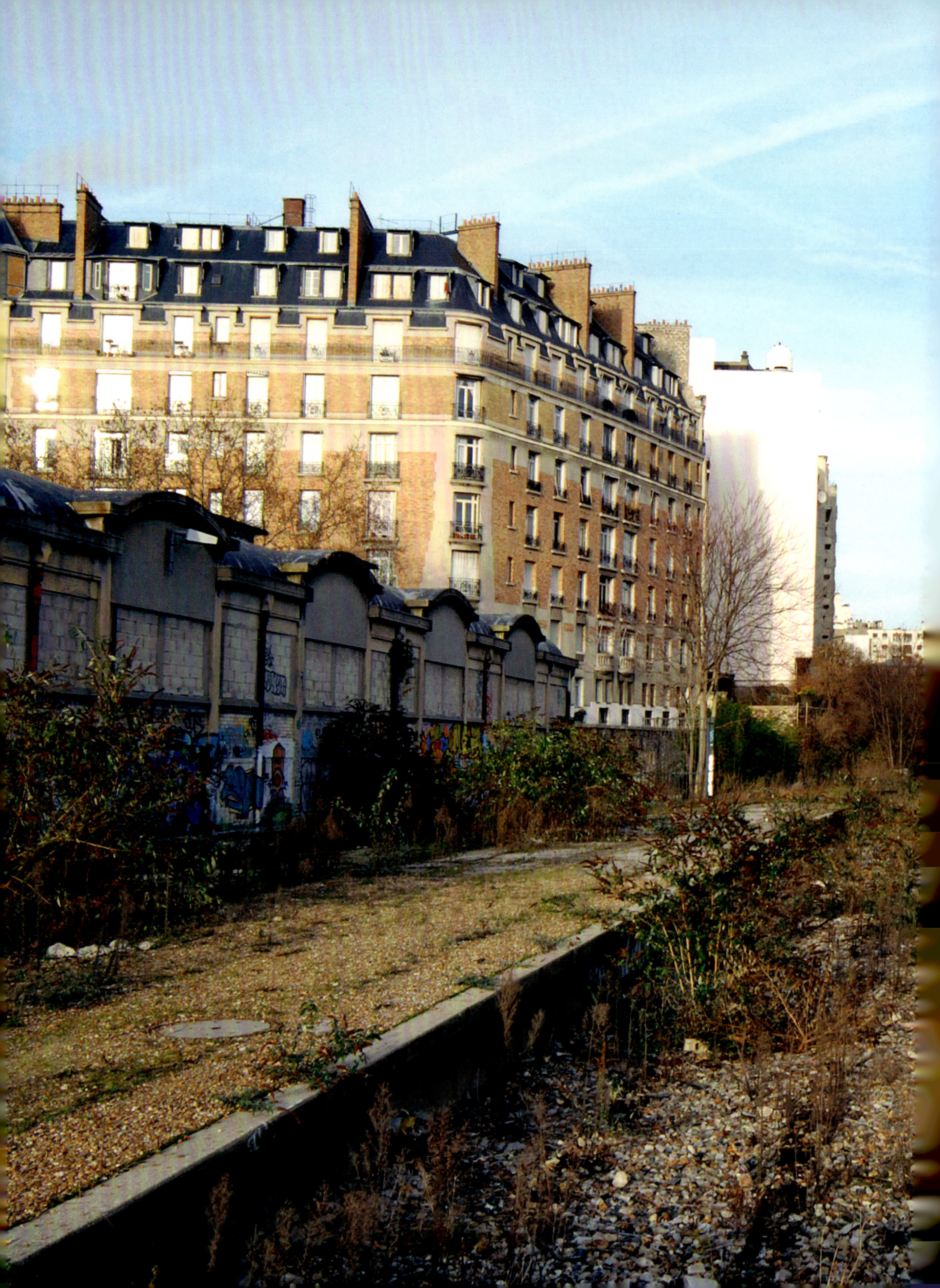

LEFT:

Petite Ceinture, Gare d'Auteuil, Paris, France
The Chemin de Fer de Petite Ceinture – the 'little belt railway' – was a circular Parisian railway that, from 1869, connected the city's main railway stations. Suffering from competition from the Paris Metro, various sections stopped running in 1924, 1934 and, finally, in 1985.

OVERLEAF:

Petite Ceinture, Paris, France
The Petite Ceinture was originally a military idea. Following the completion of Paris's 1841 ring of fortifications, a circular railway beside the walls was planned as a way of moving troops and equipment between points. The plan was later revised to link the major stations and serve civilians, while still following the path of the city walls.

Although today many of the stations lie abandoned, there is a new plan to turn the whole 14-mile (23km) line into accessible green spaces. With this in mind a pathway has already been made on one section, replacing one of the railway tracks. For the most part, however, Paris's abandoned Petite Ceinture snakes its way unnoticed along quiet, mossy cuttings, through tunnels and over bridges. And, without traffic, it has been reclaimed by animals, grass and wildflowers.

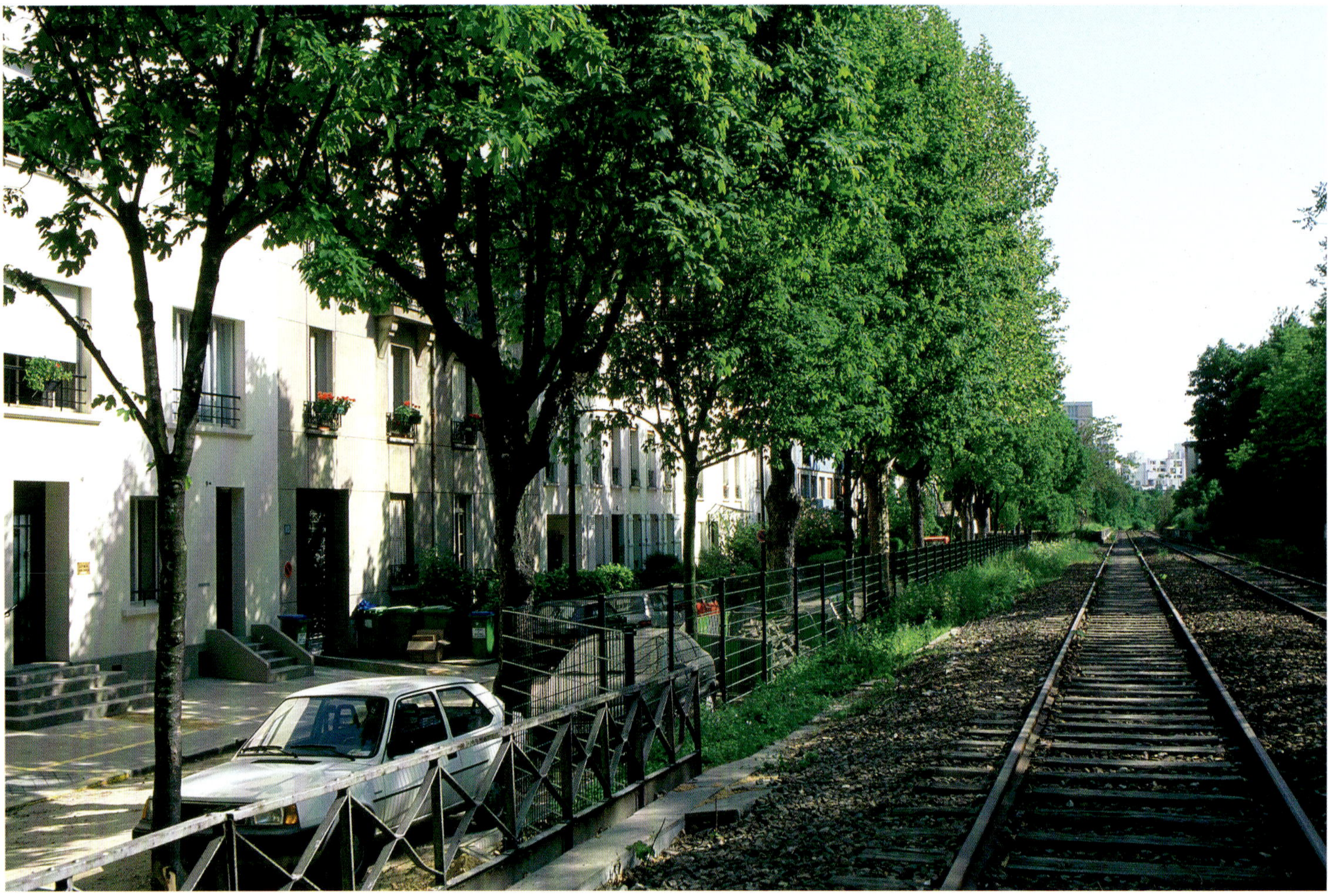

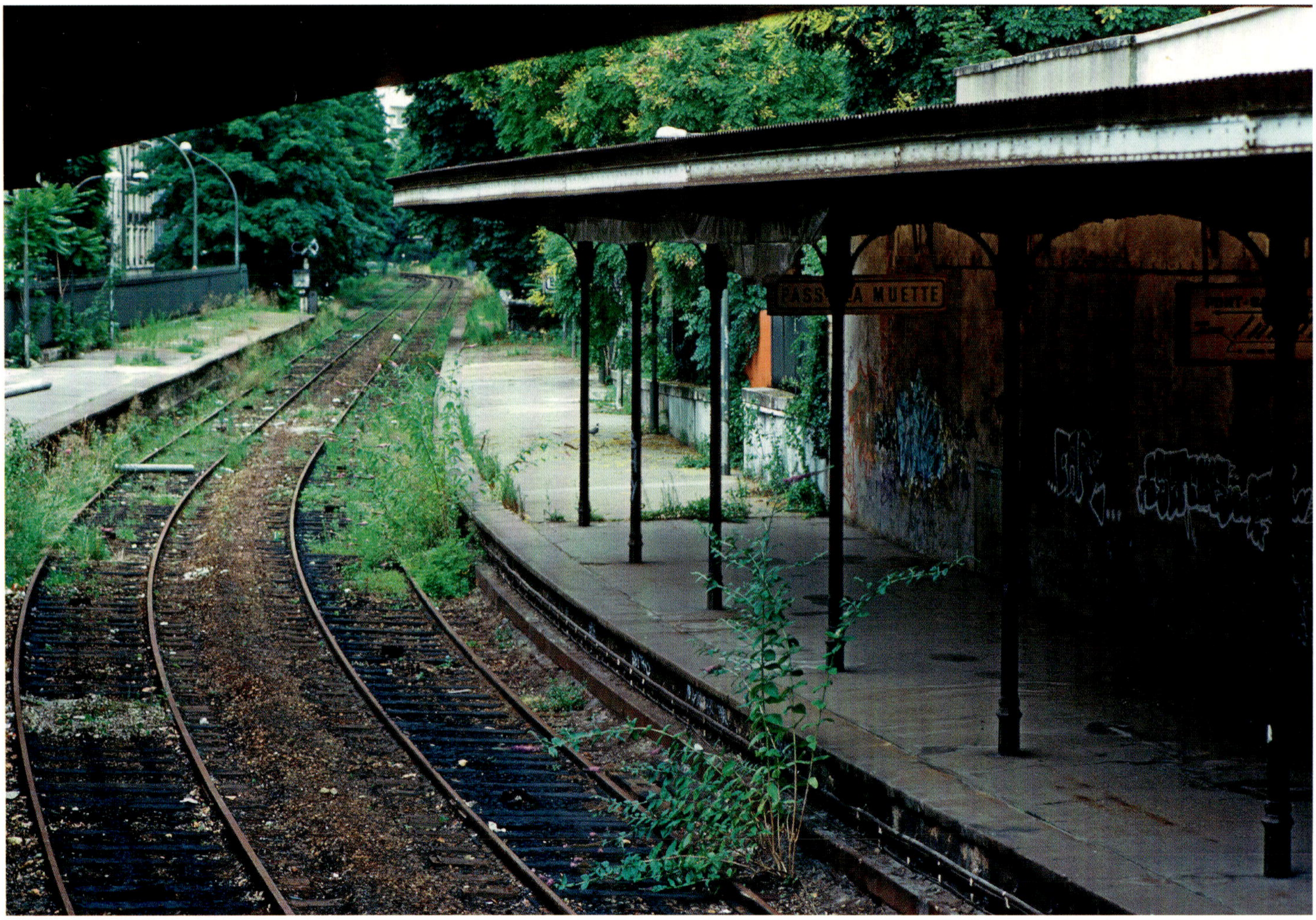
PASS LA MUETTE

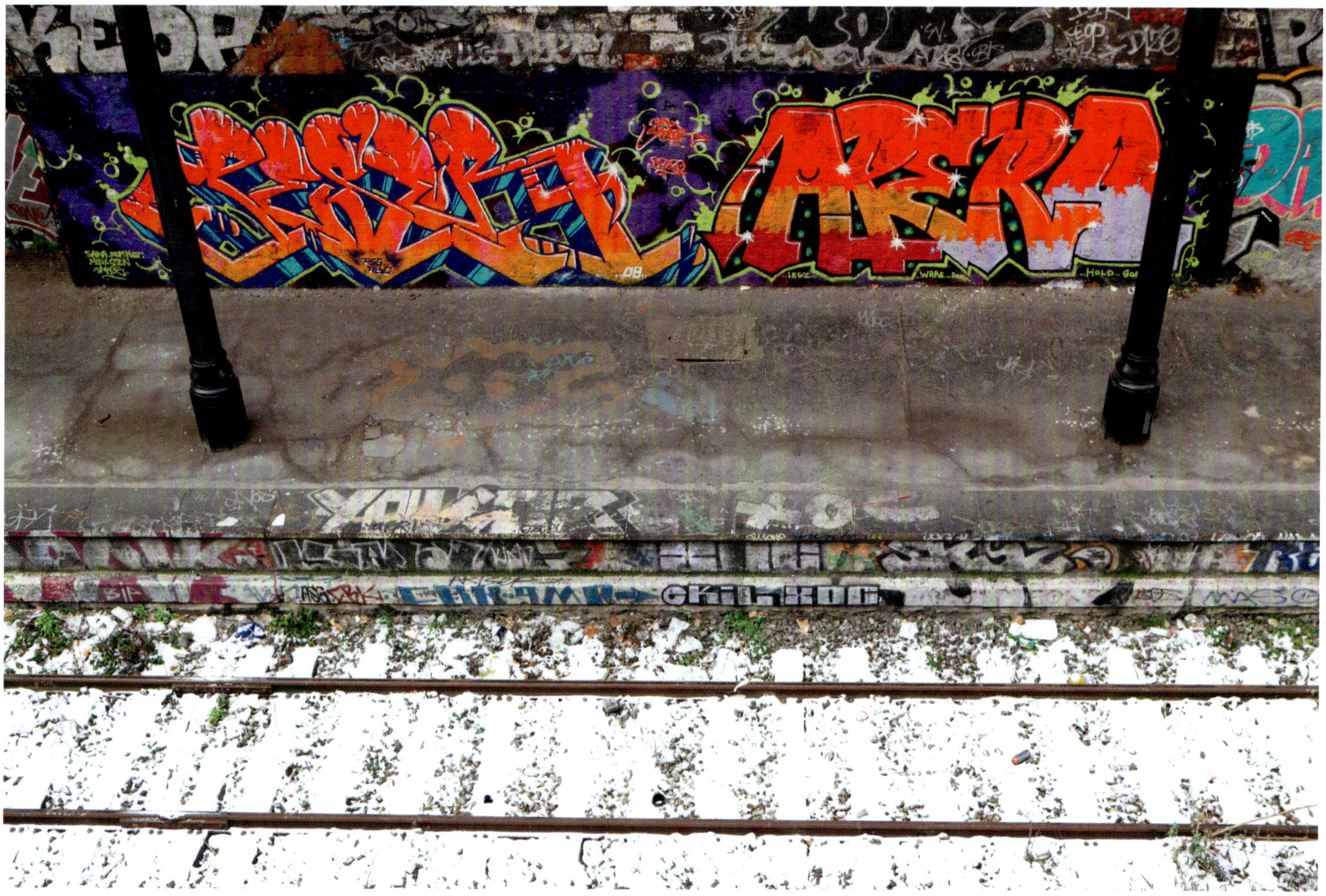

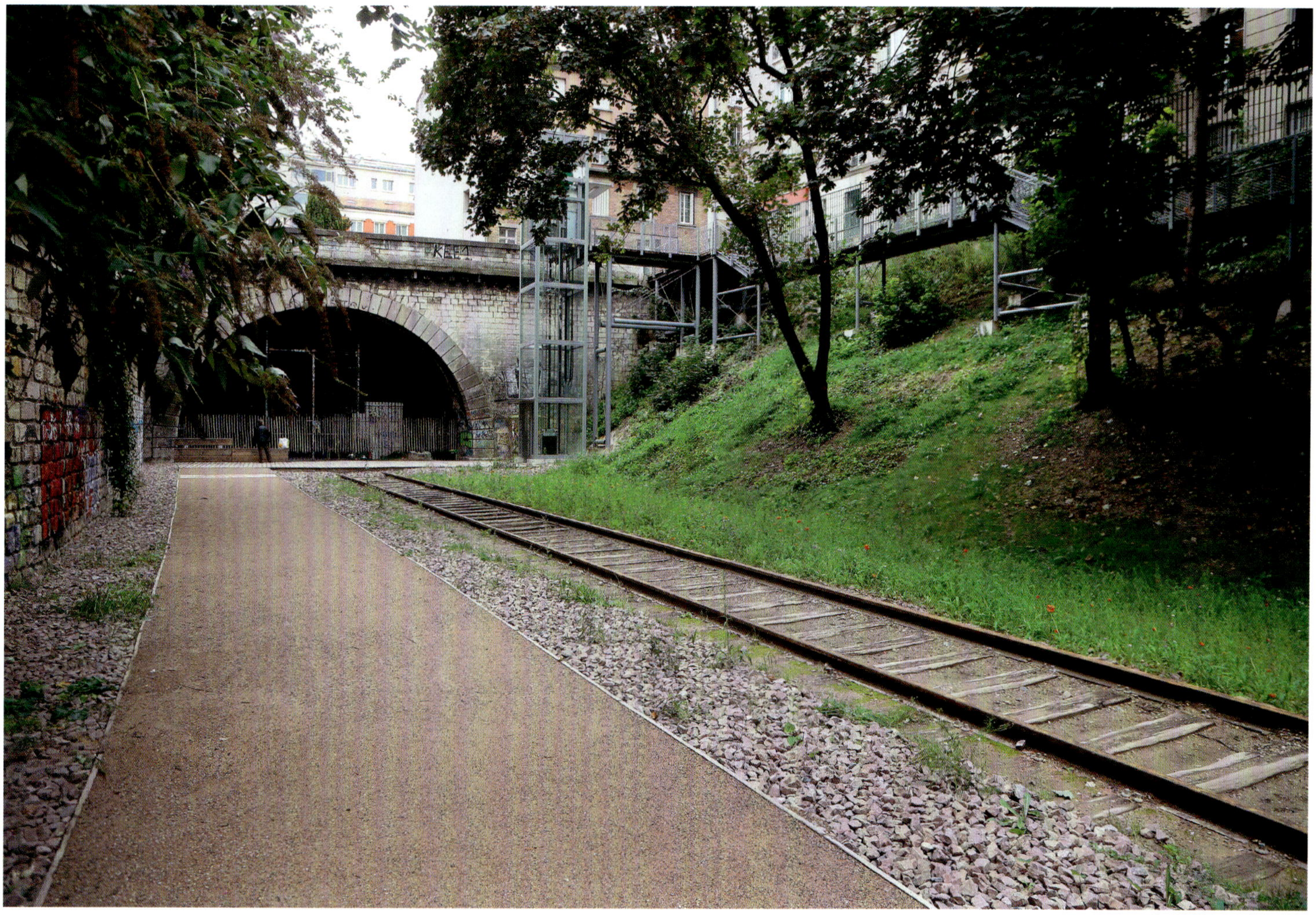

Picture Credits

Alamy: 6 (Richard Roscoe/Stocktrek Images), 8 (Simon Webster), 12 top (allOver Images), 12 bottom (Joanne Moyes), 13 top (Jim West), 18 top (Stanislav Belicka/Image Broker), 18 bottom (Simon Webster), 22/23 (Daniel Kreher/Image Broker), 32/33 (Eye35.pix), 34 top (Josh Sturgis), 35 (Julie Quarry), 36 (Catnap), 38/39 (Michael Karlsson), 40/41 (Yegorovnick), 46/47 (David Crossland/Germany Images), 54/55 (Mihai Andritoiu - Creative), 60/61 (Robert Stainforth), 74/75 (Oleksandr Rupeta), 76/77 (John Henshall), 78 (Ruchan Ziya), 80/81 (Emma Durnford), 86/87 (Leonid Plotkin), 88/89 (Robert Gilhooly), 90 both (EPA), 98 bottom (Dan Poulson/ Jaynes Gallery/Danita Delimont), 100/101 (Richard Roscoe/Stocktrek Images), 108/109 (Florida Images), 110/111 (Vassos Stylianov), 120 (Graham Whitby Boot), 122/123 & 124/125 (Jesse Alexander), 126/127 (Andreas Muhs/Agencja Fotograficzna Caro), 128-129 all (AFC), 130/131 (Ton Koene), 134/135 & 136/137(Aurora Photos), 144/145 (Inger Hogstom/Danita Delimont), 146/147 (Niebrugge Images), 152/153 (World Photo), 158/159 (CBW), 160/161 (Mmmpic), 166/167 (Jan Sochor), 168/169 (Zuma), 170/171 & 172/173 (Michael F. Mcelroy), 194/195 (Elva Dorn), 196 top (GI Photo Stock Z), 196 bottom (Jerry Dawns/Superstock), 197 top (Leon Werdinger), 197 bottom (Balan Madhavan), 198/199 (GI Photo Stock Z), 200/201 (Janice & Nolan Braud), 202 top (Pete Ryan/National Geographic), 202 bottom (Scott Downing), 203 top (Emiliano Rodriguez), 203 bottom (Pete Ryan/National Geographic), 206/207 (Michael Freeman), 208/209 (Dan Highton), 218 both (Rob Cousins), 220/221 (Luke Peters), 222 bottom (Karl Johaentges/Look Die Bildagentur der Fotografen), 223 top (Gilles Targat/Photo 12)

Corbis: 98 top & 99 top (Paul A. Souders), 116/117 & 118 bottom (Yann Arthus-Bertrand), 132/133 (Maria Tama/EPA), 138/139 (Howard Kingsnorth), 154/155 & 156 top (Julie Dermansky), 162/163 (Demotix), 164/165 (David Gray/Reuters), 174/175 (Wasawat Lukharang/NurPhoto), 222 top (Bernard Annebicque/Sygma)

Depositphotos: 7 (Vicnt2815), 16/17 (Knut Niehus), 24/25 (Prudek), 26/27 (Jorisvo), 30/31 (Tatisol), 42/43 & 44/45 (Kre_geg), 56/57 (Nikolay 100), 62/63 (Nndrin), 68/69 (Tomasz Parys), 82/83 (Herraez), 84/85 (Milla 74), 102/103 (Lachris 77), 112/113 (ABCDK), 114/115 (MIMOHE), 118 top (Yar O), 119 (Posztos), 142/143 (Karen Foley Photography), 180/181 (Alexxich), 182/183 (Inesfot), 192/193 (Fort Lauderdale Girl), 204/205 (Demerzel 21), 212/213 (Black Regis 2)

Dreamstime: 14/15 (Fotorince), 19 top (Searagen), 52/53 (Rob van Esch), 64/65 (Sean Pavone), 66/67 (Miroslav Liska), 70/71 (Ilia Torlin), 72/73 (Stephen Archer), 140/141 (Emivel), 184 (Simone Kesh), 190/191 (Elisabeth Coelfen), 210/211 (Javarman), 214/215 (Andrew Periam)

Fotolia: 20/21 (Mezzalira Davide), 34 bottom (Celso Diniz), 92/93 & 94/95 (Salajean), 104 top (Lukasz Zakrzewski)

Jack Freer: 106/107

Getty Images: 19 bottom (Alex Linghorn), 58/59 (Dimitar Dilkoff/AFP), 91 top (Air Rabbit), 91 bottom (Jeremy Sutton-Hibbert), 96/97 & 99 bottom (John Eastcott & Yva Momatiuk), 150/151 (Alex Fradkin), 156 bottom (WIN-Initiative), 157 (AFP), 176/177 (Andrew Burton), 186-189 all (Oli Scarff), 223 bottom (Jacques Demarthon)

Frank C. Grace: 48-51 all, 148, 178/179

Ingram Images: 28/29

Photoshot: 104 bottom (Joerg Heimann), 105 (Anton Yakunin)

Press Association Images: 10/11 (Carlos Osorio), 13 bottom (AP)

Stocksy: 216/217 & 219 (Victor Torres)